Introduction

With the conclusion of the War of 1812, a new spirit of nationalism swept the American nation. It had shown that America was not a weak country awaiting defeat and had helped to cast off any foreign hope that they might one day possess this land. The war had established, once again, that the victors were Americans! But how was one to define what it was to be *American*? Were Americans really that different from their European counterparts, and for that matter, their own ancestors? How did an American act? What made one an *American* lady or gentleman? Was there even such a thing as *American behavior* apart from the tendency the nation's citizenry had in imitating European behaviors and manners?

To answer these questions, American publishers turned to printing etiquette and behavior manuals. At first they were simply American reprints of European etiquette guides, usually word for word! As the demand grew for guidance on how to be a proper American, not simply an imitation of a European, during the 1830s publishers began producing their own American etiquette manuals, followed by numerous reprints. A rising set of American etiquette experts were introduced by these publishing houses and it was to them that Americans turned to inquire and learn how to behave as an *American*.

The Perfect Gentleman is one such manual. It is a gentleman's etiquette manual, not intended for a lady, and as such it provides a unique insight into the male sphere of 19th century society. Included within is the standard collection of etiquette found in most books: etiquette concerning social behavior, introductions, dress, special occasion duties, etc. However, a noted difference is to be found in this unique manual.

Compared to many of its contemporaries, this book has an extensive abundance of literary examples and suggested guidelines concerning how a gentleman is to present himself in situations which required him to speak formally; for example, when presenting a speech to an audience, when engaged in debate or when asked to give a toast at a dinner. To help aid him on his path to becoming a well-spoken

American gentleman, there is provided a wonderful collection of speeches and toasts from which a man could study, select and glean from in order to create his own eloquent words next time he was called upon to perform such honors.

In reprinting this original book from the year 1860, it is my hope that those living historians, reenactors and lovers of history who endeavor to comprehend the mind of the mid-19th century American male, may gain some new insights and draw closer to understanding him and the society in which he was to present himself as *"The Perfect Gentleman."*

Karen Donathen Duffy

Defiance, Missouri

August 2015

THE PERFECT GENTLEMAN;

OR,

ETIQUETTE AND ELOQUENCE

A BOOK OF INFORMATION AND INSTRUCTION FOR THOSE WHO DESIRE TO BECOME BRILLIANT OR CONSPICUOUS IN GENERAL SOCIETY,

OR AT

Parties, Dinners, or Popular Gatherings.

CONTAINING

MODEL SPEECHES FOR ALL OCCASIONS,

WITH DIRECTIONS HOW TO DELIVER THEM.

500 TOASTS AND SENTIMENTS FOR EVERYBODY,

AND THEIR PROPER MODE OF INTRODUCTION.

HOW TO USE WINE AT TABLE, WITH RULES FOR JUDGING THE QUALITY OF WINE, AND RULES FOR CARVING. ETIQUETTE; OR, PROPER BEHAVIOR IN COMPANY, WITH AN AMERICAN CODE OF POLITENESS FOR EVERY OCCASION; AND ETIQUETTE AT WASHINGTON. REMARKABLE WIT AND CONVERSATION AT TABLE, ETC., ETC.,

TO WHICH ARE ADDED, THE

DUTIES OF CHAIRMEN OF PUBLIC MEETINGS,

AND RULES FOR THE ORDERLY CONDUCT THEREOF, TOGETHER WITH VALUABLE HINTS AND EXAMPLES FOR DRAWING UP PREAMBLES AND RESOLUTIONS.

BY A GENTLEMAN.

SOLD ONLY BY SUBSCRIPTION.

NEW YORK:
DICK & FITZGERALD, PUBLISHERS,
No. 18 ANN STREET.

Entered according to Act of Congress, in the year 1860, by
DICK & FITZGERALD,
In the Clerk's Office of the District Court of the United States, for the Southern District of New York.

To the American Gentleman:

THE MAN WHO IS POLITE WITHOUT AFFECTATION;

PROUD WITHOUT VANITY;

DIGNIFIED WITHOUT OSTENTATION;

AFFABLE TO ALL, SERVILE TO NONE;

WHO NEVER DECEIVED HIS FRIEND, NOR TURNED HIS BACK TO HIS FOE;

THIS VOLUME IS RESPECTFULLY DEDICATED BY

THE AUTHOR.

PREFACE.

Of all that portion of this work which is devoted to the speeches, it is not the author's purpose to say anything, in the way either of explanation or apology. Let the speeches speak for themselves.

It is not claimed that all the toasts are original. Many of them are taken from such eminent sources—whether American or European—as the author had at his hand; and, whenever the phraseology suited, he adopted it without change.

Of the "*American Code of Politeness*" there is somewhat more to be said. It was not expected that much which is new could be written on this subject. The only aim has been to present the general rules of politeness and etiquette in such a manner as to render them plain and instructive, and to point out some of the absurd and conflicting rules of the fashionable code which have come into our country from different parts of Europe.

The author has had the opportunity of seeing that there are wide differences between some particular rules of etiquette as practised in America, and England, and on the continent of Europe. Some things that are orthodox etiquette in London, are gross heresy in Paris and all over the continent of Europe. A man who should conduct himself on the continent in all particulars according to the rules of etiquette practised in England, would soon find himself stared at by well-bred people, if not banished from polite society.

The author has witnessed some amusing, not to say ridiculous incidents in fashionable society in America, arising out of the fact that one party practised the Parisian code, while another persistently adhered to the English fashion, and so a social *collision*, if not an *explosion*, was inevitable.

Let a person go into company who has read only the English books on etiquette, which are quite numerously republished in this country, and meet with another who happens to have read only the French, or continental rules, and they will soon be found bumping heads with each other. A notable instance of this occurred in the city of New York within the present year, in which a lady and gentleman of considerable eminence got into an unspeaking feud with each other. They had for some months enjoyed what might be called a literary and musical acquaintance, when they one day met in Mr. Hall's music store, and the gentleman, after the English fashion, waited for the lady to recognize him; and the lady, after the French fashion, waited for the gentleman to recognize her;—and so neither could recognize the other. They had both decidedly cut each other without intending it—without knowing what they had done. And so afterwards they always passed each other like enemies in the streets, until one day the lady had an opportunity of asking for an explanation of the insult which she believed had been offered her. The gentleman denied that he had been the offending party, but on the other hand declared that *she* had refused to recognize *him*. "I waited," said he, "a long time to see if you really meant to cut me." "But," replied the lady, "it was for you to recognize me first."

And then followed a debate on the great question of the etiquette involved in the important affair, in which each, confident of being in the right, refused to give way; and the gentleman actually believed himself master of the field, until he was assured by the author that there was an overwhelming majority of the fashionable world against him.

The lady above referred to is an accomplished translator of French works, and was undoubtedly well informed in all the rules of etiquette as practised on the continent of Europe. The gentleman was equally *au fait* in the English rules. But, with sorrow be it said, neither was quite up to the generous and hearty spirit of politeness dictated by the common sense and simplicity of republican manners.

Although fashionable society in America is made up, to some extent, of people who have come from every part of the Old World, each bringing his own peculiar fashions, yet there is gradually growing up an *individuality of our own*, which happily begins to display itself in *social* and *fashionable*, as well as in political independence.

The *spirit* of politeness, like that of morality and religion, must be the same all over the world; but the artificial rules of etiquette are necessarily modified and varied by local institutions.

The stiff and stately pomp of fashion, as it comes out of the atmosphere of monarchical courts, and thence descends upon the plains of common life in those countries, brings with it much that is unnatural and grotesque, in contrast with the simplicity of republican institutions.

Notwithstanding all the books on etiquette in use in this country are either translations from the French, or republications of English books, there is, in many instances, a modification of the artificial rules of politeness they contain, in the manners of the best society in America. In a word, it is not too much to say that we are beginning to have an American code, in better harmony with the practical and enlightened common sense of democratic institutions than much that has been dictated by the pompous impudence of aristocratic exclusiveness.

The anecdotes at the end of the volume have been selected for the two-fold purpose of affording *amusement* and *instruction* at the convivial board.

Indeed, the author's aim, in every part of the book, has been to make a useful companion of the dining-room, the parlor, and of every other place where ladies and gentlemen may be properly ambitious to appear with satisfaction and honor to themselves, and pleasure to others.

The author professes that modesty alone causes him to withhold his name from the title-page. He is aware that such a remarkable degree of modesty in an author will be considered improbable, if not impossible, by the general public. But he consoles himself with the idea that, even if it shall be believed that the virtue is only an affectation on his part, he has at least set a good example, and one which is very much needed, for the benefit of authors at the present time.

CONTENTS.

	PAGE
Ariosto,	151
Amendments,	319
Adjournments,	322
Actor, Speech of an,	66
American's Toast to the Queen of England,	77
Author, Speech of an,	129
Actor's Toast,	146
Amatory Toasts,	148
Artistic Toasts,	150
American Wines,	196
Art of Drinking Wine,	198
American Code of Politeness,	200
Anecdotes, 37, 38, 47, 52, 57, 69, 76, 81, 89, 90, 91, 103,	131
American Valor,	136
Alfieri,	152
Bibliographer, Speech of a,	115
Baker's Toast,	145
Blacksmith's Toast,	146
Banker's Toast,	146
Book-keeper's Toast,	147
Burgundy,	193
Balls, in Washington,	252
Boccaccio,	150
Cervantes,	151
Cook, Speech of a,	91
Capitalist, Speech of a,	111
Chairman, Selecting a,	301
Character of a Chairman,	303
Carpenter's Toast,	146
Card-maker's Toast,	147

CONTENTS.

	PAGE
Coal Merchant's Toast,	147
Coach-maker's Toast,	147
Carving,	178
Champagne,	190
Claret Wine,	193
Catharine de Medicis,	16
Chaucer,	150
Camoens,	152
Carving Birds,	179
" Ham,	179
" Sirloin of Beef,	179
" Round of Beef,	179
" Fillet of Veal,	179
" Leg of Mutton,	180
" Fore Quarter of Lamb,	180
" Haunch of Mutton,	180
" Saddle of Mutton,	180
" Roast Pig,	180
" Fowl,	181
" Goose,	181
" Turkey,	181
Dinners, on Giving,	35
Drinking, on Honest,	46
Duel, Speech of a Man who would not fight one,	80
Distiller's Toast,	147
Dinners, Invitations to,	167
Definition of Politeness,	200
Dress,	230
Dress at Washington,	242
Dinners at Washington,	249
Deportment in the Street,	250
Dinner-Table Eloquence,	23
Dante,	150
Demosthenes,	152
Duties of a Chairman,	312

CONTENTS.

	PAGE
DEBATES,	328
EDITOR, SPEECH OF AN,	107
ENGLISH BENEVOLENCE, SPEECH ON,	120
EVERY MAN'S TOAST,	147
ETIQUETTE OF THE DINNER-TABLE,	167
EVENING PARTIES,	232
ETIQUETTE AT WASHINGTON,	242
EVENING PARTIES AT WASHINGTON,	247
FIREMAN, SPEECH OF A,	62
FIREMAN'S TOAST,	146
GEOGRAPHICAL SPEECH,	34
GREAT NAMES, SPEECH ON,	123
GLAZIER'S TOAST,	145
GERMAN WINES,	194
GENERAL RULES OF POLITENESS,	201
HOTEL, SPEECH AT THE OPENING OF,	26
HOW TO CALL ON THE PRESIDENT OF THE UNITED STATES,	253
HOW TO NEGATIVE A MOTION,	320
HOW TO VISIT OFFICIAL PERSONS IN WASHINGTON,	253
HANDEL,	151
HERODOTUS,	152
HOGARTH,	152
INTERRUPTION IN DEBATE,	331
IMPUDENT MAN, SPEECH OF AN,	101
INVITATIONS TO DINNER,	203
INTRODUCTIONS,	227
JOHNSON, DR.,	15
JUDGE, SPEECH OF A,	51
JESTER, SPEECH OF A,	100
LASSES, LOVER'S SPEECH ON THE,	41
LAWYER, SPEECH OF A,	53
LOVER, SPEECH OF AN OLD,	72
LOUD LAUGHER, SPEECH OF A,	75
LACONIC MAN, SPEECH OF A,	90

	PAGE
LITERARY GENTLEMAN, SPEECH OF A,	109
LITERARY TOASTS,	150
LOPEZ DE VEGA,	151
MILLER'S WIFE, THE,	39
MODEST WOMEN,	40
MUSICIAN, SPEECH OF A,	88
MERCHANT, SPEECH OF A,	94
MAN OF HONOR, SPEECH OF A,	98
MARRIAGE, SPEECH AT A,	103
MISCELLANEOUS TOASTS,	153
MASONIC TOASTS,	159
MANNERS AT TABLE,	168
MARRIAGE,	228
MOZART,	151
MONTAIGNE,	151
NAVAL AND MILITARY TOASTS,	140
NIAGARA FALLS,	137
ON GIVING DINNERS,	172
ON CARVING,	178
ON INTRODUCTIONS,	227
ON DRESS,	230
ON EVENING PARTIES,	232
ON MARRIAGE,	228
OPINION OF LORD BYRON ON EATING,	27
ORIGINAL MOTIONS,	317
ON MOTIONS,	316
OUR LAKES AND RIVERS,	137
POET, SPEECH OF A,	48
PUNSTER, SPEECH OF A,	55
PRIZE-FIGHTING, SPEECH ON,	64
POOR MAN, SPEECH OF A,	75
PATRIOT, SPEECH OF A,	81
POLITE MAN, SPEECH OF A,	89
PUBLISHER, SPEECH OF A,	105

CONTENTS. 13

	PAGE
PATRIOTIC TOASTS,	134
PRINTER'S TOAST,	146
PLUMBER'S TOAST,	146
PAINTER'S TOAST,	147
PORT WINE,	189
POLITENESS,	200
POLITICAL DINNERS IN THE UNITED STATES,	17
PETRARCH,	150
PLUTARCH,	151
PHIDIAS,	152
PLAUTUS,	152
PREVIOUS QUESTION,	321
QUESTIONS OF ORDER,	334
RIDDLE INSTEAD OF A SPEECH,	33
RED-HEADED MAN, SPEECH OF A,	70
ROAD-MAKER'S TOAST,	147
RULES FOR PRESIDING AT TABLE,	19
ROGER BACON,	150
ROBERT HERRICK,	151
RABELAIS,	151
RAPHAEL,	151
ROBERT FULTON,	153
REMOVING A CHAIRMAN,	333
RAISING OBJECTIONS,	313
RIGHT OF REPLY,	326
SPEECH OF THE CHAIRMAN,	315
SPEECH OF A MAN WHO DOES NOT MAKE SPEECHES,	32
SOBER MAN, SPEECH OF A,	37
STRONG-MINDED WOMEN,	38
SAM SLICK'S SPEECH ON THE CLERGY,	43
SONG INSTEAD OF A SPEECH,	59
SAILOR, SPEECH OF A,	60
SHOEMAKER, SPEECH OF A,	87
SCANDAL, SPEECH ON,	93
SOLDIER, SPEECH OF A,	96

CONTENTS.

	PAGE
Surgeon's Toast,	145
Saddler's Toast,	147
Sherry Wine,	195
Sir Walter Scott's Rules for Presiding at Table,	21
Sir Joshua Reynolds' Opinion of Wine at Table,	30
Sidney Smith,	36
Scolding Wife,	39
Sir Humphry Davy,	150
Tailor, Speech of a,	61
Tallow-Chandler, Speech of a,	86
Toast-master's Companion,	133
Toasts for all Professions,	145
Tinker's Toast,	146
Talking in Company,	224
Table Wit,	255
Titian,	156
Thespis,	152
The Well-Bred Man,	168
Treatment of Servants,	171
Taking the Chair,	312
Undertaker, Speech of an,	85
United States and Central America,	126
Vandyck,	151
Voting on Original Motions and Amendments,	326, 330
Wine Merchant, Speech of a,	29
Wag, Speech of a,	57
Wine-bibber, Speech of a,	58
Wedding of Mr. Grave,	63
Wine at Table,	182
Wine, How to Know Good,	188
Wine, Art of Drinking,	198
Wits and Wine,	29
Watchword of America,	139
William Caxton,	151

THE PERFECT GENTLEMAN;

OR,

ETIQUETTE AND ELOQUENCE.

THE SUBJECT.

If a literary gentleman, and a scholar, needed any excuse for writing a book on the eloquence and etiquette of the dinner-table, beyond that one which is readily appreciated by all authors—*the price it brings him*—he would find it in the fact that great men, in all ages, have given their *countenance* to this subject. The subject has been amply canvassed by such men as Dr. Johnson, Voltaire, Sir Humphry Davy, Lord Bacon, Jeremy Bentham, Lord Byron, and an innumerable list of philosophers, wits, and poets of all nations.

Sidney Smith says: "An excellent and well arranged dinner is a most pleasing occurrence, and a great triumph of civilized life. It is not only the descending morsel and the enveloping sauce, but the rank, wealth, wit, and beauty which surround the meats; the learned management of light and heat; the silent and rapid services of attendants; the smiling and sedulous host, proffering gusts and relishes; the exotic bottles; the embossed plate; the pleasant remarks; the handsome dresses; the cunning artifices of fruit and farina! The hour of dinner, in short, includes everything of sensual and intellectual gratification, which a great nation glories in producing."

The accomplished Scargil wittily writes: "There is an attraction of affinity effected by cookery: they who dine much together generally assimilate much in opinion. It is not an easy matter to dine frequently with a man, especially if he have a good cook, without coming into some or most of his ways of thinking. How observable is the unanimity produced by a public dinner. It seems an established fact—a generally recognized opinion—that the people may be dined into anything. They are dined into liberty; they are dined into loyalty; they are dined into charity; they are dined into piety; they are dined into liberality; they are dined into orthodoxy; they are dined into heresy."

So well is this great gastronomic pacificator understood by statesmen and politicians, that nearly all matters of state and diplomacy are discussed and settled at the dinner-table. The empress Catharine de Medicis, who was called "the mother and the wife of kings," used to descend to the kitchen to superintend the dinners prepared for those whom she would control, and dipped in rich sauces the hand which held the reins of government, and which Roussard compared to the rosy fingers of Aurora. This great empress declared that "the highest thing to be said in praise of woman is, that she can cook a good dinner." It was over the conciliating odors of a rich dinner, superintended by her own hand, that she drew the Duke of Alba into the fearful plan of the massacre of

St. Bartholomew. With such a tremendous *fricandeau* before our eyes, we surely cannot underrate the power of the dinner-table.

When Henry of Valois, the son of the famous empress Catharine de Medicis, ascended the throne, he followed in the culinary footsteps of his mother, and it was at the beginning of his reign we have to date the invention of the Fricandeau, which some authors have, without good reason, accredited to the Swiss. Henry of Valois was the Columbus of the new world of *sauces*—a world which has had more admirers, and played a far more important part in the history of diplomacy, than this other *saucy* new world discovered by Columbus the Spaniard.

From that date the dinner-table has been the common ground where kings, ministers of state, presidents, governors, diplomats, and all the descending scales of politicians, have met to scheme, plot, and settle terms of peace, and whatever else the intricacy of diplomacy may contain.

The dinner-table is one of the political institutions of the United States. Nothing is settled until it has been dined over by the leaders of parties. And as a very considerable number of our politicians spring from the ranks of the uneducated and the uncultivated, much that is grotesque, and that is even offensive to refined society, is apt to make its appearance on these occasions. A coarse and clownish man is quite as great a nuisance at the dinner-table with gentlemen, as a pig would be in a lady's drawing-room. Nearly all of the exquisite relish of the table depends upon the observance of those delicate rules of etiquette and politeness which give to civilization its immense social advantages over savage life. A man who can appear well at the table will always be judged a gentleman by well-bred people. On the other hand, the man who appears ill there, has the mark of vulgarity indelibly impressed upon him.

The presence of one clown at the dinner-table would spoil the comfort of every well-bred guest. And, for this reason, those who are at all careful of the customs of good society, rigidly abstain from inviting such persons to meet parties at their tables. Where ladies are invited this rule is never, under any circumstances, deviated from. But, where no ladies are to be present, and the dinner is given exclusively to gentlemen, for political purposes, it is customary, in this country, to invite a mixed crowd of guests, without any reference whatever to their social equality; and no gentleman, at such a time, can object to sit at table by the side of a fellow who shovels the victuals into his mouth with the knife, or blows his nose in the napkin, or squirts a stream of tobacco juice over his shoulder at the fire-place. There is a necessity for this wide deviation from the ordinary laws of social respectability: the unrefined man is invited because he has influence with a class of men whose votes are sought for by the gentleman, or by the party, for whose political interests the dinner is given. On such occasions it would be a great impoliteness for any gentleman in any way to notice the vulgarities of this man. He has not pushed himself into the company, but he has been invited there because he is a man of influence with his class; and being thus invited, he is entitled to the same attention and respect from all the other guests as though he had enjoyed equal advantages of education and refinement with them.

RULES FOR PRESIDING AT TABLE.

A great deal of the pleasure at table depends upon the person who is called upon to preside.

If the dinner is given by a society, or a committee, or by an institution, the president or chairman will of course preside; and when a gentleman gives a dinner, for political or any other purposes, he will take the chair himself.

At dinners given by individuals to the public press, or on any occasion where there is no one upon whom the duties of presiding already devolve, it is customary for the party giving the dinner to invite some gentleman to take the chair (the head of the table); or in case he does not do that, the guests themselves indicate one of their number for that post.

The chairman remains standing until all the other guests are seated, and when he takes his seat it is a signal that the party is ready to be waited upon, and the feast opens.

The chairman is waited upon last, and as the dinner progresses he will carefully, but very quietly, see that none of the guests are neglected by the waiters.

If the chairman has occasion to give any direction to the waiter, he does not speak to him loud enough to be heard by the rest at table, but calls him quietly to his side, and gives his instructions in an undertone.

It is when the *toasting* and *speaking* commence that the chairman's most important duties begin. His office is that of a moderator. He will call the table to order at the reading of each toast, and will see that proper silence is preserved while responses are being made.

Though wine is a mighty quickener of men's tongues, the well-bred man will neither talk aloud nor whisper while another guest is making a speech. The chairman will see that none break this rule.

The experienced chairman will allow plenty of time between the toasting and speaking, for the guests to chat, and laugh, and joke together. However vigilant he is in pushing round the bottle, he takes care that the speeches do not come too fast, nor occupy too much of the time.

A gentleman wishing to propose a sentiment may either repeat it himself or hand it to the chairman to be read. If he repeats it himself, he will say, " Mr. chairman, have I your permission to offer a toast?" The chair will give his consent, and say, " Gentlemen will please to come to order, and listen to a sentiment from Mr. ———."

It is the duty of the chair to take notice that each gentleman is helped to the wine that he prefers, and that the bottle does not forget him in its rounds.

When any gentleman is called upon to respond to a

toast, the chairman will use his endeavors to get a speech from the party thus complimented. But if it shall be evident to the chair that the gentleman is suffering under a real embarrassment, in being thus called upon, he will relieve him from his dilemma by some ingenious turn that will let the victim off from a speech, and that, too, if possible, without mortifying his vanity. No case could occur where an adroit chairman would not be able to do this.

Sir Walter Scott has left the following rules of presidency at the table:

"1*st*, Always hurry the bottle round for five or six rounds, without prosing yourself, or permitting others to prose. A slight filip of wine inclines people to be pleased, and removes the nervousness which prevents men from speaking; disposes them, in short, to be amusing, and to be amused.

"2*nd*, Push on, keep moving! as young Rapid says. Do not think of saying fine things; nobody cares for them, any more than for fine music, which is often too liberally bestowed on such occasions. Speak at all ventures, and attempt the *mot pour rire*. You will find people satisfied with wonderfully indifferent jokes, if you can but hit the taste of the company, which depends much on its character. Even a very high party, primed with all fashionable folks, may be stormed by a jovial, rough, round, and ready president. Choose your text with discretion; the sermon may be as you like. Should a drunkard or an ass break in with anything out of joint, if you can parry with a jest, good and well; if not, do not exert your serious authority, unless it is something very bad. The authority even of a chairman ought to be very cautiously exercised. With patience you will have the support of every one.

"*3rd,* When you have drunk a few glasses, to play the good fellow and banish modesty (if you are unlucky enough to have such a troublesome companion), then beware of the cup too much. Nothing is so ridiculous as a drunken president.

"*Lastly,* Always speak short, and *skeoch doch na skiel* —cut a tale with a drink."

SPEECHES AT THE DINNER-TABLE.

To speak really well at the convivial table requires considerable and varied talent, reading, and observation. To shine on such occasions, it is necessary that one should possess wit, a command of language, and a good degree of taste and judgment. Unless a man is armed with some of these gifts, at least, it will be a hazardous thing for him to undertake a regular speech at the dinner-table.

If, however, a man is called up at table, he must say something, if it is no more than to apologize for not responding in a speech. And even this little matter may be done so gracefully and good-naturedly that he will sit down amid the applause of the whole table. If he feels himself totally unable to make any kind of a speech, he may resort to some such little trick as saying, that his friends knew very well when they called him up, that he had conscientious scruples against speech-making at any time, and especially at such a dinner as this, where there is so much good victuals and wine to be enjoyed. He would, therefore, content himself with thanking the gentlemen for their kindness, and leave them to the uninterrupted enjoyment of the good wine spread before them, until some gentleman shall be called up who will make a speech worthy of the great treat to which they have been invited. Any good-natured turn like this is infinitely better than a dull speech at table. Besides, it is not expected, nor desired, that every person who is called up at table should make a speech. It is customary to extend the compliment to all, but it is not expected that those will inflict a speech who are incapable of making one. But every one ought to be able to return his thanks to gentlemen gracefully, or perhaps to tell some appropriate story to set the table in a roar.

The eloquence of the dinner table should always be of a quiet tone of voice, with a pleased and friendly countenance, and very little, if any kind of action or gesture, should be indulged in. Loud and boisterous declamation at such times would be both out of place and ridiculous.

Good jokes and merriment are always in order at dinner, but the mirth and hilarity must be tempered with good sense and a delicate observance of propriety. All strained attempts at facetiousness by one who has not a natural talent for it, are sure to end in making him ridiculous. Therefore, let no man venture upon gay sallies at dinner unless they so press forward to his lips as to escape almost in spite of him. One gains far more credit by showing that he duly appreciates the wit of others, and genially laughing in the right places, than he can by vain attempts of his own. Dr. Johnson says, we take no more pleasure in seeing a man strive to be witty and fail, than we should in seeing him attempt to jump over a ditch and fall into it.

It is often the case that those who converse well at table still make the worst of *speeches* at the convivial meeting. What a pity that a man who is good in conversation should destroy his influence by bad speeches! When one who is called up at table finds himself confused and unable to give utterance to his ideas, as is often the case with the inexperienced, the only thing for him to do is to stop at once, and resume his seat before he makes himself ridiculous. The following specimen of an after-dinner speech is not worse than is quite often heard at the merry table : " This I may, gentlemen—that is, perhaps, I may be allowed to observe—to remark, rather as remarkably expressive of my feelings on this occa—on the present occasion—that is, gentlemen—that I consider this I am sure I need not say—and I say it without hesitation—that this is the proudest moment of, as I was about to say, my life (pause). For as the fabled bird of poetry, the phœnix of our immortal bard, derives new vitality from the ashes of, if I may be allowed the expression, an expired, an extinct existence, so does the calm serenity of age emanate from the transitory turbulence of youth (pause). And, gentlemen—gentlemen, I need not add—need not add, as it were, in a manner provided, on the present occasion, as I was about to say, that language is inadequate, inadequate to express, to utter the sublimity of my emotions." Many a man of pretty good sense may make as incoherent and ridiculous a speech as this under the nervous excitement produced by being unexpectedly called up at table.

We have often seen distinguished statesmen make sorry enough failures at the dinner-table, by attempting those graceful sallies of levity which are not in their vein. On this account, great men are often great bores at table. When Dr. Johnson was asked why he was not invited out to dine as often as Garrick was, he answered, with characteristic ill-nature, " Because great lords and ladies don't like to have their mouths stopped." Well, who *do* like to have their mouths stopped ? The man who is in the habit of stopping people's mouths ought never to be invited to dinner, where good nature, amiability, and a moderate degree of self-satisfaction are desirable in all.

Avoid by all means occupying more than your share of the time in talking. A quiet deportment and an unembarrassed modesty, are at all times indicative of the well-bred man. Very loud talking is especially unbecoming at table— it will impress gentlemen that you are more familiar with the manners of the bar-room than with the habits of polite society. Whispering at such times is quite as great a breach of etiquette.

Long speeches are almost always a bore—a man must be invariably facetious who can with impunity spin out a speech of more than ten minutes' length at dinner. A few amiable words of thanks to the gentlemen who have called him up, a pleasant allusion to the host, or to the occasion in honor of which the dinner is given, and, if he is equal to it, some good-natured and telling hit at somebody, or something, is all that should be attempted. To " set the table in a roar," and not to set it *gaping*, should be the object of the convivial orator.

Always before you go to a dinner where speaking and toasting is likely to be the order of the day, be careful to arm yourself with at least one good toast and some anecdote suitable to the occasion. With a good toast and an anecdote at your tongue's end, you can hardly fail to make a respectable response to whatever call may be made upon you.

SPEECH AT THE OPENING OF AN EATING SALOON OR HOTEL.

Some people, who are very ambitious to shine at table, are in the habit of carefully preparing a little speech, and then writing a toast to call it out, which they hand to a friend, with the request that he will offer it, at a proper time, and call upon them to respond to it. At a splendid feast which was given to the press on the opening of Taylor's grand saloon on the corner of Broadway and Franklin streets, a gentleman said to another as he entered, " You will be invited to take the chair—here is a *toast* which I want you to read when we have got a little warmed with wine, and call on me to respond." In due time the following toast was read: "*To all good eating and good eaters—as on the present occasion, where the latter exist may the former never be wanting.*" And M—— was asked to respond, which he did nearly as follows: "Mr. Chairman, as that toast is one to which any *well* man might heartily respond, I shall not consider that any especial reference to my *eating ability* was intended by my being called up to respond. I acknowledge a fair appreciation of good eating, and I am always happy to associate with good livers—*especially at meal times*—(laughter and applause), and my experience has led me to adopt the idea of Lord Byron, who said that he 'had generally found good livers to be amiable gentlemen and good friends.' The Duke of York pronounced the *Almanack for Gourmands* the most delightful book ever issued from the press, and I must say that I have rarely known a great man, a man of vigorous brain and well-sustained mental powers, who was a despiser of good living. The ancients were not so much to be laughed at, who considered the stomach the seat of our noblest faculties and affections. Old Persius called it 'the dispenser of genius,' and the Hebrews regarded it as the head-quarters of intellect, while the Hindoos, to this day, hold it to be the seat of all the delightful affections; and, if we wanted further proof, we have it in the delight and enthusiasm with which the learned guests at this table are addressing themselves to this intensely active fountain of *their* genius—(laughter and applause). Eating, gentlemen, is a great spur to industry, and a mighty pusher of commerce. Could we live without eating, all the world would be idle, and the ships, which now fly before the winds on every sea, would fold their wings and drift listless and empty along the desolate shores. It is *eating* which rears such magnificent palaces as this, which gives employment to so many millions of men and women all over the world, in coining brick out of the earth, hewing stone from the quarry, gathering timber from the forest, constructing these superb decorations of art, and finally, in meting out the delicate fruits and luxuries which will be served within these walls to the thousands who will come here to forget care, and to refresh themselves with renewed joy and vigor to meet the shock of their daily toils. One man, who rears a temple of luxury like this, does more for mankind than the *whole tribe* of vegetarian, anti-eating, lean-stomached and leaner-brained reformers, who have dragged their sluggish beings across the earth since time began—(great applause). So, sir, allow me to vary your toast by wishing that *the shadows of good eaters may never be less, and may bad eaters have no shadows at all.*"

This speech was delivered in a careless, half-waggish style, which well suited the temper of a party of intelligent men who had just partaken of an extraordinarily fine dinner, and were sufficiently warmed with generous wine to render them appreciative of anything which could be said in praise of good living.

SPEECH OF AN OLD BACHELOR.

An old batchelor, who was toasted at a party of merry friends, by way of twitting him of his obstinate celibacy, replied, that he was not so far gone as to have any word to utter in praise of his condition, especially in the presence of so many gentlemen who luxuriate in the *sweets of matrimony*. He should attempt no eulogy of his misfortune, but must defend himself from any suspicion that he was indifferent to the charms and excellencies of the fair sex. He remembered a celebrated wit, who, when he was asked why he did not marry a young lady to whom he was attached, replied, "I know not, except the great regard we have for each other."

Any happy turn like this is always in good taste, and is sure to put the table in excellent temper. It turned the banter upon the married guests without the bad taste of railing against marriage.

SPEECH OF A WINE-MERCHANT.

At the opening of a feast the following toast was offered : "*At this table, as ever, may wine be the whetstone of wit;*" and a celebrated wine merchant, who was present, was called up to respond. He stated that in the presence of such excellent livers, and before so many gentlemen of taste and wit, good wine needed no eulogy. Great wits were always appreciators of good wine. Goldsmith called it "the philosopher which drives away care, and makes us forget whatever is disagreeable." Sir Joshua Reynolds maintained that wine "improved conversation and benevolence." "I am," said he, "in very good spirits when I get up in the morning; by dinner-time I am exhausted; wine puts me in the same state as when I got up, and I am sure that wine makes people talk better." The famous solicitor Spotiswoode once declared at a public dinner-party, that "wine makes a man better pleased with himself." Dr. Johnson replied, "and to make a man better pleased with himself, let me tell you, is doing a very great thing." Sir William Forbes wittily remarked, that "a man warmed with wine was like a bottle of beer, which is made brisker by being set before the fire." Burke was a lover of generous wine, and when Dr. Johnson, who was always trying to disagree with everybody, gave the following scale of liquors, "claret for boys—port for men—brandy for heroes"—Burke replied, "Let me have claret, then: I love to be a boy; to have the careless gayety of boyish days again." Wine has, in all ages of the world, been a classic bond of good-fellowship between heroes, philosophers, and great men. Sir Joshua Reynolds declared, that "At first the taste of wine was disagreeable to me; but I brought myself to drink it that I might be like other people. The pleasure of drinking wine is so connected with pleasing your company, that altogether there is something of social goodness in it." But the highest thing to be said in praise of wine—and one which I know this party will appreciate—is, that it has immemorially been associated with the beauty of women. "Woman and wine" are twin words which go hand-in-hand together, and everywhere warm the coldest hearts with the glow of feeling and gush of hope that form the sweetest ingredients in the cup of life. Byron's famous toast—

> "Give us wine and women—mirth and laughter,
> Sermons and soda-water the day after—"

will never want for admirers. What poet has not celebrated the pleasures of wine? But for wine much of the sweetest poetry of the world were unsung. The sweet songs of Anacreon, of Harfez, of Burns, of Moore, and a glorious list of bards too numerous to mention, were all unsung but for the charms and inspirations of wine. Gentlemen, I have ventured to dwell so long upon this subject because I supposed that to praise wine in your presence was like entertaining a lover with a eulogy on the charms of his mistress. And in taking my seat, allow me to give you a sentiment which I beg you will not consider as *professional*—"May we never be out of *spirits*."

There are several good points in the above speech: the opinion of celebrated men on the use of wine is classical and interesting; the language is easy and natural; there is no straining after effect, or vain reaching after wit and humor; and yet there is considerable pleasant and genuine humor in it, which could not fail to put the company in a pleased and satisfied frame of mind.

A SILENT MAN'S SPEECH.

On another occasion, a talking man had made a dashing, flowery speech, in extravagant praise of the host, the dinner, and everything at the table, and finally sat down, by calling upon a gentleman, in a bantering way, who was known for his extreme silence, to get up and say something in praise of such an excellent feast. The person thus rallied rose very slowly, and with a quiet and good-natured leer replied that, for his part, *he believed* all that the eloquent gentlemen who had just taken his seat had said; a fact which reminded him of an old Athenian, who was deficient in eloquence, but whose bravery was never doubted,—and when one of his competitors, in a long and flowery speech, made great professions of what he would do, arose and said, "Men of Athens! all that he has promised, *I* will do." The silent gentleman took his seat amid a general roar and laughter of applause.

SPEECH OF A MAN WHO DOES NOT MAKE SPEECHES.

We were once at a dinner-table in Philadelphia, when the business of speech-making and story-telling was pushed, almost with annoying haste, and where one gentleman, more silent than the rest, was continually bantered and pushed up to say something. At length the host laughingly declared, that he should either make a speech, or tell a story, or leave the table. The gentleman rose and replied, that he had found the host's wine too good to lose time in talking, but as he had been commanded so emphatically to speak, he did not feel at liberty to refuse any longer, especially as the object of so much speaking might be to save wine, for men can't drink while talking. He remembered a story of the wife of the great Dr. Bentham, who asked a person that applied for the place of footman in her family, if he could whistle. "Why is that necessary?" said the man. "Because," said the lady, "I expect my footman to whistle all the time he is in the cellar, to be certain he is not drinking the wine." "Now," added the gentleman, "as I am not a speech-maker, I will whistle my portion of the time, in order to make the rest of you sure of your portion of the wine."

I need not say that this set the table in a roar, and was " the speech of the evening."

A RIDDLE INSTEAD OF A SPEECH.

I once knew a man to make himself agreeable at table by telling a riddle; which shows that, if a man cannot make a speech, nor tell a story, nor sing a song, he at least may go armed with some such little thing as a pleasant riddle, which will enable him to contribute his share to the general fund of the entertainment. The gentleman, though a fine scholar, was so little gifted in speech that he could not even tell a story respectably, and when rallied upon his silence, and asked if such fine wine did not inspire him either to talk or sing about it, he replied, that he neither sung nor made speeches, but he could tell them an Italian riddle about wine, which was, "*Per mancamento d'acqua bevo del acqua; se io havesse acqua beverei el vino*"— "For want of water I am forced to drink water; if I had water, I would drink wine." After every gentleman at the table had tried in vain to solve the riddle, the explanation was given. It was the speech of an Italian vineyard-man, after a long drought and an extremely hot summer, that had parched up all his grapes, and thus a want of water had forced him to drink water, by destroying his wine crop.

A GEOGRAPHICAL SPEECH.

At a dinner-party lately given to several learned gentlemen in New York, the conversation became heavy with a prolonged discussion on the comparative merits of different geographical works, when a facetious guest put a stop to the tedious discussion, by saying, "Now, gentlemen, I protest against all this; I am a geographical disciple of a jocular member of a literary club which existed in London at the period of our Revolutionary war, who contended that it 'is now become ridiculous to adhere to the old divisions of the globe. The name of Europe reminds us of the indelicate story of Europa and the bull Jupiter; Asia of luxurious nabobs; Africa of the guinea coast, at a time when, alas! guineas are as scarce as Roman coins; America of those unnatural children who are fighting with their mother.'"

It need not be said that this ingenious turn put a stop to the dull geographical controversy.

SPEECH ON GIVING AND EATING DINNERS.

At a feast where the following toast was offered, "*To all who give good dinners, and to all who are invited to them,*" the gentleman called upon to respond remarked, that this sentiment was a very comprehensive one, embracing the two great divisions of polite society; in one or the other of which the greatest names of history might be classified. For instance, at the head of the list of eminent dinner-givers we may arrange such a name as that of Lord Chancellor Erskine, who, while sitting upon the bench, used to amuse himself in sketching turtles upon cards, with a certain day and hour written upon the margin, which he was in the habit of passing to his friends in court, as dinner invitations. And then, at the top of the list of celebrated diners-out, is the great Doctor Johnson, of whose discourses, sayings, and repartees at table, Mr. Boswell has made a big book. No doubt if all the learned, wise, sharp, pungent, and witty speeches and sayings which have been made at table were collected into books, they would form a library, which for wisdom and number of volumes, would outrival the famous Alexandrian. At table men forget their formal philosophies and stilted opinions, and come down to the simplicity of nature itself; and there is, therefore, good reason for the custom practised by all polite nations, of settling nearly all affairs of public or private interest by calling the parties most concerned together for a free and friendly intercourse at dinner. Rev. Sidney Smith, when dining with a party of literary gentlemen, compared Mr. Canning, who was then in office, to a fly in amber. "Nobody," said he, "cares about the fly; the only question is, How the devil did it get there? Nor do I attack him for the love of glory, but for the love of utility, as a burgomaster hunts rats in a Dutch dyke, for fear it should flood a province. When he is jocular he is strong; when he is serious he is like Samson in a wig. Call him a legislator, a reasoner, and the conductor of the affairs of a great nation, and it seems to me as absurd as if a butterfly were to teach bees to make honey. That he is an extraordinary writer of small poetry, and a diner-out of the highest lustre, I do most readily admit. After George Selwyn, and perhaps Tickell, there has been no such man for this last half century." Nowhere but *at dinner* could so free, and racy, and unstudied, and witty a criticism have fallen from the lips of even Sidney Smith. Therefore, gentlemen, in an intellectual, social, and critical point of view, you do well to toast those who give and eat good dinners.

SPEECH OF A SOBER MAN AT A DRINKING-PARTY.

I was, a few years ago, dining with some merry fellows, mostly military men, in the city of Baltimore, who were quite uproarious with deep drinking and loud laughter; all but one gentleman, who was of a less excitable temperament than the rest, and who to a late hour remained comparatively sober. Of course all pitched at him. One called on him for a speech. Another said, "No, he is not drunk enough to make a good speech; but he shall tell an anecdote;" and so "Anecdote!" "Anecdote!" rung from a dozen voices. "Well," said the quiet gentleman, "your complaint of my want of merriment reminds me of an anecdote of the famous General Gustavus Adolphus, who impetuously overran the greatest part of Germany, and surmounted every obstacle opposed to his arms. When he was besieging Ingolstadt, his horse was killed under him by a cannon ball. His chancellor entreated him not to risk his life so often. Gustavus replied with warmth, "You are always too cold; and you stop my progress." "True, sire," said the chancellor, "I confess I am cold; but if I did not sometimes throw a little of my ice into your fire, you would be burnt to ashes." "Now, gentlemen," said he, laughing, "what would become of this party if I did not keep sober? The way you go on storming this army of bottles, your legs will soon be under your bodies, very much in the condition of General Adolphus' horse under its rider, at the battle of Ingolstadt, and then I shall be here like the chancellor to support the fallen heroes."

SPEECH ON METAPHYSICS.

At a dinner-party in Boston, where two or three men of learning monopolized the whole time in talking metaphysics, one of them at length banteringly asked a young gentleman who had just graduated, if he could favor the company with a metaphysical speech; whereupon the rest began thumping the table and calling "speech!" "speech!" The graduate got slowly up, and said that he felt honored in being called upon to make a speech on metaphysics, especially in the presence of so many learned metaphysicians as he saw before him. He had listened attentively to their learned and *interesting* conversation, which had reminded him of a Scotch blacksmith's definition of metaphysics, which was as follows: "Twa fouk disputin' thagither; he that's listenin' disna ken what he that's speakin' means; and he that's speakin' disna ken what he means himself; that's metaphysics."

This palpable hit produced an uproarious laugh, and the student had the tact to sit down in the midst of it, for nothing that he could add would increase the reputation which he had in a single minute gained as a wit and a man of sense.

SPEECH ON STRONG-MINDED WOMEN.

At a late anniversary dinner of one of the New York societies, the following volunteer toast was offered:

"*Strong-minded women—may their shadows ever be less.*"

The gentleman who volunteered to respond, said there was a remarkable propriety in the language of the latter clause of this toast, as the strong-minded women are undoubtedly a *shadow*, instead of a warm and cheerful fire-light, upon the domestic hearth. They are indeed *shadows*, and not sun-beams, in the path of life, and on the threshold of home. In their coarse and clamorous demand to be allowed to mix in elections, how unlike the virtuous and exemplary Madame de Longueville, who, when she was advised to appear at Court in order to set the courtiers an example, replied, "I cannot set a better example than to stay at home, and not go to Court at all." For women past their prime, for old termigants, or those of a cracked reputation, women's-rights meetings are natural places enough; but, for a fair and virtuous young girl to be seen there, is as ungraceful a sight as it would be to see a bunch of June roses growing in the midst of the *geese* and *pigs* of a barn-yard. I remember a song which used to be sung when I was a boy, and it was an old song then, called the "Miller's Wife," which was a faithful portrait of our modern convention scolds:

THE MILLER'S WIFE.

"The miller leads a noisy life
 E'en at the very best;
But should he have a scolding wife,
 He's sure to have no rest:
Her tongue, unlike the mill,
 Does never motion lack,

> For that is sometimes still,
> But she goes always clack,
>> Click, clack!
>> Click, clack!
>> Good lack!
>> Good lack!
> No rest her tongue e'er finding,
> 'Tis always, always grinding;
>> Clipper, clapper,
>> Clitter, clatter,
> For all the world like my mill hopper,
> And the devil himself can't stop her."

SPEECH ON MODEST WOMEN.

When the following toast was proposed, "*Our wives and sweethearts—may the love which was won by their beauty be kept fresh and perennial by the modesty that adorns their lives,*" a gentleman remarked that this sentiment, like the toasts given to presidents and kings, should be drunk *standing* and in *silence*. Modesty is a jewel beyond price, and beyond the power of description. In men, it is the shadow of a noble mind; in women, it is the light of a pure soul. St. Bernard happily styles it, "the jewel of manners, the sister of chastity; the guardian of reputation, the portion of all goodness." Diogenes, the cynic philosopher, called the blush of modesty, "*the color of virtue.*" Rowe says:

> "From every blush that kindles in thy cheeks,
> Ten thousand little loves and graces spring
> To revel in the roses."

Allow me, gentlemen, to vary the language of the toast, so that it shall read, "*May the modesty of our wives and sweethearts never fail to keep the footprints of our affections from being discovered beyond the sacred domain of home.*"

SAMUEL LOVER'S SPEECH ON THE "LASSES."

I had the pleasure to be present at the grand centenial festival which was given in Glasgow, and which occasion was also celebrated all over the civilized world, in honor of Scotland's immortal poet, Robert Burns. Towards the close of the magnificent feast, Samuel Lover, the Irish song-writer and singer, who now resides on a small estate near Glasgow, came forward and said: "At a very short notice I am called upon to propose a toast; but it is one that no man could probably be asked to propose without feeling that a great compliment and a great privilege had been granted to him. That toast is 'The Lasses.' (Cheers.) Ladies and gentlemen, it seems a sort of practical pun that the lasses should be proposed by a Lover. (Laughter.) But I hope the ladies that are here will believe that an Irish lover is never deficient in paying his homage to what has well been called the most beautiful half of the human race. (Cheers.) Ladies, in your smile exists the poet's inspiration, and in your smile exists the poet's reward. There never was a poet yet that didn't worship women

—(hear, hear)—and preëminently the bard, whose name we have met this day to honor, worshipped 'the lasses, O!' (Loud applause.) But the greatest poet in the world, whatever may be his power—and the power of making love was very great in Robert Burns—can never make love by himself. He must have a lady to help him (laughter); and, I must say, that from all my experience, very good helps they are. (Renewed laughter.) Shakespeare has comprised under one head the lunatic, the lover, and the poet; and when I first became a lover, I felt convinced that Shakespeare was right in saying that a lover was a lunatic—(laughter)—for I was perfectly mad. (Much laughter.) But that took place a long time ago---about half a century—but I began very young. (Roars of laughter.) And, Mr. Chairman, ladies and gentleman --for I wish to call as many witnesses as I can to this fact—I found madness so delightful that I think I never have been right in my senses since—(great laughter)—but if ever I have had a lucid interval, it has only been to sigh for Bedlam again, and call upon Cupid for my keeper. (Cheers.) A very interesting document has been placed in my hand to read to you to-night. It is an additional verse to 'Green grow the rashes, O,' composed by Robert Burns, the son of the great Robert Burns. The lines were presented by Mr. Alexander Maclagan, author of "Poems and Songs," to be repeated. In reading it, I shall give as much attention as I can to your Scottish dialect, and if I make mistakes, pray forgive a stranger." Mr. Lover then read the following verse, which was received with applause; the talented reader's manner in setting off the Scotch words creating considerable amusement:

> "Frae man's ain side God made his wark,
>   That a' the lave surpasses, O;
> The man but lo'es his ain heart's bluid
>   Wha dearly lo'es the lasses, O!"

Mr. Lover concluded by saying, "After this, of course, it would be trespassing on you to say one word more than to give the toast, and I hope that my fair hearers will believe me when I say, that never had they a truer, or a warmer, or a more gallant lover than the one that addresses them." (Loud cheers.)

SAM SLICK'S SPEECH AT THE BURNS CENTENNIAL IN GLASGOW.

At the great Burns Centennial at Glasgow, Judge Haliburton (Sam Slick) was called upon to read the following toast: "*The Scottish Clergy.*" In doing so he said, "I have accepted the invitation to appear here to-night with peculiar pleasure. A hundred and fifty years have elapsed since my family left the borders of Scotland to seek their fortune in the wilds of America, and I am the first of that family that has made his appearance in his fatherland—(cheers)—and that you have been so good as to call me hear to-night, as your guest, overpowers me in a way that I cannot well express. I have been honored by being requested to propose a toast, which, I am sure, every one who hears me will receive with a most cordial and affectionate response, since it is the clergy of Scotland. When it was first proposed to me to give this toast, I confess that I was considerably embarrassed. It did not appear to me particularly appropriate that so venerable, so pious, so zealous, and so learned a body as the Church of Scotland should be given by the humble author of Sam Slick. (Laughter and loud cheers.) I thought perhaps that it might have been given more appropriately by one nearer home, and better able to do justice to such a subject; but a moment's reflection taught me that nothing was required of me but to propose it, because it was a toast that spoke for itself, as the clergy had their bond of union with the country in the feelings, and sympathies, and hearts of the people. Nothing, therefore, remained for me to do but to propose it, for their eulogium is like that beautiful inscription, sublime from its simplicity, in the crypt of St. Paul's Cathedral—the inscription to the immortal architect who raised it—*si monumentum quæris, circumspice.* (Cheers.) In like manner, the eulogium of the clergy of Scotland is best found in the character of its people, in the institutions they have fostered, in that comprehensive system of education they have encouraged, which has made Scotland preëminent among the nations. Having said thus much, I should feel that I have done all that is required of me; but the clergy of the Church of Scotland are not the whole Scottish clergy, for there is a very large body of Scottish clergymen whom they have sent abroad, as learned, as pious, as laborious, as self-denying, and as useful as any, in British North America." The Hon. Judge proceeded to describe the arduous labors and trials of the Scottish clergy in the vast territory of British North America, covering as it did a ninth part of the surface of the globe, and proceeded to say, "It is easy to draw delusive pictures, as I saw one drawn the other day by a skilful artist, who, addressing the working-classes of Glasgow, bade them go to a country where they would have a vote in the representation, with the safeguard of the ballot-box, where there were no taxes, and where they would have a happier home in the wilderness. These are such very pretty pictures, that it is a pity they are fancy sketches, and not realities. (Laughter and cheers.) The poor settler that goes to that country, you hear from when he succeeds; but do you ever hear from the hundreds who perish by the way, who carry a broken heart, broken hopes, and a broken constitution to the grave? You hear not from them: all you know is, that they have gone to America, and that they have not written, or that their letters have not reached you.

"I am delighted to see here the venerable and learned head of the University of Glasgow—a university so renowned throughout the world, which has produced so many statesmen, poets, judges, lawyers, and able men; and I am delighted also to see the Rev. Dr. M'Leod, whose acquaintance I had the honor and pleasure of making on the other side of the Atlantic, where the amenities of his manner, and the eloquence of his pulpit oratory will long be remembered by the population through whom he passed. (Cheers.) I am delighted to see him here, further, because he can bear witness that wherever there are Scottish clergymen, you find under their care a body of men distinguished for moral and religious feeling, for frugality, industry, and general respectability. (Cheers.) I am glad to see them, further, because it tells me that by the end of a century there has been time enough to weave that cloak of charity which we are told covers a multitude of sins. (Cheers.) If that cloak had not been woven by this time, I would think little of the clerical or lay weavers of Glasgow. I beg leave to propose to you *The Scottish Clergy, present and absent, those here and those in North America.*"

SPEECH ON HONEST DRINKING.

At a dinner-party of deep drinkers in Cleveland, Ohio, the following toast was proposed: "*To all honest drinkers.*" A gentleman of New York, who was present, remarked, that the phrase *honest drinker* was a westernism, which he supposed meant a man who filled every time the bottle went round, and who drank to the bottom of his glass at every round. This, he declared, as a test of honesty and good-fellowship, was not quite fair, as the quantity of liquor a man could drink depended somewhat upon the size of his stomach.

A man cannot well drink more liquor than he can hold—unless he be a Dutchman, who is supposed to hold an uncomputable amount; at least he had heard of one who was capable of containing eight hundred cubic inches more of lager-beer than the measurement of his whole body! He was, some years ago, with a party of New York politicians at a State Convention at Syracuse, where they drank steadily from nine in the evening until four the next morning. The beer was served in those high glasses which are about ten inches in length, and he estimated that the party of eight persons contained about four thousand six hundred and ninety-eight feet of lager. But he confessed that he began to entertain conscientious scruples against keeping such imbibing company much longer. He doubted if this 'honest drinking' was a very *honest* thing after all. He was not sure if any one man had a right to consume so much of life's good stuff. For his part, he was more inclined to the opinion of king James I., who, when a fellow was brought to him as a curiosity because he could eat a whole sheep at a meal, asked, "What else can he do more than other men?" "Nothing," was the reply. "Hang him, then," said the king, "for it is a pity a man should live who eats the share of twenty men, and can do no more than one."

This little speech, altogether, was pleasant and humorous, and the anecdote of king James and the sheep-eater produced so decided a laugh that it was impossible for the gentleman to do better than to stop there. Had he attempted to make an application of the anecdote to the company, all the humor would have evaporated. The application was too palpable to need explanation.

SPEECH OF A POET.

At a dinner-party of literary men in New York, a young versifier, who was perpetually talking about the '*art* of poetry," and who had often been engaged in controversy with a gentleman who was at the table, in relation to the comparative merits of *art* and *nature* in poetry, offered the following toast: " *The art of poetry —may poets never forget that it is an art.* The gentleman, who was known to be an advocate for *nature*, was called upon to respond. He said that he felt his inability to do justice to the toast. He realized that true poetry was something beyond *art*. If it was only an *art*, it was, comparatively, an easy thing to be a poet—a little book of a hundred pages might contain it all, and the ten thousand ambitious versifiers, who vainly try to scale the Parnassian heights, might then really make themselves poets. But alas, to write good verses and to write good poetry is not necessarily to do the same thing. The verses, so far as *art* is concerned, may be very good, and the poetry very bad. It is well for the poet to use art, but it is not well to let art use him: if he does, it will soon enough use him up. How long will it be before *art* will produce such songs as " John Anderson my Jo, John," and "Woodman, spare that tree"?—when the evanescent meteors that fall through the damp darkness of night become fixed stars in the heavens! To be a poet, a man must be something more than a good philosopher, good historian, good grammarian, or good rhetorician—he must know the very inmost recesses of nature, represent the passions in all their intricate and various windings, and want nothing that humanity is capable of receiving. In him, as in a mirror, nature shows herself. The most of what is called *art* in poetry is a distortion of nature. "Fie, my friend! Could a poet paint the glories of the rising sun by looking at it through a smoked glass?" It is given to no man to view nature with the eye of a poet, except the man whom nature has made a poet; and no man was ever a poet who viewed her, as Dryden expresses it, "through the spectacles of books." The *vis poetica*, or "fine frenzy," as Shakespeare calls it, was never born of books. A hundred years ago a poet came out from behind his plow on the mountainside, above the banks of the Doon, in Scotland, and, defying the disadvantages of writing in a rude northern dialect, sung such songs as the world has been glad enough to listen to ever since. What could art do for a genius like that? The *art* that he used was born in him. Nature spoke to him in her own language, and he uttered what she told him, as best he could, in the unadorned simplicity of nature herself. When art makes a Robert Burns, it will be time enough to read this toast. No, gentlemen, let us give up this foolishness of persuading all the drudging students of Iambics and Spondees that they are poets. The ancients held poetry to be the language of their gods —let us not degrade it by admitting it to be the language of mere rhetoricians and verse-mongers. Let us believe something better of the God-gift than to say he has it who only writes some verses, and runs away with his neighbor's wife. To be a *poet* is to stand in the inner temple of nature and see how the world is made! It is to hear whispers from the sky, and converse alone, face to face, with the angel forms of truth.

Tell me not that this sallow-visaged fellow, who comes this way, with a face " thatched all over with impudence "—this mere word-juggler and rhyme-gingler —is a poet. He has disowned nature, and nature disowns him. The Greeks called their poets *creators*, and in England, as late as Ben Jonson's day, the bard was called "*the maker.*" And this was not understood to mean a mere maker of *rhymes* and *mischief*, but a sublime creative genius, who was supposed to approach nearer than any other mortal to the creative power of divinity. The office of the poet is thus set forth by Hesiod:

> "Tis ours to speak the Truth in language plain,
> Or give the face of Truth to what we feign."

All the great poets of antiquity regarded the ability to do this as an INSPIRATION, rather than an *art*. Cicero called it "*Mentis visibus, excitara divino spiritu afflati.*" And this intellectual enthusiasm, this spiritual and divine afflatus is what *art* can never teach. But there is a sense in which art belongs to poetry, and in which the poet must use art to transmit, in pleasing forms, the sublime and beautiful ideas that are flashing through his brain. But the way that " God-made " and " book-made " poets employ art is as different as NATURAL from *artificial* flowers. The latter may have a resemblance to the former, but it has nothing of its *aroma*. The one throws roses on his precepts to conceal their harshness, while the other scatters his precepts in the midst of roses. The one gives us delightful images which teach nothing, and are, therefore, insipid, just as beauty, without sense, leaves disgust behind it ; the other puts truth into delightful images to charm us. His images are not made to instruct, but he puts instruction into them to please.

Thus, gentlemen, you may as easily know the true poets from their counterfeits, as you can distinguish roses, growing in their native fields, from the gaudy paper flowers which are hung up to catch flies in summer.

SPEECH OF A JUDGE.

At a public dinner in New Orleans, the following toast was proposed : " *The judiciary—may it ever remain the independent palladium of justice, and the sure support of the liberties of the people.*" A distinguished judge was called up to respond. He said that too great importance could not be attached to the sentiment proposed. Whatever tended to render the judiciary dependent upon the favor of individuals, or upon the varying caprices of partisan politics, was a step towards its depravity, and opened the way for assaults upon the spirit of enlightened liberty. There is much in the ancient history of courts of justice which may teach us to shun some of the quicksand upon which the judiciary barque is in danger of foundering at the present day. When Cleon was chosen judge in Lacedemon, he sent for all those with whom he had contracted particular friendship, and told them he must renounce all especial intimacy, as it was impossible that such friendship should not bias the mind and render it less stern in the execution of justice. When Aristides the Just sat as judge in a cause where the plaintiff, to prejudice Aristides in his favor, began with saying that the defendant always acted in opposition to Aristides, Aristides interrupted him, saying, "My friend, you forget yourself; state your case; for it is *your* case I am to try, and not my own." When this just judge, Aristides, once issued out a process against an adversary, the judges condemned the accused without hearing him speak, on account of the spotless character of the plaintiff; but Aristides himself remonstrated, and threw himself at their feet, entreating them not to wrong the laws, or do anything by way of compliment to him, which might be used as an example to pervert justice. Brutus put his two sons to death who had broken the laws, in order to show the Romans that the sword of justice should know no partiality. It is for this reason that the goddess of justice is painted as blind, with a sword in her hand, to signify that she knows not her favorites, but inflexibly strikes for the just cause. When the poet Simonides went to Themistocles while he was sitting as judge and asked him something that was not just, Themistocles replied, " Thou wouldst be an ill poet if thy lines ran contrary to the rules of art, and I should be an ill governor if I granted what was contrary to the laws." To dispense justice without fear and without partiality is the highest duty a mortal can be called upon to perform. And the less you make that high and responsible office dependent upon the fickle and selfish accidents of mere partisan will, the safer will be the liberties of the people.

SPEECH OF A LAWYER.

When "*The legal profession*" was given as a toast, a lawyer remarked that there was no profession which had been the victim of so many jibes and taunts as the legal. There is an old saying, that

> "No rogue e'er felt the halter draw,
> With good opinion of the law."

And he supposed that no man ever felt the halter draw, with good opinion of the *lawyers*. That might be the reason why lawyers had been so much abused. But it was certain that no other profession had ever contained anything like the number of great and just men that the legal profession can boast of. To go back to ancient days, Moses was the first lawyer of the Jews, Trismegistus of the Egyptians, Solon of the Athenians, Lycurgus of the Lacedemonians, Anacharsis of the Scythians, Numa Pompilius of the Romans. Indeed, nearly all the great names in the history of all nations were lawyers. And what would the history of our own country be worth if we were to strike from its pages the names of all who were members of the legal profession? Our Adamses, Jeffersons, Websters, Calhouns, Clays, were lawyers. There was a time in the early history of our country, when comparatively few were sent to our legislatures except lawyers. Compare the character of our legislation then with what it is at the present day. New laws now come upon us thick and fast, and quite as destructive of private and public property as the vermin that once descended upon the domains of King Pharaoh in Egypt. The Locrians ordained a statute, that any man who should offer to introduce a new law should come into the marketplace with a rope about his neck, and repeat before the people what new law he proposed; and, if not agreed to, he was immediately strangled for his arrogance. Now would not this be a good way to rid our country at once of the legion list of new and pernicious laws, and of the illiterate raggamuffin mob who make them? Think of the time it takes to qualify a man to become a competent expounder of the law, and then judge of the learning and wisdom which the law-makers should possess! The fearful extent to which law fails in this country is undoubtedly owing to the ignorance and partisan recklessness of our legislative bodies. The remedy which I propose, gentlemen, is, that our legislatures should have a larger infusion of lawyers, and a less number of tinkers and political charlatans. It is the legal profession which has in all ages shed the greatest lustre upon social philosophy and legislative science. Lord Bacon was a lawyer. So was Sir Edward Coke, whose sturdy opposition to a despotic king preserved the purity of the laws and transmitted them to us in his immortal "Petition of Rights;" and in his digests are decisions which will be lights to latest posterity! Sir William Jones was a lawyer, and so was Sir Samuel Romilly. Indeed, in past ages, as well as at the present time, the greatest and purest minds of all nations have belonged to the legal profession.

SPEECH OF A PUNSTER.

At a table of merry wags, a famous punster was called upon for a speech on *the morality of punning*. He began by saying he could easily enough prove the morality of punning, because all morality depended upon the just *punishment* of those who broke the laws; but, while he could do this, he could not make a speech—he never attempted to make a speech in all his life, and he felt very much as he should think a fish would feel out of water; in fact, it was a very *scaly* business in those who had forced him to try to make a speech." And then, fixing his eye upon a spot of grease on the chins of two or three of the party, he added, "it is especially too bad to expect a poor unlearned man like me to make a speech to such a body of learned Grecians as this." "What! we Grecians?" exclaimed several of the party. "Yes," said he, "some of you, at least, are Grecians, for I see it in your faces!" "Oh! oh!" cried the party, "that won't do—that is too far-fetched." "No," said the punster, "it cannot be very far-fetched, for I made it *on the spot*, and I am sure that it was not *fetched* farther than from the kitchen, as I could prove if you would allow me to summon the cook. But then I will not insist upon this, for cooks are, for the most part, a *saucy* people, and this one might take it into her head to give us a *taste* of hers; and besides, in this *summer weather*, the smell of cooks is not always the most agreeable." "This summer weather!" exclaimed the party, "how do you make that out in the middle of December?" "Why," said the wit, "from the very great number of *swallows* I have seen here I thought it must be summer." "So-so," said one of the imbibers, "you mean to *haul us over the coals* for drinking so much!" "Oh, no," replied the wag, "I would not do that for the world, for then *the fat would be all in the fire*, and, as this is only Monday, that would be cruelly anticipating the awful unlucky *fry-day* which you have such good reason to dread; I say to dread, gentlemen, for if your past career has been like your present conduct (fixing his eyes on the carcasses of a brace of ducks), you must have practised a great deal of *foul play* in your time.

SPEECH OF A WAG.

At a dinner of some of the merriest of the students at New Haven, when the hour was late, and most of the company had each "slain his man," or drank his full bottle, story-telling was the order of the night; and, as is usually the case at such times, the party was easily pleased, and applauded every story with the most uproarious laughter. But there was one serio-comico-faced wag who did not seem to find much to laugh at in the stories which were almost splitting the sides of all the rest. His noisy companions bantered him with being "stupid," and with having "no appreciation of wit and fun." To which he waggishly replied, that, if they would explain to him the *ponits* of their jokes he would laugh too. They reminded him of an anecdote of the student of St. John's college, in England, who heard a wit say to Archbishop Herring, as he happened to slip and fall into a muddy ditch, "There, bishop *Herring*, you are in a fine *pickle* now." The student went on to his school, laughing immoderately at the joke, and when his fellow-collegians inquired the cause of his merriment, he, still laughing himself out of breath, said, "I never heard a better thing in my life. Bishop Herring fell into the ditch, and his friend said, as he lay there sprawling, 'Why, *Herring*, you are in a fine *condition* now.'" "Why," said his companions, "where is the wit of that, pray?" "Well," said the laugher, "I am sure it was a good thing when I heard it." "So, gentlemen," said the wag, "it is possible your stories were very good when you heard them, but that was probably so long ago, that I expect the fun has pretty much all evaporated now. Fun don't keep well in some people —like wine, it easily spoils in bottles that are loosely corked."

SPEECH OF A WINE-BIBBER.

A famous wine-bibber, who was called upon to favor the company with a speech on "the drink of the gods," declared that no mortal lips could ever describe the joys of good wine. For his part, he was not rash enough to attempt it, but with the permission of the company he would recite Cowley's exquisite tipsy logic in praise of drinking:

> "The thirsty earth soaks up the rain,
> And drinks, and gapes for drink again.
> The plants suck in the earth, and are
> With constant drinking fresh and fair.
> The sea itself, which, one would think,
> Should have but little need of drink,
> Drinks ten thousand rivers up,
> So filled that they o'erflow the cup.
> The busy sun, (and one would guess
> By 's drunken fiery face no less,)
> Drinks up the sea, and when he 's done,
> The moon and stars drink up the sun.
> They drink and dance by their own light,
> They drink and revel all the night.
> Nothing in nature's sober found,
> But an eternal health goes round.

Fill up the bowl, then, fill it high,
Fill all the glasses there,--for why
Should every creature drink but I?
Why, men of morals, tell me why!"

A SONG INSTEAD OF A SPEECH.

Nothing enlivens a dinner-party more than an occasional song, especially when the company is so well warmed with wine as to become a little impatient at the restraints necessarily imposed in listening to speeches. Under such circumstances we once heard the following song sung by a western Member of Congress, at Willard's, in Washington :

"Do not ask me, charming Phillis,
    Why I lead you here alone,
By this bank of pinks and lilies,
    And of roses newly blown:
'Tis not to behold the beauty
    Of those flow'rs that crown the spring—
'Tis to—but I know my duty,
    And dare never name the thing.
'Tis, at worst, but her denying,
    Why should you thus fearful be?
Ev'ry minute gently flying,
    Smiles and says, make use of me.
What the sun does to those roses,
    While the beams play sweetly in;
I would!—but my fear opposes,
    And I dare not name the thing.

Yet I die if I conceal it,—
 Ask my eyes, or ask your own;
And if neither can reveal it,
 Think what lovers do alone.
On this bank of pinks and lilies,
 Might I speak what I would do,—
I would!—with my lovely Phillis,
 I would!—I would!—Ah! would you?"

SPEECH OF A SAILOR.

A facetious sea-captain, an old tar withal, who was asked to respond to a toast which was complimentary to a sea-faring life, began by saying that he "had not much to say in favor of the sailor. He is a quarrelsome fellow at best, who only studies to *dispute* with the tempests, and is of such a rank and brackish disposition that he is always in a *pickle* with his best friends. He is a mere time-server, too, always on the watch for a *fair wind*, and his ambition is more restless than that of a scurvy politician, for he is always *climbing* and striving to get above his equals. He is a self-contradictory creature, too; for, although everybody knows him to be *brave*, yet he is ever *flying* before his foe, and dreads nothing so much as to have his adversary *head* him off, and meet him in the face. And though his heart is as warm as noon in the tropics, yet the intelligence that guides his actions is so cold that it points only to the north. Though he is proud of his country, he is always abandoning it for other lands; and, although he is vain of his honor, he rides only a wooden horse into every port. But he is a hearty friend, a zealous lover, and will never forsake one in distress so long as he can keep his deck above water."

SPEECH OF A TAILOR.

In order to call out a witty tailor, this toast was offered: "*The ninth part of a man.*" He said that "to call a tailor the ninth part of a man was to make all other men a still smaller fraction, for the tailor is powerful enough to make even the *proudest* of men serve his interest; and he is cunning enough to *thrive* even upon other men's *vanities*. His charity, like the mercy of heaven, *covers* a multitude of sins, and his profession le**a**ds him, as far as possible, to *hide* the faults of mankind. Those whom nature has slighted he makes perfect. He has such an eye to beauty, that even in his *bills* he imitates the birds of Paradise, and is so virtuous, withal, that he turns even the *extravagance* of other men to good *account*. What indecent spectacles all men would be but for the tailors! What more can be said in praise of tailors, than the fact that they flourish most in those communities which are celebrated for their civilization and respectability. His profession, too, is the oldest on earth; as it dates as far back as the garden of Eden, where, after the devil had ruined our first parents, by exposing their nakedness, a tailor did all he could to *repair* the mischief, and make them as decent as possible, by ingeniously constructing garments out of fig-leaves. Finally, gentlemen, so good a man is the tailor, that if his yard-stick sometimes interferes with the rights of others, he does not selfishly confine the benefits to himself, but does all in his power to satisfy the reasonable wants of those who appeal to him for charity. He endeavors to *sheer* out of the way of sin, to *cut* bad company, and devote his life to the study of *men* and *measures*.

SPEECH OF A FIREMAN.

A fireman, who spoke in response to a toast to the fire department, said, that there is no profession in which everybody ought to feel a deeper interest than the fireman's. He is the city's sentinel, that keeps watch over life and property while others sleep; and if he should "kick the bucket," nobody could sleep in safety. The firemen are a volunteer army, who shed no blood and share no spoils, and yet they conquer the most terrible and *unquenchable* foe that ever a soldiery met in battle array. The "machine" is the most glorious piece of workmanship ever invented, for it preserves what all other machines produce. It "throws cold water" on *incendiary* strife, and *quenches* the *flames* that are kindled by malice and revenge. But for the fireman's *hose* even the fair ladies would not long have *hose* to wear, and that I expect is the reason why every fireman is so quick to obey the call of the *belles*. But, as I am no speech-maker, gentlemen, allow me to close by repeating this well-known fireman's toast: "May his coat be water-proof, his flesh be fire-proof, his bones be fracture-proof, and his *spirits* be *fourth-proof*."

SPEECH AT THE WEDDING OF A MR. GRAVE.

In the year of our Lord 1858, a Mr. William Grave, of Mobile, married his cousin, a Miss Melinda Grave, of some town in the interior of Alabama. After his marriage, and on his return to Mobile, he gave a splendid feast to several of his bachelor friends, at which a gentleman, celebrated for his wit, was called up for a speech. With a solemn face he commenced rebuking the party for manifesting such irreverent mirth on so *grave* an occasion as the one which had called them together. The extraordinary marriage of our friend teaches us the great lesson, that history is always reproducing itself,—for, more than a century ago, a Capt. William Grave, of the British army, married a Miss Grave, and a wag of that day honored the occasion with the following epigram:

"The graves, 'tis said, will yield their dead,
  When the last trumpet shakes the skies;
But, if God please, from Graves like these,
  A dozen *living folkes* may rise."

Now, my friends, while you seem inclined to be merry, I assure you that I feel like speaking reverently and hopefully of the blessed memory of our departed *bachelor*, who has found an *early* and an *honored grave;* and, what seems a contradiction, like the patriarch of old, was '*translated* without seeing death.' We trust that our worthy friend fully obeyed the sublime injunction contained in the closing lines of Bryant's "Thanatopsis:"

> " Go, not like the quarry-slave at night,
> Scourged to his dungeon; but, sustained and soothed
> By an unfaltering trust, approach thy *grave*,
> Like one who wraps the drapery of his couch
> About him, and lies down to pleasant dreams."

Gentlemen, allow me to propose a sentiment: "To the memory of our departed *bachelor:* peace be to him in the bosom of the grave."

This toast was drank with all the honors; after which the devout company sang these two lines:

> " Thou hast gone to thy Grave,
> But we will not deplore thee."

And then, we are glad to say, they went home.

SPEECH ON PRIZE-FIGHTING.

The sentiment of "*The manly art of self-defence*" was given at an entertainment, where, as there was no professor of that art present, a gentleman was called upon who was celebrated for his learning on almost all subjects, and for a remarkable faculty of blending instruction and amusement in his speeches. He remarked, that "it is very difficult to see any propriety in calling that art '*manly*' which is practised mainly by *thieves* and the most brutal type of midnight *bruisers*. If it is *manly* to be able to strike the hardest blow, then the jackass might bear the palm out of the prize-ring, for his *hoof* has a blow which may easily put to shame the *fist* of any king of the fancies. And yet, there is, at least, a kind of retrospective truth in the sentiment of the toast. In the early ages of the world, *muscular prowess* was the only defence upon which mankind relied in public or private war. At that time the *gymnasia*, and all the variety of boxing and wrestling institutions, were a greater necessity than our military schools are to us. They were established, not for places of brutal and vulgar *amusement*, but for the public benefit, and all the boxing sports were designed to qualify the youth for warlike exploits, and to make them successful defenders of the State. It was on this account that the greatest honors were bestowed upon the victorious combatants.

"The gladiatorial sports arose out of the barbarous custom practised in all ages of antiquity, of sacrificing captives or slaves at the funerals and tombs of their great heroes. The Romans, as they advanced a little in refinement, abolished this type of butchery, and commanded those thus doomed, to kill each other in gladiatorial conflict. Their first gladiators were either slaves by birth, captives of war, or malefactors, condemned by the laws to death. Thus the slaves and captives of war fought for liberty, and the malefactors for life. The éclat which followed the victors in these conflicts so intoxicated those in better life, that gradually persons of distinction were induced to enter for gladiatorial prizes. The tyrant Nero once compelled a thousand *knights* and *senators* in one day to grace his shows, and to cut, slash, and slay one another for his amusement. Modern civilization, or rather *uncivilization*, is indebted entirely to the English for raising from the dead an amusement which was born of barbarism, and died with barbarism. It lay buried for centuries, until the refined English nation happily accomplished its resurrection into the *prize-ring*. It is the refined English nation that now dictates the laws of this genteel and pleasant amusement, which, indeed, is practised nowhere out of Great Britain, except in the United States; and in this country it is confined to a few foreign thieves in our largest cities, and to the Congress of the United States. A gentleman from Virginia, and one from Wisconsin, lately attempted to revise the code of the congressional prize-ring, but without much success; and England—proud England—still remains the happy lawgiver to the gladiators."

SPEECH OF AN ACTOR.

A celebrated American actor, who was invited to speak in response to a toast to his profession, declared.

that it was impossible for him ever to think of his profession without experiencing mingled feelings of pride and pain; of *pride* at the glorious origin and early triumphs of the stage, and of *pain* at much of its later history. There is no profession that ought to command more respect and admiration than that of an actor; for there is none that requires a greater assemblage of all the powers of genius. To be a great actor, a man must possess the taste and feeling of the poet, the judgment of the philosopher, and the skill of the painter; for there is an art of coloring peculiar to poetry and acting, which, though in some respects it may be different from that of painting, is yet to be conducted by the same kind of rules. We require of each the same strength of tints and the same distinctions in the distribution of the brightness and shadows; the same caution in the softening of lights, and the same art in throwing objects to a distance, or in bringing them immediately under the eye. The actor, especially, like the painter, must be a master of this ingenious theory of shadows, the skilful application of which is, by an insensible gradation, to conduct the eye from the first and most striking part of the picture to whatever lies obscured in shades behind. Like the painter and the poet, the player must have address and precision to give the true strength to every passage in his part, and to convey the sentiments delivered to his care in their proper force and beauty; nor are these qualifications less necessary to him in dictating the proper gestures which are to accompany the expression, and in forming not only his countenance, but his whole person, according to the nature of the age, station, and character of the person he represents. What is an actor but a *painter of character?*—the tones of his voice, the expressions of his face, his gestures, and the attitudes of his body, being the lights and shades with which he accomplishes the difficult task of finishing his picture? What feeling, what taste, what imagination, what judgment, are necessary for so great an undertaking? Shakespeare was an actor, and in classic antiquity, men of the first rank in life, the masters of all the polite arts of learning, were often actors. Nor did some of their principal poets, though they were the first men of the age, think it beneath them to go upon the stage and take parts in their own plays. It was something to be an actor when Tully patronized the stage, and plead the cause of Roscius, and when Æsopius was sought after by the society of the wise and great.

It is not a place here to trace out the causes which have led to a decline of the stage; enough to say, that those causes lie outside and back of the stage, in the character of society itself. The stage is always what the popular taste makes it. Although it may exert a power upon the popular taste, yet popular taste is omnipotent, and exerts a greater power upon it. Financial success is the touchstone by which everything in life is tried. If the theatrical manager puts his pieces upon the stage in a style above the general popular taste and morality, he makes as great a mistake, financially, as if he fell below the popular standard. His object is to hit the middle ground, and to make his theatre just as moral as the average taste of society requires. To succeed, the door of the theatre must be built upon a level with the door of the church. The same people support the one that support the other. There may be fractions of society who fancy they go above, and other fractions who fall below the great medium standard of taste and morality; but it is to the *masses* that all institutions have to look for support—the *church*, not less than the *theatre*. And, it is undoubtedly more from a spirit of rivalry than anything else that the two are arrayed in such violent opposition to each other. It is a misfortune to society that this is so, for the theatre might be, and ought to be, an omnipotent support to the cause of virtue, by ridiculing and scourging the vices of the world. As a teacher and director of the popular taste, the theatre possesses every advantage over the pulpit, not only because it speaks six times as often, but every department of logic and eloquence is open to its use, while the pulpit is limited to the single range of formal and dignified utterance. A clergyman once asked Garrick how it was that actors controlled the sympathies of their audience so much better than clergymen. "Because," replied the actor, "we utter fiction as though it were truth, while you utter truth as though it were fiction."

SPEECH OF A RED-HEADED MAN.

At a drinking-party of merry friends, where one of the number was a man of wit and learning, and red-headed withal, the following toast was given : "*To the man with the most brilliant head.*" And the party to whom the sentiment was directed instantly rose and said, "I have to thank you, gentlemen, for the very great compliment of being designated *the brilliant* man of such a company of wits and scholars as I see before me. And I suppose I am indebted for this distinguished favor, in part, to the brilliant color of my *hair*, which has, in all ages, been held such a sign of certain mental and physical activities, that it has always been coveted and envied by those who have been less favored by Providence. In classic antiquity *red hair* was deemed an indispensable accompaniment to the highest gifts of genius and beauty. It was held by the classic poets to be the chief ornament of the fair sex. It was supposed to give a lustre to all other accomplishments in nature, and was so admired and coveted that every one strove to imitate it by art, where nature had not bestowed it on them. All the first eminent painters, as Appelles, Euchion, Melanthus, and Nichomachus, prized this color for the hair, in their portraits of fair and beautiful women, above all others. The *red hair* of the stately Sabina Poppea, who was held the most accomplished and beautiful woman in the world, in her day, was considered the chief ornament of her beauty. The great queen of beauty, Cleopatra, had her charms illuminated by this high tint of nature's preferences, as Lucian testifies in his Pharsalia:

> "Laden with pearls, the rich sea-spoilèd store,
> On her *red hair*, and weary neck she wore.
> Her snowy breasts their whiteness did display,
> Through the thin Sidonian tiffany."

Red hair was in such repute in Turtullian's time, and in the days of St. Hierom, that even artificial *red* was resorted to, just as people of bad taste fly to black dyes now. Publius Lentulus, in his famous epistle to the Roman Senate, written from Jerusalem, among other bodily perfections which he assured them were possessed by our Saviour, described his hair and beard as being *red;* and I recollect that one of the most learned of the Spanish theologians argued, from this color of the Saviour's hair, that he was undoubtedly alluded to in the following passage in the book of Isaiah: "Who is he that cometh from the *Red Land?*"

And, gentlemen, are we to suppose that the Creator's hand has not labelled his works correctly? Does he not *brilliantly* label the most *brilliant* pieces of his handywork? Do not the excellencies of the creation resemble the *red head* in the brilliancy of their *tints?* Is not *fire*, the most aspiring and agile of all bodies, *red?* Is not the sun, the sovereign physical majesty of the material heavens, clothed in the same transcendent brightness? And, when it puts on its most triumphant glory to greet the rising moon, and again to bid good-night to the departing day, does it not array itself in robes of *gorgeous red?* What is the color of the June roses? of the most odorous pinks? of the charming flowers that load the air with perfume in summer? *Red!* What are the distinguishing tints of the *rainbow*, hung in the heavens as a sign of safety to man? *Red*, gentlemen!

On the other hand, let me ask you, gentlemen, of what is *black hair* the emblem?—of the grave! of death! of mourning! It is the garment of cats! of crows! and is the color of mud! Among what nations do *red heads* most prevail? Among the intelligent Germans, the artistic French and Italians, the refined English and Americans! Where are black heads universal? Among the cannibal Negroes of Africa and the Tartars of Asia! Whoever saw a *red-headed negro?* except where the fellow's thievish mother found an opportunity to steal the color from the head of some white man! Nobody, gentlemen. *Red* is the color for *heads*, for *roses*, as well as for the cheeks of *maidens*.

This speech, of course, could not fail to set the table roaring, especially as the wit had been rallied upon the color of his hair.

SPEECH OF AN OLD LOVER.

A man, sixty years old, who was about to marry a young lady of twenty-six, was called out to respond to the following toast: "*The delights of love—may we never be too old to enjoy them.*" He said, "Age has less to do with the capacity of *loving* than we imagine.

At any rate, youth is not the period for the enjoyment of the highest and most substantial delights of love. The love of youth is like green fruit, which has not yet obtained its best flavor, and easily spoils after it is plucked. It is with the faculty of *loving*, as with all our other faculties, best when ripe. In youth the heart is too full of curiosities, vanities, adventures, and a thousand little weaknesses, to be singly devoted to any one passion. Love has to take its chance with the rest; and it is generally a great vagabond then, which spends its time roving about, like the discontented fairy, who no sooner found one flower than it left it to run after another, and so never stopped long enough to enjoy any. And then some are constitutionally devoid of the faculty of loving. They have not the tenderness and delicate susceptibility in which love delights to dwell. Their natures are too hard, and too selfish. They can love as the lower animals love, but not otherwise. The passion is a mere property of their *bodies*, without the sanctifying blending of the soul. It is an *appetite* which leaves nothing to be enjoyed the moment it is gratified. It is but one-half of love, and that the lowest half. It is a great *cheat*, for it cheats itself and its victim. One minute it thinks itself immortal, and promises to last forever; but in an hour it has vanished like a shadow, and left nothing but a little satiety behind it. But all this is less than one-half of that delightful passion which God has ordained to be the bond of union between two kindred hearts. The highest thing to be said in praise of this passion of love is, that it has never, and can never, be described. Language is too gross and heavy to define so ethereal a flame. It is like *light*, a thing which everybody knows, but which nobody can explain. An old artist tried to paint a *sigh*, but nobody ever attempted to draw the passion of love. We may say it is an expanded softness of the heart, drawn out and kept alive by a consciousness of sympathies congenial with our own! We may say it is like *bliss set to music*—where two hearts, like two exquisite lyres, strung to the accompaniment of one delightful sound, vibrate in delicious harmony. But all in vain! The greatest orator, the most enraptured poet, is incapable of describing *love*, as even the humblest swain may be capable of feeling and enjoying it. And this love, gentlemen, has no such tedious calendar of time as you call *years*. It is in the *soul*, and the soul is immortal. Instead of dying out with age, it becomes settled and fixed in the heart, like the steady light of a fixed star. Love in an old man is not like *hot fire* in the veins, burning up the blood, but like *wine*, coursing up and down through all the channels of being, like rivers of delight. In Knowles' play of "The Wife," there is this passage, descriptive of the supreme reign of love in the faithful heart:

Ferrardo. Lives he of whom you speak, in Mantua?
Mariana. In Mantua, he told me he did live.
Fer. What! know you not the place of his sojourn?
Mar. Yes, where he still sojourns, where'er he is!
Fer. What place is that?
Mar. My heart! Though travels he
　　By land or sea—though I'm in Mantua,

And he as distant as the pole away—
I look but into that, and there he is,
Its king enthron'd, with every thought, wish, will,
In waiting at his feet!

Gentlemen, the snows of sixty winters have fallen on my head, but no frost has ever yet touched my heart.

SPEECH OF A POOR MAN.

In response to the toast, "THE HONEST MAN, THOUGH POOR," a scholar and a man of genius said: "It would be a needless piece of folly in any man who should attempt, especially in these days of the triumphant reign of wealth, to eulogize the condition of poverty. And yet, in the days of *great men*, it was not always so. Aristophanes said, 'Poverty is the mistress of manners; and, severe and harsh as she seems, the school of virtue, in her state, is chiefly kept.' And Euripides declared that 'Riches bring on vices, but poverty is oftener attended by wisdom; and the most truly brave and worthy men were content with having only the necessities of their life supplied.' Aristides the Just was once the poorest man in Athens; and when his virtues and genius raised him to the highest honors, he refused the friendship of Calhas, the richest citizen in Athens, because he laid claims to consideration on account of his wealth. The poverty of Diogenes was the cause of his beginning his study of philosophy, by which the world has been rendered so much his debtor. Pythagoras was so poor that he could not afford to eat bread, but lived on fruit. The great Philoxenus was as poor as a beggar; and when, in consequence of his virtues, the Athenians sent him to a town in Sicily, where a splendid mansion, full of luxury and gold, was provided for him, as soon as he perceived that pride and indolence were stealing on his soul, he threw up all, and returned penniless to Athens, saying, "*'Tis better to lose all than myself!*" Cleanthes, the philosopher, was so poor that he was obliged to grind corn for his daily support. When Antigonus, the king of Macedon, was told of this, he sent for him, and asked him if he found the wonderful things he wrote in a millstone. 'No, my lord,' said the philosopher, 'but while laboring with my hands for my livelihood, the eyes of my mind are bent on subjects more sublime, and what I reflect on in the day I write down in the night.' A father asked Themistocles to which of two lovers he should marry his daughter—whether to a poor man of merit, or to a rich man of ignorance. 'Were I in your place,' said Themistocles, 'I should prefer for my daughter a man without money, to money without a man.' It is something worth saying, that nearly all the poetry, philosophy, and literature of the world, has come down from those mountain heights of intellect, where the heavy weight of gold rarely ascends. 'I wonder,' said a rich ignoramus to an author of genius, 'why you men of genius are most always so poor.' 'Charge the difference between us to our Maker,' said the author; 'for, had I bestowed the same attention upon making earthen pots that you have, I should have your money ; but no amount of application on your part could ever enable you to write my books.' This agrees with Dean Swift, who said that 'A man of wit is not incapable of business, but above it. A sprightly, generous horse is able to carry a pack-saddle as well as an ass, but he is too good to be put to the drudgery.' After all, gentlemen, much of the advantages of riches over poverty is only arbitrary and imaginary. Who will tell us how much better off the rich man is, who can drink *champagne*, than the poor man, who can drink only *cold water?* What are the precise advantages of broadcloth over satinet?—of a marble palace over a wooden cottage? Much of the pride of the rich is as conventional and as ridiculous as the vanity of the Khan of Tartary, who lives in a cabin, and when he has finished his noon-tide meal, which consists of such great luxuries as milk and horse-flesh, he orders a proclamation to be made by his herald, that all the emperors and kings of the world have his permission to go to dinner."

AN AMERICAN'S TOAST TO THE QUEEN OF ENGLAND.

Several years ago an editor of Philadelphia was in Montreal, Canada, when a dinner was given to the press of that city, and he received an invitation to be present. But when he arrived in the anteroom, he was informed by the friend who had been instrumental in having him invited, that an objection had been raised to him in consequence of his having, some two years before, recommended in "The Nineteenth Century" (a quarterly magazine) a plan for the invasion of Canada by the Irish of the United States, and of achieving its independence of Great Britain. "Very well," said the Philadelphian, "I will withdraw, then; but the article of which they complain was intended to ridicule the folly of the immense subscriptions then going on in the United States to free Ireland." A gentleman of the Montreal press, who overheard this conversation, immediately caused the objection to be withdrawn, and a handsome apology was made to the American editor for the annoyance to which he had been subjected. At the dinner, the first toast in order was, of course, to the Queen; and, as the last mail from England brought the news that her Majesty was expecting every day to be confined with a fifth child in the same number of years, the *Queen's health* was particularly a pertinent sentiment. The privilege of proposing this toast was allowed the American gentleman, which he discharged as follows: " Gentlemen, whatever prejudices I may have entertained against the form of the British government, I can sincerely say that I have never been blind to the truly *feminine* virtues of your noble Queen; and, with all my heart, I give you—'The Queen of England, beautiful as a star in one of the heavenly constellations; and, like the star, always in the *milky-way*.'"

It is needless to say, that this "palpable hit" set the table in a roar, and made the American all right for the remainder of the feast.

SPEECH OF A LOUD LAUGHER.

A gentleman, with a very loud laugh—a sort of Stentor-leather Lungs, Esq.—being at a dinner, where personal hits seemed to be the order of the day, was called out to respond to this sentiment: "*The blessings of silence.*" He said, "Being an honest man, and being ashamed of nothing, and having nothing to conceal, I confess that I cannot so fully appreciate this sentiment as you, gentlemen, appear to. Our appreciation of *silence* depends entirely upon what we wish to do. If I were about to commit a theft, or, what the present company will better understand, to steal into the bedchamber of my neighbor's wife, I have no doubt that I should pray for silence as a blessing to cover my deeds! All rogues have a great horror of noise. The bloody Macbeth exclaims:

"How is't with me when every noise appalls me?"

I have read of a thieving Jew, who found his *way* into an *out-of-the-way* hedge ale-house, where he found a rasher of bacon. Being excessively hungry, he thought he might venture on the forbidden food in this obscure place; but just as he was lifting the first bit to his mouth, a loud clap of thunder made him drop it in dismay. 'Here's a pretty racket (said he) about a morsel of bacon!' And that, gentlemen, is about as tender as I suppose all rogues to be on the subject of noise; but as you, gentlemen, are better judges of this than I, I leave the whole matter with your wisdom."

SPEECH OF A MAN WHO WOULDN'T FIGHT A DUEL.

A gentleman who had refused a challenge to a duel was at a dinner party, where the following toast was offered as a compliment to him: "*To the man who is so brave that he dare refuse to fight a duel.*" In response, the gentleman said: "I am of the opinion that accepting or refusing a challenge to a duel has very little to do with a man's courage. A great coward may challenge, and a great coward may accept a challenge, but it is certain that a wise and honorable man will do neither. Scipio Africanus and Matellus were as brave as any men that ever lived, and both of them often refused to fight duels. Theophrastus maintained that he who lost his life in a duel robbed his country of what he had no right to dispose of. When Marc Antony challenged Cæsar, the latter replied, 'My life is of too much consequence to my subjects to hazard it ingloriously.' And it is, I think, a dictate of common sense, that no man, who feels that his life is of any importance to his family or his country, has a right to run the risk of **throwing it away in a duel.**

If a question of honor is between two men, how does it settle the question for one to shoot the other?

"A revolutionary mob once seized the Abbé Maury to put him to death. 'To the lantern with him,' was the universal shout. The Abbé, with great coolness, said to those who were dragging him along, 'Well, if you hang me to the lantern, will you see any the clearer for it?' This wit saved the Abbé's life.

"When a Greenlander receives an affront, he gives notice to his adversary that at a particular time and place he will recite a satire against him; and if the other party does not appear and make some answer to the satire, he is regarded as a poltroon; and he who keeps up the *badinage* longest and best, is, by the numerous bystanders, pronounced victor.

"Now this strikes me as a more sensible way of settling personal quarrels than the one which is practised in the Congress of the United States. The only objection I can see to it is, that possibly it may require a degree of wit and smartness that our Congressional savages do not possess. But then, if thus challenged, they might get the same men to write their satires that do their speeches. Why not?"

SPEECH OF A PATRIOT.

At a recent dinner given at the house of a United States Senator in Washington, the oldest gentleman present was called up to respond to the following toast: "Our country and our countrymen." "The sentiment," said the venerable Senator, "embraces the highest considerations that a good man can wish to live for; and in it will be found the sublime motives which have devoted the lives of the greatest men to death. It includes all that is most blessed in the home of our parents and our children. Our country is *ourselves*, for we are all but parts of the public system, which constitutes the grand edifice of our social and political lives. The man who even dies for his country, dies for himself, for his children, and for the honor of his forefathers. And what are a few days added to a man's life, compared to the glory and progressive stability of those institutions which are to be the abode of all the descending generations of our offspring? Only as a minute compared to a thousand years. It is of little moment whether I go hence to-day or to-morrow; and every act of mine, that bears upon my country's weal or woe, is something infinitely greater than my life.

"When I was a young man, long before I entered into public life, the history of the noble Saint Pierre, who devoted his own life to save his countrymen, made an impression on my mind that has never, to this day, been erased. It is more than fifty years since I copied his last speech; I think I have it with me now, and I shall beg to read it on this occasion. You remember the history, gentlemen—that when Edward III., King of England, laid siege to Calais, that city made an almost miraculous resistance to the invading foe. But at length famine did what the arms of Edward had failed to do, and the inexorable Edward, in his wrath at the determined resistance which had been offered to him, resolved at first to put every man, woman, and child to death; but at length consented to pardon the mass, on condition that they should select six of their principal citizens, and send them to him, with halters about their necks, to be executed. When Sir Walter bore this terrible message to the people of the distracted city, who were all assembled in the great square, Saint Pierre, getting up to a little eminence, addressed the assembly in these immortal words:

"My friends and fellow-citizens, you see the condition to which we are reduced; we must either submit to the terms of our cruel and unsparing conqueror, or yield up our tender infants, our wives and chaste daughters to the bloody and brutal lusts of the violating soldiery. We well know what the tyrant intends by his specious offers of mercy. It does not satiate his vengeance to make us merely miserable,—he would also make us criminal. He would make us contemptible; he will grant us life on no condition, save that of our being unworthy of it. Look about you, my friends, and fix your eyes on the persons whom you wish to deliver up as the victims of your own safety. Which of these would you appoint to the rack, the axe, or the halter? Who, through the length of this inveterate siege, has not suffered fatigues and miseries a thousand times worse than death, that you and yours might survive to days of peace and prosperity? Is it your perverseness, then, whom you would destine to destruction? You will not, you cannot do it. Justice, honor, humanity, make such a treason impossible. Where then is our recourse? Is there any expedient left whereby we may avoid guilt and infamy on one hand, or the desolation and horrors of a sacked city on the other? There is, my friends, there is an expedient left,—a gracious, a God-like expedient! Is there any here to whom virtue is dearer than life? Let him offer himself an oblation for the safety of his people—he shall not fail of a blessed approbation from that power who offered up his only Son for the salvation of mankind. I doubt not that there are many here as ready, nay, more zealous for this martyrdom than I can be, however modesty and the fear of imputed ostentation may withhold them from being foremost in exhibiting their merits. Indeed, the station to which Lord Vienne has unhappily raised me, imparts a right to be the first in giving my life for your sakes. I give it freely, I give it cheerfully: who comes next? 'Your son!' exclaims a youth, not yet come to maturity. 'Ah, my child!' cried Saint Pierre, 'I am then twice sacrificed; but, no, I have rather begotten thee a second time; thy years are few, but full, my son.' Who next, my friends?—this is the hour of heroes! 'Your kinsman,' cried John de Aire; 'your kinsman,' cried Peter Wissant! 'your kinsman,' cried James Wissant! 'Ah!' exclaimed Sir Walter Maury, bursting into tears, 'why was I not a citizen of Calais!'

"The sixth victim was still wanting, and so many were the candidates who rushed forward eager for the glory, that it had to be determined by lot; and these six brave and virtuous citizens were led out, and died a sacrifice for their country's safety. What an example! and how worthy the admiration of all good men as long as the world stands! What a rebuke to the factious ambition of those who would distract and divide and destroy their country on mere abstractions and partisan vanity! Somebody has profanely said, that the race of great men is gone. I hope no one has ventured to say that the race of *patriots* is gone! And yet, when I think of history, I am frightened. When I think of what our fathers suffered, to bestow upon us such a glorious inheritance as our country, and then see for what baubles and abstractions many would recklessly throw it away, I am frightened. I can almost say that I have seen the glorious sun of our Republic *rise*, and I pray God that my children may never witness its *setting*."

SPEECH OF AN UNDERTAKER.

A merry undertaker, who had become rich by a diligent attention to his calling, was present at one of the sumptuous feasts which used to be given by the Ten Governors of the city of New York, and was called upon to speak upon this toast: "*The Undertaker*—may it be long before he *overtakes* us." "I can," said he, "heartily respond to that toast, gentlemen. I am in no hurry, for I am sure of the *game* at last, and can well afford to wait until you are better prepared to be *overtaken* by me than you are at this sitting. I speak to you *gravely*, and to you only on this subject; and I pledge you my word, that when I have *tolled* your sad fate to those who *follow* you, I shall make no allusion to your vices and dissipations. The undertaker is the most charitable of men, for it is his business to *cover up* the faults of mankind, and *to put to rest* a great deal of strife and wrong. And if St. Paul may be taken as authority, there is no better Christian than the undertaker, for to him *death is great gain*. And no man possesses a kinder heart, for every *passing belle* fills him with the tenderest emotions.

SPEECH OF A TALLOW-CHANDLER.

A witty tallow-chandler, whose profession was toasted at an anniversary dinner of one of the mechanic's associations of the city of Newark, responded as follows: "I thank you, gentlemen, in behalf of the numerous and *enlightened* members of the profession which you have toasted. We are a merry set of fellows, who continue to *make light work* of even the heaviest duties of life. None are more amiable and fascinating, especially to the ladies, than we, for we never fail to have *a melting way*, however cold and ungenial the whole world around us may be. We, too, practise the Christian virtues, and were never known, even in the most profane and infidel times, to *hide our candle under a bushel*. We send a hospitable guide to the bewildered traveller, to show him the way through the darkness of night. We enable the philosopher to pursue his studies, whenever the sun of heaven fails him. When darkness covers the earth, we send thousands of suns into the gloomy abodes of men. The king and the beggar are alike dependent upon us; and it is we who have the honor and happiness to light millions of beautiful girls to bed every night of their lives. But I must stop this, gentlemen, or you will all be rushing into the profession, and spoil the business. And if you were to, you would not find us—like the members of other over-crowded professions—gloomy and morose, for we should *make light* of our misfortunes, and still toil on, endeavoring to *throw light* upon the darkest hour of adversity."

SPEECH OF A SHOEMAKER.

In response to this toast—" The Shoemaker—may he stick to his last, and may his customers stick to him,"—a member of the craft said: "There is every reason in the world why his customers should *stick* to him, not only because he is generally well *waxed*, but because they are under the strongest obligations to him for the good condition of their *understandings*. Men's very *soles* have to look to the shoemaker for protection and salvation. It is he who helps men to become wise, by impressing them with the everlasting truth of such immortal maxims as, 'a stitch in time saves nine.' It is he who enables men to go abroad, amid the snows of winter, and over the burning sands of summer. How fatally would all the social and commercial intercourse among men be interrupted, if not entirely destroyed, but for the shoemaker! The philosopher, the poet, the statesman, the hero, the beautiful maiden, all ranks and conditions in life— from the king to the beggar—pay tribute to the skill and industry of the shoemaker. He is one of the most useful, as well as ornamental, members of society. While the importance of all other trades may be computed by inches, his is reckoned by *feet*. And when all other trades fail, his will survive, for at the end of the world the shoemaker will be the *last* man."

SPEECH OF A MUSICIAN.

A musician, who was called upon at table to respond to a toast, complimentary to his profession, said: "I thank you, gentlemen, in behalf of the musical fraternity, which you are not to consider as a mere ornamental and amusing profession, but as one eminently philosophical, useful, and instructive. No profession has been more wronged by public opinion than ours, which is regarded as vain, idle, reckless, envious, and unprincipled. But, to the direct contrary of all this, the musician is one of the most industrious men in the world, always endeavoring to *lose no time;* and so prudent, withal, that he *keeps time*, which everybody else allows to keep them. He is so honest, that he will do every thing in his power to make every *note* of his good; and so benevolent, that he will sacrifice his own ease to establish *harmony* among men, and *bar* out *discord* from the family circle. He is the only man who can get *crotchets in his head*, without destroying his practical usefulness. Our childhood's primer taught us that—

> 'Time cuts down all,
> Both great and small.'

And the voice of experience has said, that 'Time conquers all,'—all but the musician, gentlemen, but he *beats time*. And although he often proves a *thorough-bass fellow*, yet that is of *minor* importance, since his good qualities are *major*."

SPEECH OF A POLITE MAN.

A gentleman who was called upon to speak upon a toast in favor of politeness, for some time remained silent, while the party continually cried, Speech! speech! At length he said: "Gentlemen, we shall better show our appreciation of the sentiment of the toast by silence than by speaking. Politeness requires that we shall talk no more than is necessary, and that we should, on all occasions, make the least possible display and ceremony. When Louis XIV. was told that Lord Stair, the English ambassador to the French court, was the best bred man in Europe, he said, 'I will put his politeness to the test;' and asking Lord Stair to take an airing with him, he desired him to walk on ahead and enter the royal carriage first. Lord Stair obeyed. 'The world is right,' said the king, 'in the character it has given of this nobleman; a person less polite than he would have teased me with ceremony.' I can say nothing, gentlemen, that will add to this test of true politeness laid down by the *grand monarque*. In true politeness there is the least possible pretension, ceremony, or display. Every thing is done to make people at ease and satisfied, and nothing that can have a tendency to disquiet and displease. It is the easiest thing in the world for a man or woman, with a good heart, to be polite, but no amount of art and education can ever make a bad-hearted and ill-natured person truly so."

SPEECH OF A LACONIC MAN.

A gentleman remarkable for his brevity was toasted in this manner: "To the man who says the best things in the fewest words." He said: "Gentlemen, I thank you," and took his seat. But the party clamorously cried "A speech! a speech!" "No," said he, "gentlemen, brevity, like great deeds, does not tolerate much speaking. History gives us memorable examples. When William the Conqueror set his foot on English ground, he burned his ships and cried: 'Soldiers, behold your country!' Henry IV. of France was about as brief. On going into battle he said to his troops:

'I am your king; you are Frenchmen; behold the enemy.' At the great naval engagement at Trafalgar, Nelson said: 'England expects every man to do his duty.' Napoleon's speech to his army in Egypt was: 'Soldiers, forty centuries look down upon you from the tops of these pyramids.' The great Roman's bulletin of the battle he had won was: 'I came, I saw, I conquered.' King Henry IV. once met an ecclesiastic, to whom he said: 'Whence do you come? Where are you going? What do you want?' The ecclesiastic replied instantly: 'From Bourges—to Paris—a benefice.' 'You shall have it,' replied the monarch. But, gentlemen, let me not spoil your excellent toast by prolix illustrations. I have done."

SPEECH OF A COOK.

A celebrated cook, who had also some pretensions to learning, and was a good deal of a wag withal, was called upon to speak to a toast in praise of his profession. He said: " Gentlemen, the cook's profession is one of which any man may be justly proud, for the most distinguished men of all ages have expended their best *taste* upon it. Nearly all the celebrated wits of the age of Louis XIV. were excellent cooks, and were prouder of their skill in compounding sauces than they were of their literary fame. Boileau was a famous cook; so was Sir Humphry Davy. Talleyrand was quite as proud of being a great cook as he was of being a great statesman. Lord Byron pronounced Gouthier d'Andernach the greatest man of his age, because he invented, in less than ten years, seven cullises, nine ragouts, thirty-one sauces, and twenty-one soups. A celebrated member of the French Academy said: 'I regard the discovery of a dish as a far more interesting event than the discovery of a star; for we have always stars enough, but can never have too many dishes; and I shall not regard the sciences as sufficiently honored until I see a cook in the first class in the institute.' The great Earl of Peterborough was quite as fond of cooking as he was of war. It was his custom to assist in preparing the feast over which he was to preside; and when at Bath, he was often seen in the streets, in his blue ribbon and star, carrying a chicken in his hand, and perhaps a cabbage under each arm. I have often seen Alexander Dumas presiding over the smoking viands of his kitchen in Paris. Voltaire had so much respect for a good cook, that the worst thing he could say of an enemy was to call him *fricasseur!—a mean cook.* Men of genius in all ages have held the gastronomic science in greatest respect. Shakespeare must have been a famous cook, especially of beefsteaks, as we infer from the following excellent receipt for cooking one, which he puts into the mouth of one Macbeth, a well-known butcher of Scotland, in the time of King Duncan:

"'If it were *done,* when *'tis done,* then 'twere well
It were *done quickly.*'"

SPEECH ON SCANDAL.

When the following toast was proposed, "To the man who thinks the most good, and speaks the least ill of his neighbors," a gentleman remarked that a good man rarely *thinks* ill of his neighbor, and the well-bred man *never speaks* ill of him. Scandal is too mean a vice to find a place anywhere but in the meanest soul. It is generally the companion of ignorance and self-conceit. Those who are guilty of it, seldom have any correct idea of right or wrong, but censure indiscriminately everything in others which they do not possess themselves. For this reason the good and wise are as apt as any others to be the victims of it. Seneca said, "It is enough for a man to have an exalted virtue to draw on him a deep weight of scandal and detraction."

Demosthenes observed, that "Ill tongues are busy only with those who deserve praise; but as a worthless person is beneath scandal, all truly meritorious people may feel themselves to be above its reach." It was singular advice which Demaratus gave his friend when about to marry, to make choice of one for his wife who was most generally spoken ill of by her own sex. Slanderers generally betray the vices which they are inclined to themselves, by the faults which they suspect in others. The horse-thief naturally suspects the man he meets by the wayside to be a *horse-thief*; the liar believes no man's word, and the woman of impure thoughts suspects the chastity of every other woman. I have a friend who lately came near marrying a young lady who possessed considerable beauty and accomplishment, but she knew so much ill of her neighbors, and had such a horror of unchaste women, that she frightened him out of all his matrimonial intentions.

As good people do not speak ill of others, they do not make much ado when others speak ill of them. Conscious innocency is a door that shuts out all fear and anxiety as to their good name. When Philip, king of Macedon, was told that the Greeks spoke ill of him, he calmly replied, "Then it is my business to live in such a manner as to prove them to be liars."

SPEECH OF A MERCHANT.

A merchant was complimented with this toast, "*The merchant—may he ever be exchanging for the better.*" He responded by saying, that if the merchant's exchanges did not better himself, they were sure to benefit others. For it is the merchant who causes the chief value of all the goods and commodities in the world. It is the exchange of the fruits of industry that gives them their highest price. The farmer, the mechanic, the artisan— all are indebted to the merchant for the wealth and luxury which their productions bring to their doors. The merchant takes the farmer's produce, and the mechanic's wares, and gives him in exchange for them money, silks, sugars, teas, and the fruits of all climes. And it is this principle of *exchange* which so immensely increases the prices of all kinds of productions, that it is the mighty mainspring of the wealth of the world.

It was out of trade and commerce that the grandeur and freedom of the English nation arose to such gigantic proportions. It was trade and commerce that raised, by insensible degrees, her navy to be the master of the seas, and enabled her to leave the foot-prints of her civilization on every shore. It will be the marvel of posterity that a little island, not larger in territory than one of our States, whose only produce was a little lead, tin, fuller's earth, and coarse wool, should become so powerful by its commerce as to dictate terms to the civilized and savage world. It is not the nobility but the merchants of England who have made her what she is. A lord is a powdered puppet, who can tell you at what time the monarch arises and goes to bed, who gives himself airs of grandeur and state through an idle and gouty life, while the merchant enriches his country, dispatches orders to the ends of the earth, and perpetually contributes to the felicity and progress of the world. If our country is richer now than in earlier days, look to our merchants for the immediate cause of its progressive development. It is to them that we are indebted for the convenience of railroads, steamboats, telegraphs, the sinews of war, and the luxuries of peace. It is the merchant who enables the farmer to live like a king, and the mechanic to dress his wife and daughters in silk brocades. Nearly all the advantages of civilization over savage life come to the people through the hands and enterprise of the merchant. The phrase "merchant princes," therefore, gentlemen, conveys no exaggerated idea of the usefulness and importance of the mercantile profession.

SPEECH OF A SOLDIER.

A military gentleman of considerable repute, being present at a public dinner, was called upon to speak in response to a toast complimentary to the military profession. He remarked that the profession of a soldier, to be appreciated, must be looked at historically. We must regard it, not in the light of its abstract deeds of carnage and destruction, but in the protection it gives to the institutions of state and the rights of our country. As it was by war that our liberties had to be achieved, so by war they may have to be defended and protected. That has been the history of all time. It was by war that the foundation of the mighty commonwealth of Rome was laid, and it was by war that it was raised to its lofty pitch of glory. In vain had Numa taught her people the arts of peace, and its holy rites and ceremonies, if Tullus Hostilius had not also taught them the arts of war. Both the literature and religion of antiquity proclaim the warlike arts as descending from the gods. Jupiter himself was of little account without his thunder, and the disarmed Apollo was an object of commiseration. Mars had to be invoked to defend both Jupiter and Vulcan against the Giants. And all this was but a fable of what all history has been enacting ever since, and will continue to enact to the end of time. The giants still survive, and Mars and Victoria must ever be in readiness to meet them in battle array.

Lycurgus, the Lacedemonian legislator, thought the art of war so necessary, that he forbade the citizens to learn any other business, and continually employed them in the exercise of arms. And this he did, not because he desired war, but because the terror of men so skilled in the martial science might preserve peace in his republic. The greatest generals have generally been the most humane of men, carefully avoiding giving any more suffering even to the enemy than was necessary for the cause of victory. That great and terrible captain, Narses, who subjugated the Goths, conquered the Bactria, and overcame a great part of Germany, never gave battle to his enemy without passing the foregoing night in tears before the altar. The emperor Theodore, whenever he besieged a town, gave his soldiers orders never to open any battery against the walls until they had waited ten days to allow them time to capitulate. Washington, we know, was one of the most humane of men. The courage and greatness of soul with which the martial science ought to inspire the commander, naturally renders him superior to the low passions of cruelty and revenge. Sylla, Tiberius, Caligula, and Nero, were butchers, not generals; while Augustus, and Trajan, and Antigonus, and Phocian were as great in mercy as they were powerful in arms. The really great military commander is as anxious to avoid the calamities of war as that great general of the Athenians, who did all he could to prevent them from declaring war against the Macedonians; and when some who dissented from him in opinion, asked him when he would have them make war, he replied: " When the young men shall become grave and deliberate, when the rich shall voluntarily contribute to relieve the necessities of the poor, and when orators shall refain from speaking in public." I join the great Athenian, gentlemen, and pray that we may never be involved in war again until these impossible things are witnessed in our midst.

SPEECH OF A MAN OF HONOR.

At a party of literary gentlemen and merchants, one of the number, who possessed the reputation of being a man of the greatest degree of honor, was called up in response to the following toast: "*May honor and virtue ever guide the footsteps of ambition.*" He said: "The ancient Romans, having erected two temples, one dedicated to Honor and the other to Virtue, joined the passage from one to the other in such a manner that none could enter that of honor without passing through that of virtue. Many are the lessons which ancient history teaches us of the love of honor and the practice of virtue, which may be studied profitably by modern Christian nations. Julius Cæsar, in his youth, happening to see a statue of Alexander the Great, which seemed to have been made for him when he was about the age of twenty-four, fell to weeping, and said: 'How miserable am I, to have done nothing worthy of memory! and this prince, even at so few years, merited to have his figure perpetuated.'

"When Pompey the Great vanquished Tygranes,

king of Pontus, and took him prisoner, he restored him to his dignity and his liberty, preferring to make him a friend and ally of the Romans, rather than to carry him to them in triumph, saying, ' The glory of an age is more valuable than that of a day.'

"The practice of suicide, so common among defeated warriors in ancient times, illustrates the fact that they preferred honor and glory to life. And this was shown not only by male heroes, but was practised also by the women, who, like the chaste Lucrece, refused to survive the loss of her honor; or, like the beautiful Aminthea of Macedonia, who, having been caught in adultery, refused an offered pardon, declaring that she would wash away her guilt and shame in death. And how numerous are such instances at the present day, of fallen but heroic women, who prefer death to dishonor! It is one of the proofs of the dignity of human nature, that the principle of honor is, among all nations, savage and civilized, worshipped as a divinity. Their notions of it may, oftentimes, be erroneous and absurd, but the human heart everywhere bows to the principle, according to the light it enjoys. A savage negro of Guinea will be killed himself, sooner than give up a white man, who is a guest in his hut, to the violence of the mob.

> "Honor, that spark of the celestial fire,
> That above nature makes mankind aspire;
> Ennobles the rude passions of our frame
> With thirst of glory, and desire of fame,—
> The richest treasure of a generous breast,
> That gives the stamp and standard of the rest."

SPEECH OF A JESTER.

When the following toast was offered, "*May we never give way to melancholy, but always be merry in the right places*"—a gentleman, who was well known for his jests, remarked, that it is not easy to know for a certainty the right place for jesting. In the reign of Edward the Fourth, a citizen in Cheapside, London, was executed as a traitor, for saying that he would *make his son heir to the crown*, meaning his house, which had a crown for a sign. That proved a very ill-timed jest, certainly, for the innocent wag.

The temptation of a merry fellow to crack his jokes is so very great, that we must not wonder if he often cracks them in the wrong place. The greatest of men have often been jesters. *Dulce est desipere*, says Horace—"'Tis delightful to play the fool." Scipio and Cato were as frolicsome and full of jests as boys. Nor were they always so careful about the time and place either.

Jesting in illness, or at the point of death, is reckoned almost profane, and yet we have many illustrious examples of death-bed jesting; as Sir Thomas Moore, for instance, who jested upon the scaffold, in desiring the executioner to put aside his beard, saying, "It has not committed any treason." When the beautiful and accomplished Stella was in a dying condition, her physician, to encourage her, said, "Madam, you are certainly near the bottom of the hill, but we shall endeavor to get you up again." With great difficulty she could barely articulate, "I am afraid, doctor, I shall be out of breath first." These illustrious persons certainly did not think that, because we came crying into the world, it is a good reason why we should go whining out of it. If you ask me my opinion, gentlemen, as to the proper time and place for jesting, I should reply in the language of a famous old glee, set to music by Dr. Arne:

> "Which is the properest day to drink,
> Saturday, Sunday, Monday?
> Each is the properest day, I think,
> Why should I name but one day?
> Tell me but yours, I'll mention my day,
> Let us fix on some day:
> Tuesday, Wednesday, Thursday, Friday,
> Saturday, Sunday, Monday."

SPEECH OF AN IMPUDENT MAN.

A gentleman who was called out to speak in defence of impudence, said that he took great pride and pleasure in discharging the duty which their partiality had assigned him. He had good examples before him. Orators and men of wit have frequently amused themselves in maintaining paradoxes. Erasmus wrote a panegyric upon *folly*. Montague said fine things about *ignorance*, which he somewhere calls "The softest pillow a man can lay his head upon." But it is astonishing that nobody has done justice to *impudence*, since more than two-thirds of all the success in the world is due to naked, unblushing, uncompounded *impudence*. What is a politician, for instance, without impudence? A spider without legs, a gun without powder, a stomach and mouth without hands to feed them! "Impudence," says Osborn, "is no virtue, yet able to beggar them all."

> "For he that has best impudence,
> To all things has a fair pretence."

It is as useful in the professions as armor in a camp. Set the man of *wisdom* and the man of *impudence* to running a race for office or wealth, and see who shall come out first. To talk of a lawyer without impudence, is to talk of a body without breath. And as for doctors, Pliny affirms it to be "The prerogative of the art of healing, that any man who professes himself a physician, is instantly received as such."

How many a worthless, idle fellow gets a rich and industrious wife by dint of pure impudence? And, perhaps, it is well that he does, for it would be an alarming sight to see a *thriftless* man marry a *shiftless* woman! The impudent man faithfully follows that scripture which commands him not to hide his candle under a bushel; and, to be as literal as possible, the smaller his candle, the higher he generally holds it. Office somehow seems to stumble upon him, because he is always in the way. And then, gentlemen, as this is an impudent world, it will be found very hard getting along in it without a considerable share of the popular material. Impudence can be successfully met only with impudence, as is illustrated by an anecdote of an

Oxford scholar, who called one morning on another, before he was out of bed, and hallooed into his room—

"Jack, are you asleep?"

"Why?"

"Because I want to borrow half a crown of you."

"Then I am asleep."

SPEECH AT A MARRIAGE.

At a marriage dinner, where the following toast was offered, "*The present happy occasion*," a gentleman said, It is an occasion which brings happiness to all parties:

I. To our friends who are just married it is a divine time, when faith is lost in sight, and hope in fruition.

II. To those who have been long married, it brings back a memory of the blessed time when they were joined in wedlock.

III. To those who are not married, it carries their thoughts forward, in blissful anticipation of the time when they hope to be.

So all are, or ought to be, happy on the present occasion. I beg pardon; there is one class, which I trust, however, is not represented here—I mean old bachelors, that is, incorrigible old bachelors, who not only *are* not, but never mean to be married—malicious despisers of life's lawful sweetness, and contemners of the divine rights and diviner charms of woman. By the Roman laws, all such were punished as criminals, and were prohibited from holding any public office. Augustus

Cæsar laid a heavy tax on all who were found unmarried after the age of twenty-five. By the laws of Lycurgus, all the men who refused to marry were debarred from appearing at the public games; which interdiction was considered the greatest ignominy, and the greatest deprivation, too, for at these games the young and beautiful damsels displayed their charms in various feats of agility and gracefulness. Simonides said that the man who does not marry, shows himself to be so selfish a coward that he shrinks away from the most sacred responsibilities of life. So, if this famous old poet, Simonides, is right, the man who gets married is as brave as a soldier. In fact, he is so much of a soldier that he impatiently *flies to arms* in times of the profoundest peace, and is never happier than when he is at the head of the *infantry*. And this married soldier, being no longer sent to the *outskirts*, is fortunately kept on duty in the *home* squadron for life. Middleton, in his play entitled "Beware of Women," has drawn the following exquisite picture of wedlock:

> "I scent the air
> Of blessings when I come but near the house.
> What a delicious breath marriage sends forth.
> The violet bed's not sweeter. Honest wedlock
> Is like a banqueting house built in a garden,
> On which the spring's chaste flowers take delight
> To cast their modest colors; when base lust,
> With all her powders, paintings, and best pride,
> Is but a fair house built in a morass."

SPEECH OF A PUBLISHER.

At a convivial party, where the modern devices of publishers to get rid of their wares were made a subject of remark by some merry authors, a well-known New York publisher said, "Gentlemen, it is not for you to blame the 'tricks,' as you call them, which publishers sometimes resort to in order to sell a respectable edition of their books. If tricks have to be employed to sell books, it is the *authors* and not the publishers who should be laughed at. It is our business to make the most we honestly can out of an author's brains; and when they supply us with a respectable amount of that commodity, no tricks are necessary to prevent losses. Good books are always sure to find a large sale in this country; and there is no part of the world where the publishing business is carried on with less dependence upon what are called 'tricks of the trade,' than in America. There is a great deal of cant, not to say ignorance, in the talk about 'modern devices of booksellers.' Why, even in England, which has always been the teacher of the arts of humbug to other nations, the trade has discovered very little that is new in the science of pushing the business for the last hundred years. As long ago as Walpole's time, that great man remarked, that 'The manœuvres of booksellers are now equal to the stratagems of war. Publishers open and shut the sluices of reputation, as their various interests lead them; and it is become more and more difficult to judge of the merit of recent publications.' Does not this sound very much like our modern grumblers, gentlemen? When Simon Colinet, a publisher, in Paris, first printed the Colloquies of Erasmus, he threw off an edition of eighty thousand to begin with, and circulated a report that the Colloquies had been interdicted, which caused such a demand for the work that the whole immense edition was soon exhausted. Talk of the modern devices of booksellers! no, gentlemen, instead of these characteristic complaints, you and the public ought to be profoundly grateful to the publishers for the employment which they give to talent, learning, and genius. But for us what would become of men of talent? There is no opening for them in politics, for the political field is already crowded with pugilists, thieves, gamblers, and adventurers, of all conceivable stripes, and let a man of real ability dare to appear, even on the outskirts of the political arena, and the whole band of infuriated ignoramuses will make common cause against him. At a time when men of ability are not wanted for official stations, there is nothing left for them but to write books, especially since what are called 'the learned professions' are also crowded with *un*learned practitioners, who can afford to do the business at such prices as drive out men of genius and talent. Such men must write books; but what could the writer of books do without the publishers? It is the publisher, gentlemen, that keeps the intellect of the world moving. He diffuses the principles of civilization and science throughout the world, and enables the unlearned masses to instruct themselves with the wisdom of the wise and the virtues of the good. And there can never be any termination of the publisher's toils, for when he ceases his labors, Solomon will be convicted of an untruth, for he has said that 'in making many books there is no end.' This passage of Scripture also furnishes presumptive evidence that the book-trade was considerable of a business, as long ago as the days of King Solomon. It is an ancient and most respectable business, gentlemen, which not only gives the highest cash value to intellect, but it is the sole banker of genius, the founder and supporter of the mental currency of the world."

SPEECH OF AN EDITOR.

An editor, who responded to this toast—" *The editor, the defender of the rights of the people, and the right hand of great men* "—said : " Your toast stops short of the mark, gentlemen, for the editor is often a good deal more than the *right hand* of the great man,—he is his *brains*, too. Many a great man, who shines high in the firmament of political fame, was made by the editor. I have, in the course of my political life, made a good many great men, and oftentimes, I am sorry to say, I had only the meanest of stuff to make them of; and sometimes, when I had blown them up into fame, it took all the wind I could raise to keep them from collapsing and falling back into nothing. But, let me tell you, gentlemen, that this business of making great men is, generally, a thankless and an unprofitable one. It don't pay. Though the press is the mighty power that keeps the political forces of the country in motion—though it controls the fate of parties and of individuals, yet how seldom do we see the men who wield this power profiting by their own labors! Not many years ago there was an editor, of character and ability, who was a candidate for the office of a United States Marshal; but it was refused him, and given to an impudent ignoramus, a companion of thieves, and a pugilist. Many of the ablest men of our country have filled editorial chairs, to the great credit of themselves and their country, but in no instance have they been honored with a seat in the senate, or with a first-class mission abroad. Not long ago, in a debate in the House of Commons, Mr. Horseman addressed the following language to Mr. Walter, one of the proprietors of the London Times: "You combine in your own person the two most powerful attributes which an Englishman can possess, as a talented member of the legislative body, and the supreme head of the press which governs the world." The press of England has been honorably recognized by the Government of Great Britain, in appointing to the place of one of the Cabinet ministers, Mr. Wilson, the editor of the Examiner, a weekly paper of London. But the politicians of our country seem to be capable of appreciating the press only as a machine for elevating themselves into power and place. The gentlemen who are at the head of the political press of America are compelled to dance attendance upon a band of ignoramuses whom no gentleman would willingly invite into his parlor, nor even suffer to come within reaching distance of his hen-roost, if party considerations did not force him to it. And this state of things has operated most injuriously upon the political press of the country, by keeping, in many instances, gentlemen of striking abilities out of editorial chairs. But as it is, a considerable share of the intellect and respectability of politics must be sought for among the editors of the various partisan newspapers; although it must be confessed, that very many of our members of Congress are men of *striking* abilities, however much they may be wanting in intellectual respectability.

SPEECH OF A LITERARY GENTLEMAN.

A literary gentleman, of known ability, was called up to respond to a toast complimentary to his profession, and he remarked, that it must be confessed that the literary profession has become a sort of hospital for infirm humanity,—broken-down lawyers, doctors, ministers, financiers, and ladies whose husbands have left them, or who never came to claim them, frequently flocking into it, as the last resort for bread and clothes. But it must be confessed that sometimes valuable acquisitions have been made to the profession in this way. Hunger has in some instances proved a mighty detecter of genius. And, on the other hand, riches have often robbed the world of the brightest radiance of intellectual gifts. Anacreon once received five hundred talents as a gift from Policertes, but he became so restless with thoughts of what to do with it, that, after having kept it only eight days, he carried it back to the king, telling him that he had discovered that money was not worth the pains it costs the person who possesses it. The importance of the literary profession in our country is to be chiefly reckoned by its cash value. As a stepping-stone to political preferment, it is not to be thought of. Indeed, in that light, it is in a man's way. It is undoubtedly true that an idea prevails, that men of *thought* are not men of *action*—that the *thinker* must necessarily be deficient in practicability, and so, to be consistent, I suppose they infer that the less ideas a man has the better he is fitted to be a politician. But, fortunately, history sufficiently refutes this folly. Solon, one of the greatest legislators of antiquity, was also a great poet, and Socrates was a soldier, as well as a philosopher. Xenophon and Sophocles were as great as soldiers, as they were as men of letters. Alfred the Great, and Richard the Lion-Hearted, were as able in the field of letters, as in war and diplomacy. Both Dante and Machievelli were masters in politics as well as literature. The idea that literature and statesmanship do not often go together, had its origin in England in the days of darkness and ignorance in high places, when Dukes and Marquises could sign no other name than a mark or a cross to the most important documents. The elder Douglas thanked his God that no son of his, except the bishop, Gawaine, could write a line. But the most illustrious statesmen of England at the present day are men of letters, as, for instance, Lord John Russell, Brougham, and Gladstone. In France, in all ages, the greatest statesmen have also been men of letters, and the language attributed to Cardinal Richelieu, that "The pen is mightier than the sword," has found abundant illustration in the most brilliant periods of French history. The present emperor of France is an author, also. But, in America, it can hardly be said that men of letters have been recognized in the political arena. It is true that Irving and Bancroft once had a few crumbs thrown to them, and Hawthorne was sent abroad with a consulship as a reward for writing the only worthless romance which ever came from his pen,—the life of a president of the United States. It has become a common remark, that no really great man can be again elected to the presidency of these United States; and if men of literary ability believe in "the divinity of the maxims of the people," they will probably never seek for political distinction in our country, as long as "the governing classes" entertain the idea that learning and intelligence are not necessary qualifications for the politician and the statesman.

SPEECH OF A CAPITALIST.

At a party of so-called "Reformers," the following toast was offered: "*May the tyranny of capital, and every other tyranny soon find a grave in America,*" and a gentleman of wealth, who happened to be present, responded as follows: " In endeavoring to aid the cause of *progress*, its friends often throw the greatest obstacles in its way, by assuming extreme and untenable ground. For instance, what mischievous doctrines have been promulgated on this subject, as though there were a necessary antagonism between *capital* and *labor!* A class of restless and poorly-balanced minds have been made bitter and unhappy by being made to believe that there is really and necessarily some great wrong to labor in the possession of capital, whereas, precisely the reverse is the truth. Capital is labor's best friend, without which, indeed, labor itself is comparatively without value.

" What is 'capital'? There is no magic about it. It is nothing but hoarded labor. It is the result of all preceding labor, of which the individual, whether honestly or not, has come into possession. It represents past labor; and by that fact it becomes the remuneration of present toil. All money is but a conventionalism to indicate to us that so much toil has, by somebody or other, been already expended; and the party possessing money is recognized by society as having a property in the fruits of the labor which was so expended. Accordingly, from the very earliest times, the need of such a medium as money has been felt. The precious metals have no particular intrinsic worth, yet have, on various accounts, the recommendation of commerce for this purpose. As to intrinsic worth, if any one were to be left, like Robinson Crusoe, on a desolate island, he would find a hatchet of iron a much more valuable tool than one of gold or silver. But the proportion in which these metals are found, and a variety of circumstances, have, from an early stage of the history of mankind, recommended them for this purpose. They were used—even before governments coined them for money—by weight, as a medium of exchange.

"Nor is this the only form of capital. It exists also in the facilities for labor, formed by its means, or which may be formed directly by the agency of labor itself - in buildings suitable for carrying on different operations—the machinery which is necessary in multiplying the power of those who toil, or in cheapening the commodity they produce.

"The moment that labor realizes more for an individual than he deems needful for present consumption — the moment he begins to put something by, and applies that to the production of other results-- from that time he has capital in the world; and he would have it, though there were but one man upon earth, and he himself toiling day and night. Whatever he puts by as surplus to facilitate future operations—that, strictly and properly, is capital.

"The Indian who is disabled for the chase, but who has a bow and arrows which he lends to another, in order that he may bring him home a portion of the game he kills, is a capitalist. The farmer, who may have no cash in his pocket, but who has a loaf and a plow, and who finds a man willing to drive that plow, on condition that he may eat the loaf, is a *capitalist* in the labor market, and the plowman is his *customer*. Skill and strength are capital—they are the result of years of exertion, which has kept the muscular system in order. Bones and brains are capital, as truly as miles of dock and warehouses, fleets of ships, towering factories, or piles of gold. So that, strictly speaking, there is no person in the world but is, or may be, a capitalist, although he may be a *laborer* at the same time; and it is only in a broad way that we draw the line of distinction,---leaving on one side of it the great mass of those who toil, and on the other side of it those who, by their possession of sufficient means, take to themselves, or have bestowed upon them, in a popular way of speaking, the title of '*capitalists.*' The relation between them is constituted by the payment of wages. It is a bargain between the one and the other, in whatever form it may pass, whether merely for food, clothing, and shelter, or for the largest money-remuneration.

" We see, then, that this thing called ' capital,' which the ' progressive' journals of the day would have us believe is such a very wizard and devil, is nothing but *preserved labor*, without which there could be no reward for present toil, beyond the immediate supply of man's physical wants. Like all other great blessings, it is liable to great abuses in the hands of bad men; but to talk of destroying it on that account, would be like proposing to cut off a man's legs to rid him of a heavy pair of boots. To talk of the ' injustice of capital' because it *is* capital, is folly. To talk of *equalizing* it, is to talk of an impossibility. Equalize it to-day and it will be unequal again to-morrow; from the fact that, while one man *keeps*, another man *spends*. A silver dollar, in the hand of one man, soon becomes a gold eagle, while in the hand of another it becomes a copper cent. We see, then, how little sense there is in the philanthropy which is called 'taking sides with the poor man against the rich.' It sounds well, as all the other patent projects of philanthropy do; but if we examine it, it is without reason, and only *agitates* mankind, without proposing one practical remedy for the 'wrongs' described.

"The *dependence* between labor and capital is *mutual*, and all schemes of philanthropy which strive to draw antagonistic lines between them, wrong the laboring man, while they misrepresent the necessary force of capital."

SPEECH OF A BIBLIOGRAPHER.

At a party of literary gentlemen, where the conversation turned upon the subject of rare books, one of the number, who was known to be learned in this branch of knowledge, was called upon to respond to this toast—"*The wisdom that is in old books—May we never cease to drink at its fountains.*" He began by remarking, that their toast reminded him of this ancient verse—

"Fro out the olde feldes, as men saieth,
　Cometh all this new corne, fro yere to yere;
　And out of olde books, in gode faieth,
　Cometh all this newe science that men lere."

Old-fashioned as this language sounds, it is, nevertheless true, to an extent which few modern readers are prepared to admit. For instance, Mr. Ralph Waldo Emerson is considered one of the most original of all our modern *thinkers* and *writers*, and yet the student, who is familiar with the works of that old Greek, Epictetus, and with old Hierocles' divine book upon the golden verses of the Pythagoreans, will discover the fountains from which Mr. Emerson has drawn nearly all the beauty and freshness of his philosophy. In Epictetus, especially, he will find the very novelty of Mr. Emerson's style, which has been so much admired even by those who dissent from his opinions. I speak not this with a view to Mr. Emerson's discredit—so far from it, that I sincerely wish we had more like him, who have the learning and patience to drink from these ancient fountains of wisdom.

It is a happiness to believe that the students and lovers of ancient and rare books are increasing in numbers every year; indeed, there has never been a time when rare books and manuscripts were not enthusiastically sought for by men of taste and learning. But there have been particular periods when this remarkable demand for old books amounted almost to a *mania*. Such was the case at the close of the seventeenth century, when a desire of forming vast libraries of ancient books and rare manuscripts led them to search, not only the whole of Europe, but the East; and this was the source of many impostures and of some ridiculous mistakes. Some cheats, or ignorant persons, sent over from India to Paris a number of

Arabian manuscripts, in excellent condition, and written in a very beautiful character. They were received with profound respect by the *literati*, and were sold for immense sums to the enthusiastic bibliomaniacs; but as soon as they came to the eyes of scholars who were acquainted with the language, it was discovered that these *rare volumes* were nothing more than common *registers* and *account books* of Arabian merchants! There is no describing the chagrin of the *literati*, and the disappointment of the purchasers of these Arabian wonders. But the ever-inventive mind of the hungry authors of England caught the happy idea of forging translations from Persian and Arabian manuscripts, and several spurious books of this description were successfully palmed off upon the public. To such an extent did these impostures prevail, that when Sir William Jones published his translations from the Asiatic languages, he was obliged to take especial pains to prove that his book was not also a cheat.

Owing, partly, to the astonishing demand for old books in the United States, their prices have gone up in London nearly one-third in five years; and such is the present demand for them in Great Britain, that but few more really scarce works will reach this country, except at immensely increased prices. Hardly any gentleman in England or America will now put a new edition of a rare work in his library if an old one can be obtained. For instance, Bohn has just issued a fine edition of the works of Rabelais, which sells for two dollars, and yet the old edition, with the plates, brings readily six dollars in London. Bohn has also published a fine edition of Holbein's Dance of Death, at two dollars, but still the old edition sells quick at from six to ten dollars. A handsome modern edition of Milton's Paradise Lost can be bought for a dollar, but almost any of the editions published previous to 1790, are worth five dollars, and the *first edition*, of 1669, will bring from fifteen to thirty dollars. A fine new edition of Pope's Translation of Homer can be had for two dollars, but the first edition is worth from twelve to twenty dollars.

Col. Stanley's celebrated library of rare books, numbering only 1,136 volumes, which was sold at auction in London, in 1813, brought the immense sum of *forty-one thousand two hundred and thirty-two dollars*.

THE EDWARDS COLLECTION, which numbered only 830 books, brought, in 1815, *forty-two thousand two hundred and seventy dollars*.

And the famous ALCHORNE COLLECTION, of only 187 volumes, was sold in 1813 for *eight thousand eight hundred and fifty-five dollars*.

But I have known some curious instances of ignorance among the dealers in old books in this city. In 1852, I bought at a second-hand bookstore, in New York, a fine copy of Braithwaite's English Gentleman, published in 1630, for seventy-five cents. A copy of the same work is marked in the Bibliotheca Stanleiana at £4 4s. ($21.) Probably the learned dealer in rare books in Gotham gave some hungry man or woman about six cents for this scarce and curious book.

I knew a gentleman who bought, at a second-hand bookstore in Philadelphia, some ten years ago, a copy of the GOLDEN LEGEND, published by Wyllyam Caxton, in 1473, for the pittance of ten dollars. A copy of this scarce work was sold from the Alchorne collection for £82 19s. ($416.) Without any unkindness to Mr. Longfellow, we may say that he is not a little indebted to this book for the idea of his work of the same title.

One of the rarest of old books is "Sir John Froissart's Cronycles of Englande, Fraunce, and Spayne, translated by Syr Johan Bourchier, Lord Berners," from the press of Pynson, in 1525. At the Stanley sale this extremely rare book brought £39 17s. ($198 75.) A well-known literary gentleman, residing in one of the northern counties of the State of New York, had a copy of this scarce and curious work in a rare collection of old books, which he had been twenty years in collecting; but in a moment of misfortune, to protect his invaluable library from the grasp of rapacious creditors, he mortgaged his whole collection to *a friend*, who, having himself become embarrassed, soon conceived the idea of saving himself by disposing of said library. But when he broke open the boxes, instead of what he expected to find, viz., massive books glittering in their new gilt bindings, he was horrified at the sight of a lot of ragged, musty old books, which looked as though they had been thrown out with the rubbish from Noah's ark. He hesitated, doubted, looked thunderstruck; but not quite daring to trust his own judgment, he called in the bookseller of the village, a wise and consequential dealer in spelling-books and flash novels, who sagaciously pronounced the whole collection "*worth not over fifteen dollars.*" So here was one of the most curious private libraries in America, which had cost the collector not less than $2,000, knocked down, by the ignorance of a stupid bookseller, to the ridiculous figure of *fifteen dollars*. Although there were many books which were worth their full weight in silver, yet to these ignoramuses they did not appear worth boxing up again, and they were left open, exposed to the Goths and Vandals of a country village, where the contents of a rum-shop or a lager-bier cellar stood a much better chance of being understood and appreciated, than a library of rare books of the 15th and 16th centuries. And lo! when the literary gentleman came back for his precious tomes, they had vanished, nobody knew where, and had been used for—nobody could tell what! Thus was destroyed one of the most valuable private collections of curious old books in America.

But, notwithstanding such unfortunate cases as these, there is no doubt that there is, in our country, an increasing love of rare old books, and with this growing taste will come, at last, a genuine improvement in our own literature.

SPEECH ON ENGLISH BENEVOLENCE IN THE U. S.

At a dinner-party, where the speaking turned upon the benevolence of the English in sending funds for the aid of those who are poor and oppressed in our country, a gentlemen responded by saying that, under the circumstances, it was impossible for him to regard all such "*benevolence*" in any other light than a piece of *ostentatious impertinence*. He very well remembered that a portion of the American press was, a few years ago, vehement in its praise of the benevolence of Lady Byron for having sent a few pounds of ready cash to the people of Kansas. No doubt the cash was welcome enough there. The population of Kansas was at that time far from being a class of people that could well take care of themselves. A large portion of them did not go there, like legitimate emigrants, to earn an honest living by the sweat of their brows, but they were sent there to vote and to make laws. They did not go there to use the spade and the plow, but they were sent there to fight with Northern Sharpe's rifles and Southern bowie-knives. Bread and clothes must, in a short time, get to be very scarce with such a population. They were, for the most part, but little better than a secondary class of paupers at home, before they were induced to try their hands in Kansas at the voting and fighting business. Ready cash was, therefore, a great thing in Kansas, and we, too, sincerely rejoiced that an English lady found it convenient to help them to it. All we wished was, to have the gift called by the right name, and not to have it called exactly *benevolence*, for it comes much nearer to *fanaticism* and *impudence*. If the English ladies have cash to spare, there are the poor workers of their own country, crushed down, in dumb agony, at their own doors, perishing of cold and hunger, and drinking perpetually of a cup of want that no slave in America ever yet tasted. In the sanitary reports of the mining districts of England, we are made acquainted with a depth of misery which never before attracted the eye of civilized man. There he may see in rooms, fifteen feet square, two rows of beds, with no opening for air, where as many as fifty men sleep in sixteen beds, where there is not a flag or board on the floor, which is covered with small puddles of filthy water. Mr. Wood testifies, that in Lancashire he found forty people sleeping in the same room, where all decency and delicacy were lost in overwhelming squalor. He says the condition of the monkey-house in the Zoological Gardens is preferable to that of the laboring population. In Devonshire, his report tells us that families of six or eight sleep in one bed—father, mother, grown-up sons, and daughters. "I have found, he says, "that if a number of empty casks be placed along the street in Whitechapel, soon each will have its tenant."

A work, entitled "London Labor and London Poor," which has been republished in this country, gives us an amount of shocking detail of the condition of the poor workers of England, which the history of no other country has ever recorded.

"I attended the Garden" (Covent), said one poor man, "for a week, and lived entirely on the offal of the market." "I walked about," said another, "two days and nights, without a bit to eat, except what I picked up in the gutter, and ate like a dog - orange-peel, old cabbage-stumps, anything I could get."

"Oh, sir!" said a mother, "it is hard to work from morning until night—little ones and all—and not be able to live by it either."

Yes, it is indeed very hard to see so many English mothers starving to death, while the English ladies have plenty of cash to send out here to our robust, stalwart, fighting vagabonds of Kansas.

An English (Leeds) paper stated, that at an inquest it was asserted, and not denied by the surgeon, that three hundred children in Leeds alone were put to death yearly, to avoid the misery of their living, and the murderers were never discovered. Well enough may Carlyle thunder out at the Exeter Hall philanthropists, that "they would save the Sarawah cut-throats, with their poisoned spears, but ignore the thirty thousand needle-women, the three million paupers, and the Connaught potential cannibalism."

We in America may have many sins to atone for; but the English man or the English lady who sends his or her money here, as a charity to our oppressed, is a *good deal foolish* and *not a little impudent*, while the *American* that would ask alms of England for our poor or oppressed, forfeits his claims to respect while living, and to an honored grave when he is dead.

SPEECH ON GREAT NAMES.

A worshipper of antiquity proposed this toast: "*The great names of antiquity—May they be ever before us, to inspire us with a love of great deeds:*" and as he was no speech-maker himself, he called upon a waggish friend to speak upon it. "This toast is already realized," said he, humorously, "for the great names of antiquity *are* always before us. For instance, Cato keeps a sausage-stand in Washington market; Cæsar is a barber in the Bowery; Brutus is a pork-butcher's watch-dog in Christopher street; George Law has got Pompey in a stable on Fifth avenue; Nero is a parrot, which curses and swears in the back yard of a hotel in Brooklyn; Plato is a lap-dog, which is kissed and caressed day and night by a beautiful lady at the St. Nicholas hotel; Antony drives a fish-wagon in the nineteenth ward; the great Gustavus Adolphus is a sheriff in Buffalo; Alexander is a cook in Philadelphia; Cicero is a negro-waiter at Barnum's, in Baltimore; Horace edits a newspaper in New York; Hannibal is a candidate for the Vice-Presidency of the United States; Abraham, still abounding in faith, is running a race for a mansion in Washington, and John is travelling in the wilderness, hunting for the same place, while Stephen the Martyr yet lives in an ungodly place called Washington, which is adjacent to the United States. But, gentlemen, enough of this. I confess that I have a profound appreciation of the sentiment of the toast which has been offered by our learned friend, and I have no respect whatever for that narrow prejudice, which is based in ignorance alone, that considers the wisdom of past ages as of no importance in comparison with the achievements of the present time. The present is only a part of the past. All that our generation possesses is but the continuation, or natural growth, of what all past generations achieved. Had Greece, or Rome, or the middle ages, been other than what they were, we should not be what we are to-day. One layer of time has Providence piled upon another, for immemorial ages, and the first stratum in this mighty pile of generations is as important to the integrity of the whole as this last boasting present upon which *we* stand. We simply attest our own folly when we think the past generations of men were fools. Who hewed out the temple in the caverns of Elephanta? Who built the great wall of China? Who carved the great eagle in the Corinthian palace at Baalbec? Who lifted the masses of Stonehenge? Who reared the tower of Shinar's plain? Who built the pyramids of Egypt? Not fools, gentlemen!

Who wrote the Morals of Confucius, the Oracles of Zoroaster, the Fragments of Manetho, the Similitudes of Demophilis, the Laws of Solon and Lycurgus, and the Voyages of Hanno? Not fools, gentlemen!

Who were Pythagoras, Homer, Plato, Seneca, Aristotle, and Socrates? And who were Hessiod, Eschylus, Sophocles, Aristophanes, Isocrates, Lucian, Longinus, Euclid, Xenophon, Strabo, Plutarch, Herodotus, Demosthenes, and an innumerable company like them? Not fools, gentlemen! Ah, no; and how small are the greatest of us when measured by them! And what pigmies should we be without the wisdom which they imparted to the generations that succeeded them! After all our swelling pride, these lines of the poet are an inventory of the greatest things of which we can boast:

> "I am owner of the sphere,
> The seven stars, and solar year,
> Of Cæsar's hand, and Plato's brain,
> Of Lord Christ's heart, and Shakespeare's strain."

SPEECH ON THE POWER OF THE UNITED STATES TO LEGALLY ACQUIRE MEXICO AND CENTRAL AMERICA.

At a dinner-party of statesmen and diplomatic gentlemen, the subject of the rival interests of England and America, in the Central American, Mexican, and Cuban questions, became the subject of discussion. A distinguished English gentleman argued that America could never extend her boundaries in that direction without a breach of international law, which England would feel itself forced to interfere to prevent.

An American gentleman replied, that he was aware the American and English press had long appeared to be laboring with mutual anxiety in relation to the final settlement of this question; and there can be no doubt that a feeling of painful alarm has rested upon the minds of the more conservative people of both countries. And yet I confess myself unable to see any probable, or even possible, ground of collision between the two governments on this question. No doubt England would hate to see the States of Central America, and Mexico, and Cuba, absorbed by the United States, and it is a very great doubt if it would be for the health and happiness of our country to do it; but that we *can do it* without violating any law, or taking any step that England can rightfully object to, is very evident to my mind. Indeed, if our government pleases to be so unwisely ambitious as to treat every State on this continent as the boa constrictor treats its victims —slobber them all over, and then swallow them—England cannot, and dare not, seriously interfere to prevent us. Reasons as potent as those which made her finally hold her peace when we acquired Texas and California, would apply to every inch of territory on this continent, if we chose to make them. For it is not only the settled practice of the United States, but it is the rule of the English government itself, to acknowledge the *de facto* government of any country as its rightful government, without the least regard to its origin—without pausing to ask whether it is the child of long descent, or the offspring of recent revolution. England dare not quarrel with us for observing that rule; and, under it, we can safely acquire whatever territory may be an object of desire to us. We are speaking now, not of what would be wise for us to do, but of what we legally have the power to do.

A spirit of enterprise and adventure is the ruling characteristic of the American people, and it is not in the power of our government, if it were its wish, to prevent them from seeking their fortunes in whatever new fields may tempt their ambition. They may peaceably emigrate to any spot they please; may buy lands, or squat on unoccupied land; may multiply and attract others until they become an element of their own, and then quickly acquire a power that is necessarily in active conflict with the lower civilization of the country of their adoption, and which in time must result in *revolution,* and that is followed by *independence,* or the establishment of a new government—all of which neither America nor England can prevent. It may be sneered at as "manifest destiny," but it is *manifest destiny,* nevertheless. America has nothing to do but to acknowledge the *de facto* government, whatever its origin, and where and how could England interfere? The principle is one which England is not entitled to dispute. It is one which she has adopted and acted upon herself. And it is, moreover, a principle of unquestionable soundness and justice. Our alliances are with *nations,* not with *dynasties.* Whatever form of government a people choose, or acknowledge, that government is recognized as soon as it is *bonâ fide* established; even though it had its origin in revolution or usurpation. Thus England did not hesitate to recognize the South American Republics, when they threw off the dominion of the Spanish Crown. Thus, too, she recognized Louis Phillippe, as king of France, when the revolution of July placed him on his cousin's throne. So it also recognized that brief and abortive French Republic, which had Lamartine for its President; and soon afterwards acknowledged Louis Napoleon as Emperor, because he was so *de facto,* notwithstanding large numbers of his own countrymen, and the civilized world, persisted in regarding him as a military tyrant and usurper.

As a matter of international law, whoever becomes the governors of the Central American States, or of Mexico, or of any other States of this continent, the United States may recognize them, and thereby aid them to become permanently established, or allow them to annex themselves to us, and England has no legal right to interfere. She may bluster a little, and protest a good deal, but still we can legally go on, if we wish to, until—

"The whole boundless continent is ours."

SPEECH OF AN AUTHOR.

A popular author being almost forced up to speak, declared that he had no subject to speak upon, when one of the company said, "Why, speak about authors, and begin with a description of their modern wrongs." "And that," replied the author, "is precisely a subject on which I have nothing to say, because I do not believe there ever was a time when authors were used better than they are nowadays. Homer was a beggar, and Plautus died in jail. Tasso nearly starved to death, while Cervantes actually died of hunger, and Camoens ended his days in an alms-house. Bacon led a life of meanness and distress, and the charming

Spenser died of want and neglect. So did Collins. Milton did not receive as much for his Paradise Lost as a modern author gets for a shilling novel—he receiving for that immortal work but fifteen pounds, in three payments; and the great author finished his days in obscurity. Dryden lived in poverty and distress. Otway died in the street, of hunger. Steele's life was a perpetual warfare with the bailiffs. Goldsmith was no better off; and Fielding lies buried in a factory burying-ground at Lisbon, without a stone to mark the spot. Savage died in the poor-debtor's prison at Bristol. Butler, Churchill, and Chatterton were little better off. Colton, the author of Lacon, etc., blew out his brains in a fit of madness produced by absolute want. What a tale of poverty and misery is the life of Ben Jonson! Shakespeare, and the great authors of his time, did not sleep on beds of down, in gardens of roses. The bright and beautiful Shelley led a life of unrest and sorrow.

"Now, gentlemen, how shall we talk of the wrongs of *modern* authors, whilst these terrible facts are scowling upon us out of the past?

"The only reward which Theodore Gaza received from Sixtus IV. for his dedication of the Treatise of Aristotle on the Nature of Animals, was the price of the binding of his book, which the Pope generously repaid to him, and which the author accepted. Tasso was not more successful with his dedications. Ariosto, in presenting his poems to the cardinal d'Este, was saluted with sarcasm, which will be remembered as long as his works. The old historian, Dupleix, a very clever author, presented one of his books to the Duke of d'Epernin, and that nobleman turned abruptly towards the Pope's nuncio, who was present, and remarked, 'This is one of your breeding authors; he is delivered of a book every month.'

"Burnet speaks of 'one Prior,' and Whitlock of 'one Milton, a blind man.' And yet we cannot deny that Burnet and Whitlock were men of talents and reputation themselves. But we read in Heath, an obscure chronicler of civil wars, that 'one Milton, since stricken with blindness, wrote against Salmasius, and composed an impudent and blasphemous book called Iconoclastes.'

"One of those ignorant, but successful booksellers in Paternoster-row, who published things in numbers, went to Gibbon's lodgings in St. James street, and addressed the great author as follows: 'Sir, I am now publishing a History of England, done by several good hands. I understand that you have a knack of them there things, and should be glad to give you every reasonable encouragement.'

"As soon as Gibbon recovered the use of his legs and tongue, which were petrified with surprise, he ran to the bell, and ordered his servant to 'show this encourager of learning down stairs.'

"Now, how shall we complain of a want of due respect to the profession of an author, as a modern vice, when such authors as Gibbon could be thus approached in his time?

"No, gentlemen, modern authors have no reason to complain either of the publishers or the public. If the *publishers* and the *public* are willing to hold their place, my advice to the *authors* is, to keep quiet on this subject; unless they open their mouths to say, with Juvenal, *Periturœ parcite chartœ*—'spare a few sheets already doomed to die.'"

THE TOAST-MASTER'S COMPANION.

THERE is nothing in which men more conspicuously show their wit—or their want of it—than in giving toasts at public dinners. Some sparkling wit, or some fine sentiment, is always expected in a toast. A great deal of meaning is to be conveyed in the fewest words. As a rule, it is safe to say that a toast which is not embraced in a single sentence is spoiled by being too long.

In giving a volunteer toast, do not attempt to strain to be witty, for if you do, you will probably make yourself ridiculous. Not long since, a bright genius gave the following volunteer toast, at a dinner given to a New York editor who had just arrived from Europe:

"The health of ——, who like our own eagle slumbers amidst the buzz of insects, careless of what is passing until touched on some sore spot, when he flaps his wings, screams, and scatters them to the winds."

It is hard work to conceive how the gentleman, thus complimented, could enjoy the flattering comparison which makes him sleep amidst "*insects*," until some cruel wretch touches him "*on some sore spot,*" which wakes him up, and causes him to "*flap his wings,*" and "*scream,*" and "*scatter*" the aforesaid "*insects*" about him, until the very wind of heaven is lousy with his enemies.

In giving toasts it is better to err on the side of modesty, and do too little than to attempt to much. Wit is a sharp weapon, and a dangerous one in the hands of a blockhead. The moral of the story of the monkey, who attempted to shave himself with his master's razor, applies just as well in this place:

"Though others use them well---yet fools
Should never meddle with edge-tools."

It is best for a gentleman, who is going to a dinner where toasting and drinking may be the order of the day, to arm himself with at least one good toast beforehand; so, if the occasion fail to suggest a better one, he can fall back upon the one already prepared.

PATRIOTIC TOASTS.

Our country, our whole country, and nothing but our country.

America—The birthplace of liberty, and the asylum for the oppressed of every land.

The Union—No north, no south, no east, no west, but one and indivisible.

Our Native Land—May it ever continue the abode of freedom, and the birthplace of heroes.

American Commerce—May it be universally extended.

Confusion to those fanatics who conspire against the union of the States.

The next President of the United States—under his administration may neither demagogues nor thieves find place and office.

Liberty all over the world.

Free commerce for a free people.

Liberty—May it never degenerate into licentiousness.

Disgrace to the enemies of the Constitution.

Wealth, security, and resistance to oppression.

Obedience to the laws.

Our Judiciary—The sword of justice in the hand of mercy.

Disgrace to all malcontents, and a speedy end to all dissentions.

American Heraldry—An honest heart, *with* the breast of nature's nobleman.

May foreign fashions never corrupt American manners.

May the ambitious demagogue, who strives to dissever the union of these States, succeed in rising as high as the gallows.

The Fathers of our Revolution—May their sons never disgrace their parentage.

May our love for our country be without bounds, and our love of justice without fear.

The American Eagle—May she build her nest in every forest on this continent.

American Valor—May it shine in the face of all nations.

The American People—May they ever be blessed with political peace and domestic happiness.

May every American, when his country calls, spring forth to meet his country's foe.

The Defence of our Country—May our soldiers be quick to strike, and strike home.

May all Americans share equally the blessings of liberty, and ever stand ready to contend for the rights and liberties of mankind.

May those who are discontented with their own country, leave their country for their country's good.

PATRIOTIC TOASTS.

The Boundaries of our Country—East by the Atlantic Ocean; West, as far as we can get; North, according to circumstances; and South, as far as we have a mind to go.

Niagara Falls—An emblem of the power of Americans in battle.

Our Lakes and Rivers—Inland seas that unite the commerce of our States, and forever render their separation impracticable and impossible.

The Virtue of our Wives and Daughters—May it ever remain as pure as the air of our valleys, and as firm as the rocks of our mountains.

May our sons be as honest as they are brave, and our daughters as modest as they are fair.

Our Statesmen—May they ever be distinguished for their love of liberty and true patriotism.

A hempen neckcloth for all traitors.

May he who would destroy the union of his country for a mess of pottage, never get the mess of pottage.

May he who would uproot the tree of liberty, be crushed by its fall.

May the adjective *glorious* ever be joined to the substantive *America*.

American Commerce—May it be commander-in-chief of the ocean.

The Progress of our Country—May it never be fettered by faction.

May he who betrays his country never find a country to shelter him.

Uncle Sam—May the venerable old gentleman soon sweep our legislative halls clean of pugilists, duelists, and thieves.

The Ballot-box—May the vigilance of the people preserve it from the corruption of faction.

The Tree of Liberty—May every American ever have a belly full of its fruit.

May the *liberty* we enjoy never be used to subvert the *principles of freedom.*

May the weight of our taxes never break the back of our credit.

May the Sons of Liberty marry the Daughters of Virtue.

Our Trade and Manufactures—May they never be cramped by the fetters of monopoly.

May civil and religious liberty ever go hand in hand.

May peace and plenty ever rest on the bosom of our American soil.

May those who try to enrich themselves at the expense of our country, find "the devil to pay," and plenty of "pitch hot."

The watchword of America—"Who's afraid?"

May we ever enjoy *freedom* without *faction*.

May our country never cease to deserve well of us; and may we never cease to deserve well of our country.

Where liberty dawned, may it rise to its meridian splendor.

In national disputes may we never engage in a bad cause, and may we never fly from a good one.

Our Constitution—May its unquiet foes find rest in a halter.

The spot where we were born—

"Where the women can love, and the men can all fight—
The latter all day, and the former all night."

Our American Boys—Who have *arms* for their girls, or for their country's foes.

Religion without sectarianism, and politics without faction.

The land we live in—Let him who don't like it, leave it.

The Press—May it ever be free without licentiousness, and bold without intolerance.

To the memory of WEBSTER, CLAY, and JACKSON— The *brain*, the *tongue*, and the *sword* of the Constitution.

The upright elector who never sells his vote.

The Three great American Generals—General Peace, General Prosperity, and General Satisfaction.

Success to Navigation and Commerce.

Success to the Promoters of Commerce.

May our Commerce, like our *shadows*, never be less.

American Commerce—May it never be *dull*, but always be well Japanned.

NAVAL AND MILITARY TOASTS.

Our Army and Navy—The gallant sentinels of the nation's honor by land and sea, at home and abroad.

The Army and Navy—Those twin giant defenders of our nation's rights and our nation's glory.

NAVAL AND MILITARY TOASTS.

The American Flag—May it ever wave over the home of the free and the land of the brave.

An Army to *stand*, but not a Standing Army.

Health to our Brave Sailors, and a speedy calm to the storms of life.

Health to the Gallant Officers of our Army and Navy. After the battles and storms of life are over, may they drop quietly and trustingly into the harbor of eternal bliss.

Good ships, fair winds, and brave seamen.

May the arms of our soldiers never be used except against our country's foe.

May the tar who loses one eye in defence of his country, never see distress with the other.

May the Ensigns of the American Navy ever prove a harbinger of dismay and defeat to our enemies, and of confidence and security to our friends.

May our sailors, like our ships, have hearts of oak.

The Officers and Sailors of our Navy—May their hard ships at sea prove *hardships* indeed to our foes.

Our Naval Commanders—May they ever be lords of the main.

"May the tars of Columbia triumphantly sail,
And over her enemies always prevail."

May the brave soldier, who never turned his back to the enemy, never have a friend turn his back upon him.

May American fortitude and courage ever mock at trial and danger.

May the old American tar, who has been tempest-tossed at sea, always find a welcome on his native shore.

May every mutinous spirit find no place to anchor but in the *dead sea*.

Staunch ships, well rigged, and brave tars to man them.

Health to Soldiers, Sailors, and all jolly fellows.

The American Navy—May it ever sail on a sea of glory, be wafted by the gales of prosperity, guided by the compass of justice, and enter the port of victory.

To the sweet little cherub that sits up aloft, to keep watch for the life of poor Jack.

To the memory of the Father of his Country—Washington.

The memory of those who fought and bled with Washington to secure our independence.

The glorious memory of our ancestors, who shed their life's-blood to establish our liberty.

> "The wind that blows,
> The ship that goes,
> And the lass that loves a sailor."

The discoverer of the New World—Columbus.

DRINKING TOASTS.

A friend, and a bottle to give him.

A good supper, a good bottle, and a good bed to every good fellow.

A full belly, a heavy purse, and a light heart.

A bottle at night and business in the morning.

Beauty, wit, and wine.

Clean glasses and old corks.

Champagne for our real friends, and real pain for our sham friends.

Good wine, good company, and good opportunity.

May we never want for wine, nor for a friend to help drink it.

May friendship draw the cork, and love the curtain.

May we never see a frown in a bumper of wine.

May all our cares be drowned in wine.

> "May we always mingle in the friendly bowl,
> The feast of reason, and the flow of soul."

Old wine and young women.

Here's to the heart that fills as the bottle empties.

The delights of music, love, and wine.

To the big-bellied bottle.

Wine and women—may we never be too old to have a taste for both.

One wife, one bottle, and one friend—the first, beautiful; the second, full; and the last, ever faithful.

Here's to Bacchus' blisses, and Venus' kisses.

> "Come, push the goblet round,
> And drive away dull sorrow;
> Come, push the goblet round,
> And give us more to-morrow."

Delicate wine and susceptible maidens.

> "Come, fill the bowl, each jolly soul,
>   Let Bacchus guide our revels;
> Join cup to lip, with 'hip, hip, hip,'
>   And throttle the blue devils."

May the cup flow with nectar, that is pressed by woman's lip.

May the flowing bowl be the grave of sorrow and care.

> "One bumper at parting!—though many
>   Have circled the board since we met,
> The fullest, the saddest of any,
>   Remains to be crowned by us yet.
> The sweetness that pleasure has in it
>   Is always so slow to come forth,
> That seldom, alas! till the minute
>   It dies, do we know half its worth!
> But, oh! may our life's happy measure
>   Be all of such moments made up,
> They're born on the bosom of pleasure,
>   They die in the tears of the cup."

TOASTS FOR ALL PROFESSIONS.

THE SURGEON—A man who bleeds for his countrymen.

THE GLAZIER—Who constantly takes *pains* (panes) that other people may see *clearly*.

THE BAKER—May he never be *done* so much as to make him *crusty*.

THE PRINTER—May his *form* be well *locked up* in the arms of a charming wife.
May he never know what it is to want a *quoin*.

THE TINKER—A devout man, whose life is spent in a *pilgrimage*, to *mend* the mistakes and *repair* the wastes which other people have made

THE FIREMAN—The sentinel of our homes; may he burn only with ardor to protect the property and life of the city.
May the flames of dissention never find fuel in his heart.
The Fire-Department—the army that draws water instead of blood, and thanks instead of tears.

THE CARPENTER—May he have a warm house and good *boarding*.

THE ACTOR—A bumper every night.

THE PLUMBER—Though his business is to furnish mankind with the dumb blessings of *light* and water, may he be a good *spouter*, and easily turn his *lead* into *gold*.

THE BLACKSMITH—In every speculation may he always *hit the nail on the head*.

THE BANKER—May he always *draw* upon content for the *deficiency* of fortune.

THE ROAD-MAKER—A *highwayman* who deserves well of his country.

A CARD-MAKER—May he often turn up *trumps*.

A COAL MERCHANT—May his customers ever be *grate-full*.

AN AUCTIONEER—By *knocking down* may he ever rise in the world.

THE DISTILLER—May he never be *out of spirits*.

THE COACH-MAKER—May all his *wheels* be those of *fortune*.

THE PAINTER—May he have a good *pallet*, and plenty to gratify his *taste*.

EVERY MAN'S WIFE—May the *lightning of her eye* never cause him to be *afraid of thunder*.

THE SADDLER—May he sit upon a *soft cushion*, and never have the misdeeds of others saddled upon him.

THE BOOK-KEEPER—May he faithfully **keep his** *books*, and may his books *keep* him.

AMATORY TOASTS.

The Fairest Work of Nature—Woman.

All that Love can give and the Heart enjoy.

Beauty's best Companion—Modesty.

Charms to strike the Sight, and Merit to win the Heart.

Happy Lovers and Merry Maids.

Love without licentiousness, and Pleasure without excess.

Love without deceit, and Matrimony without regret.

Love to one, Friendship to a few, and Good-will to all.

May Love and Reason be friends, and Beauty and Virtue marry.

May Love's Labor never be lost.

May the villain who robs a woman of her virtue, die without a friend.

May the Flame of Love never burn up the spark that kindled it.

May we kiss whom we please, and please whom we kiss.

The Lass that we love.

Sincerity before Marriage, and Fidelity afterwards.

> "May woman's breast be pleasure's couch,
> But free from thoughts unholy;
> May it be warm to virtue's touch,
> But cold as ice to folly."

The kiss of Love on the lip of Innocence.

The Dimpled Cheek—May it never be marked with the furrows of shame.

The Rose of the Valley—May it never be rifled of its fragrance.

The Village Maid—May she remain so till she gets a good husband.

> "A cheerful glass, a pretty lass,
> A friend sincere and true;
> Blooming health, good store of wealth,
> Attend on me and you."

May he who would plant a Thorn in the bosom of Innocence, die in a bed of Nettles.

The Cot of Content and the Bosom of Love.

"Drink ye to her that each loves best,
And if ye nurse a flame
That's told but to her mutual breast,
We will not ask her name."

KATE, in a bumper, wherever she goes.

Woman's *Lips*, and Woman's *Heart*—May the former be sealed when the latter is not open.

LITERARY AND ARTISTIC.

The father of English poetry—Geoffrey Chaucer.

The prince of colorists—Titian.

The founder of poetical romance—Luigi Pulci.

The father of experimental philosophy—Sir Humphry Davy.

The father of modern philosophy—Roger Bacon.

The father of Italian poetry—Dante.

The poet of love—Petrarch.

The father of Italian prose—Boccaccio.

The father of engraving—Albert Durer.

The first English printer—William Caxton.

The prince of poetical romance writers—Ariosto.

The prince of novelists—Cervantes.

The prince of Spanish poets—Lopez de Vega.

The father of French tragedy—Corneille.

The prince of portrait painters—Vandyck.

The prince of musicians—Mozart.

The Milton of music—Handel.

The English Anacreon—Robert Herrick.

The prince of landscape painters—Claude Lorraine.

The father of modern prose humor—Rabelais.

The prince of painters—Raphael.

The father of modern essayists—Montaigne.

The father of biography—Plutarch.

The prince of Portuguese poets—Camoens.

The prince of Italian composers—Paissello.

The prince of dramatic poets—Shakespeare.

The prince of actors—Garrick.

The father of tragedy—Æschylus.

The inventor of the stage—Thespis.

The father of history—Herodotus.

The great founder of practical philosophy—Socrates.

The prince of sculptors—Phidias.

The father of comedy—Eupolis.

The prince of orators—Demosthenes.

The father of mechanics—Archimedes.

The prince of pastoral poets—Theocritus.

The father of Latin comedy—Plautus.

The father of modern satirical painting—Hogarth.

The prince of Italian dramatists—Alfieri.

The father of French comedy—Moliere.

The prince of Scotch poets—Robert Burns.

The father of American novel-writing—Charles Brodden Brown.

The prince of American authors and humorists—Washington Irving.

The American song-writer—George P. Morris.

The inventor of steamboats—Robert Fulton.

MISCELLANEOUS TOASTS.

A warm house, a good wife, a fine horse, and a snug estate to all who deserve them.

Any tales but tell-tales.

An honest lawyer, a pious divine, and a skilful physician.

All of fortune's daughters, except miss-fortune.

To all absent friends.

A head to earn and a heart to spend.

> "A friend in the morning, a sweetheart at night,
> To fill us with pleasure and blissful delight."

A heavy purse and a light heart.

A freehold in a pleasant country, lightly taxed, and unmortgaged.

A health to those we love best.

A health to our friends, our sweethearts, and wives.

Charity without ostentation, and religion without bigotry.

> "Come, fill a bumper, fill it round,
> May mirth, and wine, and wit abound;
> In them alone true wisdom lies—
> For to be merry's to be wise."

Let dull care be drowned in sparkling wine.

Equal punishment to the ragged rascal and the rich villain.

Freedom's fire—May it never go out.

"Come, fill up your glasses and join in the chant,
For no pleasure's like drinking good ale, you must grant;
Then let this be our toast, while dull care we assail—
May we ne'er want a friend, or a glass of good ale."

Here's good health to *everybody*, lest somebody should feel himself slighted.

However rough the road of life, may we jog merrily on to the end of our journey.

Liberality in booksellers, and integrity in authors.

Lovely women—May they ever find protection and pleasure under our military and naval power.

May we be able to look forward with pleasure, and backward without regret.

May we never break a joke over the head of reputation.

May our injuries be written in sand, and our friendships in marble.

May the morning of prosperity not be forgotten in the evening of adversity.

May flattery never sit in the parlor, nor plain dealing be kicked out of doors.

May we look around us with pleasure, and above us with gratitude.

May we never swear an honest girl out of her virtue, nor an honest man out of a just debt.

May the sunshine of plenty dispel the clouds of care.

May temptation never conquer virtue.

May we never feel want, nor want feeling.

May hemp bind those whom honor and the laws can not.

May we never murmur without a cause, nor have cause to murmur.

May we never make a sword of our tongues to wound the reputation of others.

May hope be the physician when calamity is the disease.

May fortune recover her eyesight, and be just in the distribution of her favors.

May we always part with regret, and meet again with pleasure.

May prudence and temperance be crowned with length of days.

May we be able to shun law and the devil.

May we always command success by deserving it.

May all men of base principles be abandoned by their principles.

May the best day we have seen be the worst that is to come.

MISCELLANEOUS TOASTS.

May truth and liberty prevail throughout the world.

May the present meeting be oft repeated.

May love and honor be inseparable.

May we never skin our eels till we get them.

> "May those that are single get wives to their mind,
> And those that are married, true happiness find———."

May the heart never know a transport, that can never feel a pain.

May you live to be old, and I be a witness of it.

May he who is an ass, and takes himself to be a deer, find out his mistake when he comes to leap a ditch.

May we either say nothing of the absent, or speak of them like a friend.

May curses, like chickens, go home to roost.

> "May the hallowed name of wife
> Bring us rapture, truth, and health:
> Her breast our pillow, her arms our home,
> Her heart our dearest wealth."

May the man who does not love his native country, neither live, die, nor be buried in it.

May we always find a spark of youthful fire beneath the frost of age.

May our cutting satire never cut a friend.

May the flower of affection never wither or decay.

> "May this be our maxim where'er we are twirl'd,
> 'A fig for the cares of the whirl-a-gig world.'"

May we never hesitate to *cut* a friend when he *shuffles*.

> "May we with Momus and the god of wine,
> Defy old care and father time."

May genius always beam in radiance from the American stage.

May wit never raise a blush on the face of beauty.

> "May we ne'er forget the immortal poet's line,
> 'To err is human—to forgive, divine.'"

May superstition never make fools of the wise.

May every *rake* review his *progress*, and every harlot reform.

> "The man that will not be merry
> With a pretty girl in bed,
> Send him to sea in a wherry,
> And we be put in his stead."

The brave women who stood by the *guns* of our forefathers.

Woman's smile and woman's tear—one to enliven, the other to soften the heart of man.

"Here's to the maiden of bashful sixteen,
    Likewise to the widow of fifty,
Here's to the bold and extravagant quean,
    And here's to the housewife that's thrifty.
        Let the toast pass,
        Drink to the lass,
I'll warrant she'll prove an excuse for the glass."

May we never want bread to make a *toast*.

May hunger never fail to find a good cook.

May the devil turn Don Giovanni, and elope with all scolding wives.

"To Venus and Bacchus united,
    Of whom jolly mortals all boast,
May they, to our board oft invited,
    Be always the general toast."

May all single men be married, and all married men be happy.

MASONIC TOASTS.

"Let us toast every brother, both ancient and young,
    Who bridles his passions and governs his tongue."

A proper application of the 24-inch gauge, so that we may measure out and husband our time wisely.

All the friends of the craft.

All free-born sons of the ancient and honorable craft.

As we meet upon the level, may we part upon the square.

All faithful and true brothers.

All brothers who have been grand masters.

Every brother who keeps the key of knowledge from intruders, but cheerfully gives it to a worthy brother.

Every brother who maintains a consistency in love, and sincerity in friendship.

Every worthy brother who was at first duly prepared, and whose heart still retains an awful regard to the three great lights of masonry.

Golden eggs to every brother, and goldfinches to our lodge.

Honor and influence to every public-spirited brother.

May every worthy brother who is willing to work and labor through the day, be happy at night with his friend, his love, and a cheerful glass.

May all freemasons be enabled to act in strict conformity to the rules of their order.

May our actions as masons be properly squared.

> "May masonry flourish till nature expire,
> And its glories ne'er fade till the world is on fire."

May the brethren of our glorious craft be ever distinguished in the world by their regular lives, more than by their gloves and aprons.

May concord, peace, and harmony subsist in all regular lodges, and always distinguish freemasons.

May masonry prove as universal as it is honorable and useful.

May every brother learn to live within the compass, and watch upon the square.

May the lodges in this place be distinguished for love, peace, and harmony.

May peace, harmony, and concord subsist among freemasons, and may every idle dispute and frivolous distinction be buried in oblivion.

May the prospect of riches never induce a mason to do that which is repugnant to virtue.

May the square, plumb-line, and level, regulate the conduct of every brother.

May the morning have no occasion to censure the night spent by freemasons.

May the hearts of freemasons agree, although their heads should differ.

May every mason participate in the happiness of a brother.

May every brother have a heart to feel, and a hand to give.

May discord, party rage, and insolence be for ever rooted out from among masons.

May covetous cares be unknown to freemasons.

May all freemasons go hand-in-hand in the road of virtue.

May we be more ready to correct our own faults than to publish the errors of a brother.

May all freemasons live in love, and die in peace.

May love animate the heart of every mason.

May unity and love be ever stamped upon the mason's mind.

May the frowns of resentment be unknown among us.

May every freemason be distinguished by the internal ornament of an upright heart.

May the brethren in this place be united to one and another by the bond of love.

May the gentle spirit of love animate the heart of every mason.

May every freemason have so much genuine philosophy, that he may neither be too much exalted with the smiles of prosperity, nor too much dejected with the frowns of adversity.

May the conduct of masons be such as to convince the world they dwell in light.

May every brother who is regularly entered be instructed in the morals of masonry.

May no freemason taste the bitter apples of affliction.

May unity, friendship, and brotherly love ever distinguish the brethren of the ancient craft.

May we never condemn that in a brother which we would pardon in ourselves.

May freemasons ever taste and relish the sweets of domestic contentment.

May our conversation be such, that by it youth may find instruction, women modesty, the aged respect, and all men civility.

May every freemason have peace, health, and plenty.

May the foundation of every regular lodge be solid, its buildings sure, and its members numerous and happy.

May every freemason find constancy in love, and sincerity in friendship.

May hypocrisy, faction, and strife, be for ever rooted from every lodge.

May every mason's conduct be such as to have an approving monitor.

May honor and honesty distinguish the brethren.

May our evening's diversion bear the morning's reflection.

May the mason's conduct be so uniform, that he may not be ashamed to take a retrospective view of it.

May virtue ever direct our actions with respect to ourselves, justice to those with whom we deal, mercy, love, and charity to all mankind.

May no freemason desire plenty, but with the benevolent view to relieve the indigent.

May the cares which haunt the heart of the covetous be unknown to the freemason.

May all freemasons ever taste and relish the sweets of freedom.

Prosperity to masons and masonry.

Relief to all indigent brethren.

The female friends of freemasons.

To the perpetual honor of freemasonry.

The masters and wardens of all regular lodges.

To the secret and silent.

To all masons who walk by the line.

To the memory of the Tyrian artist.

To all who live within the compass and square.

> To him that did the Temple rear,
> Who lived and died within the square,
> And lies interred—there's none know where
> But those who master-masons are.

To all the fraternity round the globe.

To the increase of perpetual friendship and peace among the ancient craft.

To all upright and pure masons.

To masons, and to masons' bairns,
And all the fair with wit and charms
Who bless the master masons' arms.

To every pure and faithful heart
That still preserves the secret art.

The keystone of the masonic arch.

To all true masons, and upright,
Who saw the east where rose the light.

To masonry, friendship, and love.

The mason who knows the true value of his tools.

Come, fill up a bumper, and let it go round,
May mirth and good-fellowship always abound;
And may the world see
That freemasonry
Doth teach honest hearts to be jovial and free

ETIQUETTE OF THE DINNER-TABLE.

INVITATIONS TO DINNER.

INVITATIONS to dine, from a married party, are sent in the name of the lady, in some such form as the following: "Mrs. A. B. Smith's compliments to Mr. and Mrs. Brown—will be happy of their company at dinner, at 6 o'clock, Wednesday evening, May 9th." The answer to invitations to dine, accepting or declining, should be sent immediately, and are always addressed to the lady. If, after you have accepted an invitation, any thing occurs to render it impossible for you to go, the lady should be informed of it immediately. It is a great breach of etiquette not to answer an invitation as soon after it is received as possible, and it is an insult to disappoint when we have promised.

Invitations to dine from bachelors to a party of bachelors, may be less formal. One of the wealthiest bachelors of London, and a famous eater, always carries his pockets full of cards, of which the following is an exact copy—"Turbot and Lobster, sir, at six; shall be happy of your company." These he is in the habit of handing about very liberally.

Letters or cards of invitation should always name the hour of dinner; and well-bred people will arrive as nearly at the specified time as they can. Be sure and not be a minute behind the time, and you should not get there long before, unless the invitation requests you particularly to come early for a little chat before dinner.

Always go to a dinner as neatly dressed as possible. The expensiveness of your apparel is not of much importance, but its freshness and cleanliness are indispensable. The hands and finger-nails require especial attention. It is a great insult to every lady at the table for a man to sit down to dinner with his hands in a bad condition.

MANNERS AT TABLE.

Nothing more plainly shows the well-bred man than his manners at table. A man may be well dressed, may converse well—and these are all in his favor—but if he is after all unrefined, his manners at table will be sure to expose him. If he is "*au fait*" at dinner, he has passed one of the severest tests of good breeding.

Any unpleasant peculiarity, abruptness, or coarseness of manners, is especially offensive at table. People are more easily disgusted at that time than at any other. All such acts as leaning over on one side in your own chair, placing your elbows on the table, or on the back of your neighbor's chair, gaping, twisting about restlessly in your seat, are to be avoided as heresies of the most infidel stamp at table.

Though the body at table should always be kept in a tolerably upright and easy position, yet one need not sit bolt-upright, as stiff and prim as a poker. To be easy, to be natural, and to appear comfortable, is the deportment required.

You will sip your soup as quietly as possible from the side of the spoon, and you, of course, will not commit the vulgarity of blowing in it, or trying to cool it, after it is in your mouth, by drawing in an unusual quantity of air, for by so doing you would be sure to annoy, if you did not turn the stomach of the lady or gentleman next to you.

The reason why it is considered impolite to take soup or fish a second time, at a large party, is because by so doing you keep the rest of the company staring at you; while the second course is in danger of being spoiled waiting for you. It is the selfish greediness of this act, therefore, that constitutes its vulgarity. At a small family dinner, however, the same objections do not hold good.

It is not considered proper to use your knife to convey food to your mouth. This is one of the most arbitrary and, perhaps, least sensible rules of table etiquette. The reason for it probably is, that in conveying food to the mouth on a knife, it is in some danger of falling off and dropping back into the plate, or on the table. The *knife* is used for *cutting*, and the *fork* or *spoon* for feeding. Dr. Johnson and Dean Swift used to pay little attention to this form of etiquette; but as you are neither Dr. Johnson nor Dean Swift, it is doubtful if you can afford to disregard it.

Making a noise in chewing your food, or breathing hard in eating, are unseemly habits, which will be sure to get you a bad name at table, among people of good breeding. Let it be a sacred rule that *you cannot use your knife, or fork, or teeth too quietly*.

Avoid picking your teeth, if possible, at table, for however agreeable such a practice might be to yourself, it may be offensive to others. The habit which some have of holding one hand over the mouth, does not avoid the vulgarity of teeth-picking at table.

Neither ladies nor gentlemen ever wear gloves at table, unless their hands, from some cause, are not fit to be seen.

Avoid too slow or too rapid eating; the one will appear as though you did not like your dinner, and the other as though you were afraid you would not get enough.

It is not good taste to praise extravagantly every

dish that is set before you; but, if there are some things that are really very nice, it is well to speak in their praise. But, above all things, avoid seeming indifferent to the dinner that is provided for you, as that might be construed into a dissatisfaction with it. When the Duke of Wellington was at Paris, as commander of the allied armies, he was invited to dine with Cambaceres, one of the most distinguished statesmen and *gourmands* of the time of Napoleon. In the course of the dinner, his host having helped him to some *recherché* dish, expressed a hope that he found it agreeable. "Very good," said the Duke, "but I really don't care what I eat." "Good God!" exclaimed Cambaceres, as he started back and dropped his fork, "don't care what you eat! What *did* you come here for, then?" At the time the Duke made this shocking blunder, he was probably too much absorbed about Waterloo to know what he was saying at table.

If you ask the waiter for anything, you will be careful to speak to him gently in the tone of *request*, and not of *command*. To speak to a waiter in a driving manner will create, among well-bred people, the suspicion that you were sometime a servant yourself, and are putting on *airs* at the thought of your promotion. Lord Chesterfield says: "If I tell a footman to bring me a glass of wine, in a rough, insulting manner, I should expect that, in obeying me, he would contrive to spill some of it upon me, and I am sure I should deserve it."

ON GIVING DINNERS.

It is a mistaken idea which many people entertain, to suppose that a man can get either *reputation* or *real friends* by giving a great many expensive dinners. In the first place, if a man dines people beyond his means, he gets a very bad reputation, and even the friends who eat them go away despising the man for his folly in inviting other people to eat up his substance. A man who not long since absconded from New York, a defaulter to the Federal Government, was so famous for his splendid dinners, that even the friends who ate them were prophesying for three years that he must, in the end, come out a defaulter. While laughing over his sparkling wine, it was still impossible to keep the feeling of contempt from choking them in their throats.

The most expensive and splendid dinners are not by any means, necessarily, the most enjoyable and the most desirable. The splendid Roman banquets, so famous in history, were much more remarkable for profusion and costliness than for taste. The only merit of a dish composed of the brains of five hundred peacocks, or the tongues of five hundred nightingales, must have been its dearness; and if a mode of swallowing the most money in a given time be the desideratum, commend us to Cleopatra's decoction of diamonds, though even this was fairly exceeded in originality and neatness of conception by the English sailor, who placed a ten-pound note between two slices of bread and butter, and made his black-eyed Susan eat it as a sandwich. Capt. Morris, in one of his songs, has set the proper value on such luxuries:

> "Old Lucullus, they say,
>   Forty cooks had each day,
> And Vitellius's meals cost a million;
>   But I like what is good,
>   When or where be my food,
> In a chop-house or royal pavilion.
>
> "At all feasts, if enough,
>   I most heartily stuff,
> And a song at my heart alike rushes;
>   Though I've not fed my lungs
>   Upon nightingales' tongues,
> Nor the brains of goldfinches and thrushes.'

The vulgar notion of associating gentility with expense and mere show, does not obtain among people of substantial good breeding. The most expensive banquets are often failures. Foote thus describes such a one: "As to splendor, as far as it went, I admit it: there was a very fine sideboard of plate; and if a man could have swallowed a silversmith's shop, there was enough to satisfy him; but as to all the rest, the mutton was white, the veal was red, the fish was kept too long, the venison not kept long enough: to sum up all, every thing was cold except the ice, and every thing sour except the vinegar."

If you would really please your guests at dinner, your care should be directed, not to the expense and splendor of your china, but to the *quality* of your victuals; not so much to the number and variety of dishes, as to their goodness. A single joint well cooked, with the proper vegetables, will give better satisfaction than a dozen kinds of meats and game, badly cooked. Of all the annoyances at dinner, the sight of a rare dish spoiled in the cooking and dressing is the worst. Therefore, unless you are sure of your cook, it is the safest way to confine your feast to those plain staple dishes, in the preparation of which it is not easy to get astray.

It is always best for the lady of the house, where a dinner-party is to come off, to be dressed and ready to appear in the drawing-room as early as possible, so that if any of the guests should happen to come a little early, she may be prepared to receive them. It is awkward for both parties where visitors arrive before the lady of the house is ready for them. If it is necessary for her to keep an eye upon the dinner, it is still best that she should familiarly receive her guests, and beg to be excused, if it is necessary for her to vanish occasionally to the kitchen. A real lady is not ashamed to have it known that she goes into the kitchen; on the contrary, it is more likely that she will be a little proud of being thought capable of superintending the preparing feast.

It is not in good taste for the lady of the house,

where a dinner is given, to dress very much. She leaves it for her lady-guests to make what display they please, and she offers no rivalry to their fine things. She contents herself with a tasty *negligé*, which often proves the most fascinating equipment after all, especially, if the cheeks become a little flushed with natural bloom, in consequence of the exercise and anxiety incident to the reception of the guests.

When dinner is on the table, the lady and gentleman of the house will have an opportunity of showing their tact by seeing that the most distinguished guests, or the *oldest*, are shown into the dining-room first, and by making those companions at the table who are most likely to be agreeable to each other. The lady of the house may lead the way, or follow her guests into the dining-room, as she pleases. Among those who delight to follow the etiquette of the English nobility, the latter practice is followed. But the practice must not be considered a test of good breeding in America. If the lady leads, the husband will follow behind the guests, with the lady on his arm who is to sit at his side. The old custom is still followed to some extent in this country, of the lady taking the head of the table, with the two most favored guests seated, the one at her right and the other at her left hand; while the gentleman of the house takes the foot of the table, supported on each side by the two ladies most entitled to consideration. But this old rule is by no means slavishly followed in polite society in this country.

The lady and gentleman of the house are, of course, helped last, and they are very particular to notice, every minute, whether the waiters are attentive to every guest. But they do not press people either to eat more than they appear to want, nor *insist* upon their partaking of any particular dish. It is allowable for you to recommend, so far as to say that it is considered "excellent," but remember that tastes differ, and dishes which suit *you* may be unpleasant to others; and that, in consequence of your urgency, some modest people might feel themselves compelled to partake of what is disagreeable to them.

Never speak harshly or imperatively to your servants in the presence of your guests. It would be as annoying to your guests as it would be cruel to your servants. If they make any mistake, or break anything, you will avoid keeping the attention of the party to it for a single minute. Remember that you cannot seem to be annoyed yourself, without annoying your friends at the same time. Some men have a brutal way of scolding and driving their servants in company; but it will be difficult for such a brute to get a well-bred lady or gentlemen to his house to dine a second time. And what shall be said of the man who is in the habit of speaking ill-naturedly to his wife before her guests! There is no language that can justly describe his brutality, and we shall, therefore, not attempt it.

Avoid, by all means, everything unpleasant at table. If any of your guests so far forget the rules of good breeding as to speak disparagingly of any person, you will show your tact by instantly turning the attention of the party upon something else. A back-biter is always deemed a nuisance in really polite society, but *especially so* at table, where everything unpleasant is shunned as the bane of the common enjoyment.

It is customary in some American families to serve their guests with coffee in the parlor after dinner. But this is a European custom which is not generally practised in polite American society. When coffee is given at the close of the dinner, it is more usual to serve it before the guests leave the table. The practice of handing it round in the parlor or drawing-room, is an unnecessary inconvenience to the guests particularly, without any compensating advantages.

Finger-glasses are generally handed round as soon as the viands are removed, but they are intended merely to wet the fingers and around the mouth. The habit of rinsing the mouth at table is a disgusting piece of indelicacy, which is never practised by any well-bred person.

It is generally the custom in this country for ladies to retain their seats at table till the end of the feast. But where the dinner is of a somewhat political character, and it is expected that long and deep drinking is to follow the viands, the ladies usually retire from the table after the second or third glass; and when they leave, the gentlemen all rise, and the one nearest the door opens it for them.

The polite and noble Roman, Lucullus, said that there was as much care to be taken in the right management of a feast, as in the marshalling of an army; that the one might be as pleasing to friends as the other terrible to enemies.

ON CARVING.

A great deal of the comfort and satisfaction of a good dinner depends upon the *carving*. Awkward carving is enough to spoil the appetite of a refined and sensitive person. No matter how well the meats may be cooked, if they are mutilated, torn, and hacked to pieces, or even cut awkwardly, one half of their relish is destroyed by the carver. Formerly, in England, there were regular teachers of the art of carving, and Lady Mary Wortly Montague confesses that she once took lessons of such a professor three times a week. Besides the annoyance and mortification of bad carving, it is a very extravagant piece of ignorance, as it causes a great waste of meats. In the seventeenth century, carving was a science that carried with it as much pedantry as the business of school-teaching does at the present day; and for a person to use wrong terms in relation to carving, was an unpardonable affront to etiquette. Carving all kinds of small birds was called *to thy* them; a quail, to *wing* it; a pheasant, to *allay* it; a duck, to *embrace* it; a hen, to *spoil* her; a goose, to *tare* her, and a list of similar technicalities too long and too ridiculous to repeat.

Dr. Johnson said, that "You should praise, not ridicule, your friend who carves with as much earnestness of purpose as though he were legislating."

The best way to cut a HAM, in order that the fat and lean may be served evenly, is to begin in the middle of the ham, and cut out thin circular slices. Though good carvers often begin at the large end of the ham, which is certainly the most saving way.

In carving a roast SIRLOIN OF BEEF, you may begin at either end, or in the middle. The outside should be sliced downward to the bone, while the inside or tenderloin part should be sliced thin, lengthwise, and a little of the soft fat given with each piece. You may ask whether the outside or inside is preferred; otherwise a small bit of the inside should be served with each plate, as this is generally regarded as the most choice portion.

But little skill is required in carving a ROUND OF BEEF. It should be cut in thin, smooth, and even slices.

A FILLET OF VEAL should be cut in the same way as

a round of beef. Ask whether the brown or outside is preferred. If it is stuffed, cut deep through the stuffing, and serve each plate with a thin slice, with a little of the fat also.

In carving a LEG OF MUTTON, slice it *lightly*, for if you press too heavily the knife will not cut, and you will squeeze out all the gravy, and serve your guests with dry meat. Begin to cut in the middle, as that is the most juicy part. Cut thin, deep slices, and help each person to a little of the fat, and some of the brown or outside.

In carving a FORE QUARTER OF LAMB, separate the shoulder from the breast and ribs, by passing the knife under and through it; then separate the gristly part from the ribs, and help from that, or the ribs, as may be chosen.

A HAUNCH OF MUTTON is the leg and a part of the loin. In carving, help to about equal parts of the fat of the loin, and the lean of the leg. Cut each part directly down through in slices, about a quarter of an inch thick.

A SADDLE OF MUTTON should be cut in thin slices from tail to end, beginning close to the back-bone; help some fat from the sides.

A ROAST PIG should be cut in two before it is sent to the table. Begin to carve by separating the shoulder from one side, then divide the ribs. The joints may be divided, or pieces cut from them. The ribs are considered the finest part, though some prefer the neck end.

In carving a GOOSE, cut off the apron, or the part directly under the neck, and outside of the merry-thought. Then turn the neck-end towards you, and cut the breast in slices. Take off the leg by putting the fork into the small end of the bone, pressing it to the body, at the same time passing the knife into and through the joint. Take off the wing by putting the fork into the small end of the pinion, and pressing it close to the body while the knife is dividing the joint. The wing side-bones, and also the back and lower side-bones, should then be cut off. The best pieces are the breast and thighs.

A FOWL, OR CHICKEN, is carved by first detaching the legs from the body. Next, take off the wings, by dividing the joint with the knife; then lift up the pinion with your fork, and draw the wing towards the leg, and the muscles will separate in a better form than if cut. Then remove the merry-thought from the neck-bones, and divide the breast from the carcass by cutting through the tender-ribs. Then lay the back upwards, and cut it across half-way between the neck and the rump. The breast and thighs are considered the choice bits.

A TURKEY is carved very nearly in the same way as a chicken, or fowl.

Nearly all kinds of small game birds are carved by simply cutting them in two, from the neck to the tail, unless they are given whole.

Never pour gravy over white meat, as it would destroy its delicate appearance.

There are many little ways of seasoning meats and game, which may be done by the carver, as, for instance: before cutting up a duck, slice the breast, and pour over the gashes a few spoonfuls of sauce made of port-wine, lemon-juice, salt, and Cayenne pepper. Or, after you have cut off the apron and breast-bone of a goose, pour into the body a glass of port wine and a small teaspoonful of mustard.

WINE AT TABLE.

Almost every gentleman has wine at his table whenever he has invited guests. Indeed, wine is considered an indispensable part of a good dinner, to which a gentleman has been formally invited. Even if you are a total-abstinence man yourself, you will not, if you are really a gentleman, attempt to compel all your guests to be so against their wish. If you are so fanatical that you have what is called "conscientious scruples" against furnishing wine, then you should invite none to dine who are not as fanatical and bigoted as yourself. You must consider that a gentleman may have "conscientious scruples" against dining with you on cold water, for there are even temperate and sober gentlemen who would go without meat as soon as be deprived of their glass of wine at dinner. The vegetarian, who would force his guests to dine on cabbages and onions, is hardly guilty of a greater breach of etiquette than the total-abstinence fanatic who would compel his guests to go without wine.

If there is a gentleman at the table who is known to be a total-abstinence man, you will not urge him to drink. He will suffer his glass to be filled at the first passage of the wine, and raising it to his lips, will bow his respects with the rest of the guests, and after that his glass will be allowed to remain untouched. As little notice as possible should be taken of his total-abstinence peculiarity. And, if he is a gentleman, he will carefully avoid drawing attention to it himself.

It is not now the custom to ask a lady across the table to take wine with you. It is expected that every lady will be properly helped to wine by the gentleman who takes her to the table, or who sits next to her. But if you are in company where the old custom prevails, it would be better breeding to follow the custom of the place, rather than by an omission of what your entertainer considers civility, to prove him, in face of his guests, to be either ignorant or vulgar. If either a lady or gentleman is invited to take wine at table, they must *never refuse;* if they do not *drink*, they need only touch the wine to their lips. Do not offer to help a lady to wine until you see she has finished her soup or fish.

It is considered well bred to take the same wine as that selected by the person with whom you drink. When, however, the wine chosen by him is unpalatable to you, it is allowable to take that which you prefer, at the same time apologizingly saying, "will you permit me to drink *claret?*" or whatever wine you have selected.

In inviting a gentleman to take wine with you at table, you should politely say, "Shall I have the pleasure of a glass of wine with you?" You will then either hand him the bottle you have selected, or send it by the waiter, and afterwards fill your own glass, when you will politely and silently bow to each other, as you raise the wine to your lips.

On raising the first glass of wine to his lips, it is customary for a gentleman to bow to the lady of the house.

It is not customary to propose *toasts* or to drink deep at a gentleman's family table. Lord Byron describes "a largish party," as "first silent, then talky, then argumentative, then disputatious, then unintelligible, then altogethery, then drunk." But this was "a largish party," which, it is to be hoped, was given at a tavern; for the man who drinks to intoxication, or to any considerable degree of *elevation*, at a gentleman's family table, ought never to expect to be invited a second time.

We Americans have the name of being the greatest drinkers at dinners, but the English certainly beat us, and there is some etymological probability that the Dutch have considerable claims to the honor of being acknowledged hard drinkers. At least, many of the cant phrases used in carousing are evidently of Dutch origin. The phrase *half-seas-over* is derived from the Dutch *op zee*, which means *over sea*, and was the name given to an inebriating beer introduced into England from Holland, and was called *op zee*. The word *carouse* is derived from the name of a large glass, called by the Danes *rouse*. The famous drinking-phrase, "Hip, hip, hurra!" originated in the Crusades, it being a corruption of " H. E. P.," the initial of *Hierosolyma est perdita* (Jerusalem is lost), the motto on the banner of Peter the Hermit, whose followers hunted Jews down with the cry of " Hip, hip, hurra!"

At dinner-parties which are given to gentlemen, for the purpose of conviviality, one may indulge in as much wine as he pleases, provided he does not get *drunk*, and make a nuisance of himself. Where drinking, and toasting, and bumpers, are the order of the feast, as at a public dinner, given in honor of a distinguished man, or at the inauguration of some public enterprise, far greater latitude is allowed, in all things, than on more private and select occasions. Where mirth and general hilarity are demanded, deep drinking is expected. Wine is a great sharpener of men's wits. It was said of Addison's excellent nature, that "it ran over when heated with wine, and he shone with the wit of Terence when in company with Scipio and Laelius;" exemplifying the poet's simile of the flying-fish, which soars highest when its wings are wet.

It is, however, the first care of a well-bred man never to drink beyond his self-control at table, where the comfort of the whole party is so much dependent upon the propriety of every one present. But, whenever a gentleman has the misfortune to forget himself, as sometimes will happen, every other gentleman will do all in his power to make the best of the accident. Charles II. dined with the citizens of London the year that Sir Robert Viner was mayor, who, getting elated with continually toasting the royal family, grew a little fond of his majesty. "The king understood very well how to extricate himself in all kinds of difficulty, and with a hint to the company to avoid ceremony, stole off and made towards his coach, which stood ready for him in Guildhall yard. But the mayor liked his company so well, and was grown so intimate, that he pursued him hastily, and, catching him fast by the hand, cried out with a vehement oath and accent, 'Sir, you shall stay and take t'other bottle!' The polite monarch looked kindly at him over his shoulder, and, with a smile and graceful air, repeated this line of the old song:

'He that is drunk is as great as a king;'

and immediately returned back and complied with his landlord."

Do not praise bad wine, for it will persuade those who are judges that you are an ignoramus or a flatterer. On the other hand, avoid seeming to notice that it is bad, unless the host calls attention to it himself. There is an anecdote of a man, who, being invited by Sir Thomas Grouts, who was proud of his wine, to take a second glass of his " old East India," replied, " One was a dose—had rather not double the *cape ;*" and, at the first glass of champagne, he inquired whether there had been a plentiful crop of gooseberries last year.*

As wine is a very common subject of discussion at table, it is quite necessary that every gentleman should be able to converse understandingly upon the character and quality of the various wines in use. It is very embarrassing to be called upon for an opinion and not be able to give one; and it is still worse to betray one's ignorance on the subject of conversation. Besides, ignorance of the history and quality of wines may impress gentlemen with the idea that you have not been much in good company.

* There is a great deal of champagne made of gooseberries in England.

THE AGE OF WINES.

It is a great error, and one which prevails extensively, to suppose that great age is necessary to the goodness of wine. The quality of the vintage has far more to do with the excellence of the wine than the number of years it has been kept. Port wine, of a good vintage, is best when not more than ten years old. Hocks and clarets, indeed, will not keep till old. Champagne is best at from three to five years old. So that the phrase "old wine" has no such wonderful charm for the well-informed.

HOW TO KNOW GOOD WINE.

All wines made out of the juice of the grape possess a peculiar *bouquet*, or powerful odor, which is quite unmistakable to an experienced wine-drinker. This characteristic *bouquet* depends upon the presence of *œnanthic* ether, which is produced by the fermentation of the juice of the grape, and is, therefore, relied upon as one of the general proofs that the wine is made of grapes. By comparing the *bouquet* of a bottle of real grape wine, with one made of cider, gooseberries, or any other juice, you will soon educate your nose to be a tolerable detector of bad wine.

Immature red wines are remarkably bright and red, in consequence of the presence of phosphoric and other acids, which are subdued when the wine has obtained a proper age. In perfectly ripe wines this intense brightness is changed into a mellow, rich, and tawny hue, that is considered a sign of maturity in all red wines. But, alas! this is no longer an infallible sign, for art has discovered the means of counterfeiting the golden light and mellow brown which used to be a sure guide in the choice of port and claret. After all, an experienced *taste* is about the only sure guide to the selection of good wines.

PORT WINE.

Pure port wine is undoubtedly " one of the most healthy of all vinous liquors : it strengthens the muscular system, assists the digestive powers, accelerates the circulation, exhilarates the spirits, and sharpens the mental energies." But, alas! such a thing as pure port is *never* found in this country. It can never be had here without an admixture of brandy ; as otherwise it would not keep. A great deal of cheap French wine is sold here for port, and a great deal of a poisonous drug is manufactured here and sold under the abused and prostituted name of port wine. Doctors little imagine what they are doing when they recommend their patients to " drink port wine." There are very few of the most vigorous constitutions that can stand the assaults of the poisonous compound which is generally sold for port wine in this country. When *real* port wine loses its stringency, and acquires a slightly acid taste, it is unwholesome, and is unfit for use except by a person who is ambitious to get the gout.

CHAMPAGNE.

The faculty of Paris in 1778 pronounced champagne to be the finest and healthiest of all wines; and, except in cases of weak digestion, is, if pure, one of the safest wines that can be drank. It is the king of wines at the convivial board in the United States—so much so, that when " a bottle of wine " is proposed it is understood to be champagne, unless some other name is expressly given. " Its intoxicating effects are rapid, but exceedingly transient, and depend partly upon the carbonic acid, which is evolved from it, and partly upon the alcohol, which is suspended in this gas, being applied rapidly and extensively to a large surface of the stomach." The idea that champagne produces gout is sufficiently refuted by the fact that the disease is very little known in the province where the wine is made. But it is, undoubtedly, to be avoided in cases where the disorder already exists, especially if it has been produced by the too free use of strong liquors.

It is a mistaken idea that champagne must be swallowed as soon as possible after it is uncorked. If it is really champagne it improves by letting it stand a little, as after the gas has partly escaped it will entirely retain the body and flavor of the wine, which is, to some extent, concealed by its effervescence. Lovers of champagne do not drink it until its active effervescence is a little over. A good way to test the quality of champagne, is to let it stand till the gas has considerably escaped and see if it then possesses the rich body and aroma of wine. That fatal poison which is manufactured in such immense quantities in this country out of cider and cheap Rhine wine, and almost invariably served up as champagne at political dinners, will not stand the above test. And it is no wonder that those who have drank only this abominable drug, should hold champagne to be an unhealthy wine. The English make a tolerable counterfeit champagne of the juice of rhubarb leaf-stocks and green gooseberries.

We often hear those who are most oppressively wise, in their own conceits, attempt to display their wisdom by referring to the small geographical boundaries of the champagne country, and shrewdly deducing therefrom that not enough of champagne can be made to allow a single bottle to be imported to this country. But, for all that, the species of wine known as champagne is manufactured all over the south of Europe of as excellent a quality as that produced in the district of champagne, and a vast deal of this genuine wine is imported to this country.

One of the most distinguished political editors in

the United States, who has "conscientious scruples" against the use of wine, is in the habit of making himself agreeable at table by picking up the champagne corks and pointing out to all the guests that the name of the brand upon the end of the cork is printed in American type. At great political dinners, where a contract is made with landlords and public caterers to furnish the wine, it is very likely that the impress of American type may be found on the ends of the corks; but that does not, by any means, prove that there is not plenty of real champagne imported into this country. Just as good champagne can be found here as at Rheims. But your only protection is the character of the house of which you buy. Just as good wine can be provided in the remotest inland towns of America as can be had in Paris or Bordeaux. We have tasted as great a variety of the finest wines at the house of Thomas Andrews, Esq., in the city of Chicago, as can be found in any city on the continent of Europe. And there is one importing house in New York, Britton & Co., No. 11 Broad street, which imports, on an average, ten thousand baskets a year of the Moet and Chandon champagnes, which are, perhaps, the finest of all the various brands of champagnes; and thus here, in New York, we have the *best genuine champagnes* that are made in Europe. Of these brands the Grand Imperial, or green seal, is perhaps the finest, though many choose the Bouzy Cabinet. The Fleur de Bouzy, imported by the above-named house, sells for the same price as the Heidsick, and is a better wine than even this favorite old brand. And if a single house imports ten thousand baskets yearly, what must be the amount of *genuine champagne* which is brought to this country by all the great importing houses? Probably it is not too much to say that two millions of baskets are imported yearly.

BURGUNDY.

"Burgundy is stronger than clarets, possesses a powerful aroma, and a delicious and lasting flavor." But when it arrives in this country it is generally brandied, which is most injurious to its flavor and smell. Pure Burgundy is a very delicate wine, that is not very common in the United States. A very fine sparkling Burgundy was a great favorite at the Revere House in Boston, some years ago, but the wine is not, we think, generally known in this country.

CLARET.

Claret wine is a great favorite in this country, in hot weather especially. The slightest and most palatable and aromatic of the clarets, the St. Julien, La Rose, and Bouillac. The Châteaux-margau is a delicious claret, which has the perfume of the violet, and possesses a rich ruby color. "The Haut Brion has a powerful bouquet, resembling a mixture of violets and raspberries." La Tour and Lafitte have both a bouquet and taste of violets. Clarets are chiefly shipped from Bordeaux, and the most of those above-named are from the neighboring districts of Médoc. The unmixed Bordeaux claret is the safest and best for ordinary use : it is light, agreeable, gently exhilarating, and an excellent quencher of thirst.

GERMAN WINES.

Hock wines are great favorites in hot weather. The most popular of the Rhine wines are the Johannisberg and the Steinberg, which are alike admired for their delicious flavor and exquisite bouquet.

Among the best second class Rhine wine are the Rudesheim, Markobrunner, and Rothenberg. Hockheim, which grows on the banks of the Main, ranks equally with these. The frightful names of these German wines generally follow the cognomen of the place where they are produced.

The favorite wines of the Germans themselves are generally the delicately flavored Moselles : Grunhauser and Scharrberger are called the "Nectar of the Moselle." A very fine German wine, called Straw wine, is made of grapes so ripe that they require no pressing, but the juice distills through clean wheaten straw, and imbibes its color. It is a very expensive wine, and is not much known in this country.

SHERRIES.

Brande says, "Sherry, of due age and in good condition, is a fine, perfect, and wholesome wine; free from excess of acid, and possessing a dry, aromatic flavor and fragrancy; but, as produced in ordinary market, it is of fluctuating and anomalous quality, often destitute of all aroma, and tasting of little else than alcohol and water." Almost all the sherry wine in common use in this country is of the latter description; and those served at the hotels in *England* are, if possible, still worse, notwithstanding sherry is the favorite dinner wine of that country.

The best sherries are the pale and light golden wines, made of the Xeres grape; though it is not safe to judge of sherry by its color, for art has instructed how to give the most inferior wine the delicate hue of the genuine article. The finest sherry is the Amontillado; but it is very rare, and let no man flatter himself that he often feasts his eyes or his palate upon it, in this country. In England, sherry is the *dinner* wine, but the Americans follow more in the French custom, and use it as a *vin de liqueur*.

MADEIRA.

Madeira is a delightful wine, if we could only ever get any of it. But let no happy enthusiast deceive himself with the delusive bliss that he is drinking pure Madeira. So destructive has been the disease of the vine in Madeira for many years, that such an event as any of its charming wine reaching this country is not to be hoped for.

We are told, that when the celebrated Malmsey is stored in the cellars, the following benediction is pronounced over it: "Lord God, thou who lovest mankind, direct thine eyes to this wine, and those who shall drink it: bless our vessels, thrice blessed as the walls of Jacob, and the pool of Siloam, and as thou hast blessed this drink of the apostles. O Lord! thou who wast present at the wedding at Cana, and by changing the water into wine, revealed thy glory to thy disciples, send thy Holy Spirit on this wine, and bless it in thy name." This benediction certainly shows us the great value which is placed upon good wine in that country.

AMERICAN WINES.

An English author of an interesting work on the culture of wine, says of our American wines: "In comparing these wines with those of Europe, we must bear in mind that they are distinct in flavor from any or all of them. It is their peculiarity that no spurious compound can be made to imitate them, and in purity and delicacy there is no known wine to equal them."

Our still Catawba has the lowest percentage of alcohol of any wine in the world. The most expensive wine in Europe, Tokay, has 9.85 per cent. of spirit, while our Catawba has only 9.50.

The best champagne made in the United States is Werke's sparkling Isabella, unless it is equalled by the sparkling wine of Missouri; which is, certainly, one of the lightest and finest champagnes we have ever tasted. Werke's sparkling Catawba, which is not equal in delicacy of flavor to his Isabella, is preferred by lovers of champagne to Longworth's wine of the same name.

The El Paso and mustang wines of Texas are very fine. The mustang grape yields a wine hardly distinguishable from the best port. All the first class American wines are quite equal to the best imported wines, and they are, generally, much cheaper. Werke's sparkling wines, when they can be had, are furnished at two dollars a bottle at the hotels, while the best imported champagnes cost two dollars and fifty cents or three dollars a bottle.

THE ART OF DRINKING WINE.

The old Romans had a practice of eating cheese to bring out the flavor of the wine, a custom which prevails in England at the present time, and is not unknown in the United States.

Wine-drinkers vary their choice of wines to suit the seasons; selecting light wines for summer, and those having more body and strength for winter. Thus, in summer, hock, claret, Burgundy, Rhineish, and hermitage are generally in vogue; and in cold weather, port, sherry, and Madeira have their day.

Some are so fanciful in their use of wines, that they will drink only white wine with white meats, and red wine with brown meats; light wine with light dishes, and stronger wines with more substantial food.

At table, in France, red wines almost always precede the white. In England and America, also, red wines usually open the repast; after which the sparkling and exhilarating champagne keeps up the good temper of the merry guests. In America, especially, champagne is now always taken with the meats; and then a glass of sherry usually closes the feast, so far as the wine is concerned, unless a glass of brandy and water follows it.

If you invite a friend or two to a quiet dinner at

your hotel, or at your own house, a genteel and sufficient course of wine is to open the dinner, after the soup or fish—a bottle of claret, or any light wine, to be followed by champagne—and then close the dinner with a cup of strong coffee, without the introduction of any other kind of wine. The producing of a great variety of wines at a quiet visiting dinner-party looks like an ostentatious display, and is not usually practised by gentlemen in this country. "It is but a vulgar notion which associates expense with gentility."

Wine-coolers are indispensable in hot weather, as the practice of putting ice into the glass with the wine is sure to destroy the fine aroma and delicious taste of all the choicest wines. Claret which is kept in a cellar, needs no cooling; and in winter, wine-drinkers usually place it near the fire before uncorking, as without a moderate degree of warmth it lacks the soft and delicious flavor which makes the chief merit of this wine. Champagne, in summer, needs cooling, until it is brought to the temperature of the coldest spring water.

THE AMERICAN CODE OF POLITENESS.

DEFINITION OF POLITENESS AND ETIQUETTE.

POLITENESS has been defined as "an artificial good-nature;" but it would be better said that *good-nature is natural politeness*. It inspires us with an unremitting attention, both to please others and to avoid giving them offence. Its code is a ceremonial, agreed upon and established among mankind, to give each other external testimonies of friendship or respect. *Politeness* and *etiquette* form a sort of supplement to the law, which enables society to protect itself against offences which the *law* cannot touch. For instance, the law cannot punish a man for habitually staring at people in an insolent and annoying manner, but *etiquette* can banish such an offender from the circles of good society, and fix upon him the brand of vulgarity. *Etiquette* consists in certain forms, ceremonies, and rules which the *principle of politeness* establishes and enforces for the regulation of the manners of men and women in their intercourse with each other.

Trivial as these rules and ceremonies may appear to the unreflecting, nearly all the happiness which man derives from society depends upon them. The scholar, without good breeding, is a pedant; the philosopher, a cynic; the soldier, a brute; and every man disagreeable.

The principle of politeness is the same among all nations, but the ceremonials which etiquette imposes differ according to the taste and habits of various countries. For instance, many of the minor rules of etiquette at Paris differ from those at London; and at New York they may differ from both Paris and London. But still the polite of every country have about the same manners. The recent visit of the Japanese embassy to this country proved to us that a *gentleman* in Japan differs but little, except in trifles, from a *gentleman* in America.

GENERAL RULES OF POLITENESS.

The true aim of politeness, is to make those with whom you associate as well satisfied with themselves as possible. It does not, by any means, encourage an impudent self-importance in them, but it does whatever it can to accommodate their feelings and wishes in social intercourse. Politeness is a sort of social benevolence, which avoids wounding the pride, or shocking the prejudices of those around you.

In conversation everything should be avoided that

will have a tendency to remind any one who is in the company of past or present troubles, or which can cause uneasiness of any kind to any individual.

Any conversation (that is not interdicted by decency and propriety) which can be pleasing to the whole company, is desirable. Amusement, more than instruction even, is to be sought for in social parties. People are not supposed to come together on such occasion because they are ignorant and need teaching, but to seek amusement and relaxation from professional and daily cares. All the English books on etiquette tell you that "Punning is scrupulously to be avoided as a species of ale-house wit," and a savage remark of Dr. Johnson is usually quoted on the subject. But punning is no more to be avoided than any other kind of wit; and if all wit is to be banished from the social circle it will be left a stupid affair indeed. All kinds of wit, puns by no means excepted, give a delightful relish to social parties when they spring up naturally and spontaneously out of the themes of conversation. But for a man to be constantly straining himself to make jokes is to make himself ridiculous, and to annoy the whole company, and is, therefore, what no gentleman will be guilty of.

Whatever passes in parties at your own or another's house is never repeated by well-bred people. Things of no moment, and which are meant only as harmless jokes, are liable to produce unpleasant consequences if repeated. To repeat, therefore, any conversation which passes on such occasions, is understood to be a breach of confidence, which should banish the offender from the pale of good society.

If it is ever your fortune to confer a favor, the utmost delicacy is required in bestowing it, to prevent its being an insult to the one who receives it. You may bestow your favors in such a manner as to have it almost appear that *you* are the *obliged* party. Indeed, you may say this: "You will confer a very great favor upon me by accepting," &c. A benefit conferred as a *charity* is an insult.

If you are fond of joking, be very cautious how you let your arrows fly before you are sure of your company. Many people cannot take a joke, nor give one, and to try your wits on one so unarmed would be like offering to wrestle with a cripple. And, besides, those in the company who are constitutionally unable to comprehend a witticism would start at you with inquisitorial wonder, and if they do not annoy you, they will show that you have puzzled and disturbed them.

In a mixed company, never speak to your friend of a matter which the rest do not understand, unless it is something which you can explain to them, and which may be made interesting to the whole party.

A gentleman will, by all means, avoid showing his learning and accomplishments in the presence of ignorant and vulgar people, who can, by no possibility, understand or appreciate them. It is a pretty sure sign of bad breeding to set people to staring and feeling uncomfortable.

Do not talk too loud in company. It is presumption for you to take it for granted that everybody present is anxious to listen to you, and you may, besides, disturb the conversation already going on between others. You will also, if possible, avoid talking to any one across the room. If you have something particular to say to an individual, wait until you can get an opportunity to seat yourself by his side.

In England, it is regarded a breach of etiquette to repeat the name of any person with whom you are conversing. But the same rule does not hold in America. Here it is deemed no breach, if you are conversing with a lady by the name of Johnson, to say, " Well, *Mrs. Johnson*, do you not think," etc.

In this country, poor people often become suddenly rich ; but if they possess any of the instincts of politeness, they will carefully avoid putting on airs, or trying to show off in the presence of their former poor acquaintances. If they do so, it only proves that the acquisition of wealth has not cured them of their vulgarity, but only helped them to make a more conspicuous and insulting exhibition of it. I was once at a brilliant party in New York, where a man who had acquired great wealth by the business of a scavenger, was continually drawing comparisons between the house and furniture of our host and his own. Fortunately, I have never since met the beast in polite society. It is to be hoped that that was his first and last appearance.

Palpable flattery is, on all occasions, a great insult. And yet flattery is a great sweetener of social life, if one has the knowledge of the human heart, and the skill to use it without abusing it. Your coloring must be as subtle and delicate as the "faintest blush on the Provence rose." But there is one kind of flattery which is the most seductive, the most pleasing and gratifying of all, and which can at all times be safely used—I mean the flattery of *attention*—which is always soothing to our vanity, and is one of the cardinal virtues of good breeding.

By all means, avoid the use of slang terms and phrases in polite company. No greater insult can be offered to polite society than to repeat the slang dictation of bar-rooms and other low places. If you are willing to have it known that you are familiar with such company yourself, you have no right to treat a party of ladies and gentlemen as though they were, too.

There is no surer sign of vulgarity than the perpetual boasting of the fine things you have at home. If you speak of you silver, of your jewelry, of your costly apparel, it will be taken for a sign that you are either lying, or that you were, not long ago, somebody's washerwoman, and cannot forget to be reminding everybody that you are not so now.

There is a sort of accidental and altogether equivocal type of city women, who never get into the country, but they employ their time in trying to astonish the country people with narrations of the fine things they left behind them in the city. If they have a dirty little closet, with ten valueless books in it, they will call it their *library*. If they have some small room, that is used as kitchen, parlor, and dining-room, they will magnify it into a *drawing-room*. And a hundred other *little* signs of their *great* vulgarity they will constantly insist on exhibiting to their country auditors.

Do not *dispute* in a party of ladies and gentlemen. If a gentleman advances an opinion which is different from ideas you are known to entertain, either appear not to have heard it, or differ with him as gently as possible. You will not say, "Sir, you are mistaken!" "Sir, you are wrong!" or that you "happen to know better;" but you will rather use some such phrase as, "Pardon me—if I am not mistaken," etc. This will give him a chance to say some such civil thing as that he regrets to disagree with you; and if he has not the good manners to do it, you have, at any rate, established your own manners as those of a gentleman in the eyes of the company. And when you have done that, you need not trouble yourself about any opinions he may advance contrary to your own.

If you find yourself in a company which violently abuses an absent friend of yours, you need not feel that you are called upon to take up the club for him. You will do better by saying mildly that they must have been misinformed—that you are proud to call him your friend, which you could not do if you did not know him to be incapable of such things as they had heard. After this, if they are gentlemen, they will stop—indeed, if they had been gentlemen, they would hardly have assailed an absent one in a mixed party; and if you feel constrained to quit their company, it will be no sacrifice to your own self-respect or honor.

If you are in company with a distinguished gentleman—as a governor, or senator—you will not be perpetually trying to trot out his titles, as it would make you appear like a lackey or parasite, who, conscious of no merits of your own, are trying to lift yourself by the company of others. In introducing such a gentleman, you will merely call him "governor," or "senator," and afterwards avoid all allusion to his rank.

There is a vulgar custom, too prevalent, of calling almost everybody "colonel" in this country, of which it is sufficient to say, that this false use of titles prevails most among the lower ranks of society—a fact which sufficiently stamps upon it its real character.

and renders it, to say the least, a doubtful compliment to him who has no right to the title.

The simpler, and the more easy and unconstrained your manners, the more you will impress people of your good breeding. *Affectation* is one of the brazen marks of vulgarity.

In England, it is a mark of low breeding to smoke in the public streets. But in America the rule does not hold to quite that extent; though, even here, it is not often that you catch "a gentleman of the strictest sect" in the street with a segar or pipe in his mouth.

It is not deemed polite and respectful to smoke in the presence of ladies, even though they are amiable enough to permit it. A gentleman, therefore, is not in the habit of smoking in the parlor, for if there is nobody present to object, it leaves a smell in the room which the wife has good reason to be mortified at, if discovered by her guests. For a man to go into the street with a lady on his arm and a segar in his mouth is a shocking sight, which no gentleman will ever be guilty of exhibiting; for he inevitably subjects the woman to the very worst of suspicions.

A gentleman never sits in the house with his hat on in the presence of ladies for a single moment. Indeed, so strong is the force of habit, that a gentleman will quite unconsciously remove his hat on entering a parlor, or drawing-room, even if there is no one present but himself. People who sit in the house with their hats on are to be suspected of having spent the most of their time in bar-rooms, and similar places. *A gentleman never sits with his hat on in the theatre.* Gentlemen do not generally sit even in an eating-room with their hats on, if there is any convenient place to put them.

The books on etiquette will tell you, that on waiting on a lady into a carriage, or the box of a theatre, you are to take off your hat; but such *is not* the custom among polite people in this country. The inconvenience of such a rule is a good reason against its observance in a country where the practice of politeness has in it nothing of the servility which is often attached to it in countries where the code of etiquette is dictated by the courts of monarchy. In handing a lady into a carriage, a gentleman *may* need to employ both his hands, and he has no third hand to hold on to his hat.

The books of etiquette also tell you, that if you have been introduced to a lady and you afterwards meet her in the street, you must not bow to her unless she bow first, in order, as the books say, that she may have an opportunity to cut you if she does not wish to continue the acquaintance. This is the English fashion. But on the continent of Europe the rule is reversed, and no lady, however intimate you may be with her, will acknowledge you in the street unless you first honor her with a bow of recognition. But the American fashion is not like either of them. For here the really well-bred man always politely and respectfully bows to every lady he knows, and, if she is a well bred woman, she acknowledges the respect paid her. If she expects no further acquaintance, her bow is a mere formal, but *always respectful*, recognition of the good manners which have been shown her, and no gentleman ever takes advantage of such politeness to push a further acquaintance uninvited. But why should a lady and gentleman, who know who each other are, scornfully and doggedly pass each other in the streets as though they were enemies? There is no good reason for such *impoliteness*, in the practice of politeness. As compared with the English, the French or Continental fashion is certainly more consonant with the rules of good breeding. But the American rule is better than either, for it is based upon the acknowledged general principle, that it is every gentleman's and lady's duty to be polite in all places. Unless parties have done something to forfeit the respect dictated by the common rules of politeness, there should be no deviation from this practice. It is a ridiculous idea that we are to practise ill-manners in the name of etiquette.

The custom of *raising your hat*, or of bowing respectfully to a lady or gentleman in the streets, with your hat on, is practised equally, as occasion and convenience dictate, by well-bred Americans. By a *bow* is not meant one of those indifferent, short *nods* of the head, generally given by clowns and lackeys, but a *genuine, polite, and gentlemanly bow*, which says as much as "*your servant, madam.*"

You need not stop to pull off your glove to shake hands with a lady or gentleman. If it is warm weather it is more agreeable to both parties that the glove should be on especially if it is a lady with whom you shake hands, as the perspiration of your bare hand would be very likely to soil her glove.

The English have a rule of etiquette, that if you are introduced to a person of higher position in society than yourself, you must never recognize him when you meet until you see whether he intends to notice you. The meaning of this rule is, that you should be polite to nobody until you see whether they mean to be polite to you, which is simply refusing politeness in the name of politeness itself. There is a story of an unfortunate clerk of the Treasury, who dined one day at the Beef-steak club, where he sat next to a Duke, who conversed freely with him at dinner. The next day meeting the Duke in the street he saluted him. But his grace, drawing himself up, said, "May I know, sir, to whom I have the honor of speaking?" "Why, we dined together at the club yesterday—I am Mr. Timms, of the Treasury," was the reply. "Then," said the Duke, turning on his heel, "Mr. Timms, of the Treasury, I wish you *a good-morning.*" Though this anecdote is related in the English books as an example of etiquette, it is undoubtedly true that Mr.

Timms, of the Treasury, was the politest man of the two, for even if he had made a mistake in being a little familiar in his politeness, had the Duke been really a polite man he would have made the best of it, by returning the salutation, instead of the brutal mortification which he heaped upon the clerk of the Treasury. Every body has read the anecdote of Washington, who politely returned the salutation of a negro, which caused his friend to ask if he " bowed to a negro." " To be sure I did ; do you think that I would allow a negro to outdo me in politeness ?" said Washington. This is the American rule. Everybody in this country may be polite to everybody—and if any one is too haughty and too ill-bred to return the salutation, with him alone rests the responsibility and the shame.

If you have guests in your house, you are to appear to feel that they are all equal for the time, for they all have an equal claim upon your courtesies. Those of the humblest condition will receive *full as much attention* as the rest, in order that you shall not painfully make them feel their inferiority.

An English author has well said, that there is no more common or absurd mistake, than supposing that, because people are of high rank, they cannot be vulgar ; or that, if people be in an obscure station, they cannot be well-bred. We have seen as many instances of vulgarity in a peer as could be found in a grazier ; and have noticed as many examples of a perfect freedom from the least taint of it in persons in humble life as could be desired in a duchess. It is on this idea that the American code of etiquette is based. Pope has it—

> Honor and shame from no condition rise;
> Act well your part, there all the honor lies.

A sensible English author says: Nothing more clearly indicates the true gentlemen than a desire evinced to oblige or accommodate whenever it is possible or seasonable. It forms the broad distinction between the well-bred man of the world, and the coarse and brutal crowd—the irreclaimably vulgar—vulgar, not from their inferiority of station, but because they are coarse and brutal. Nevertheless, we often find persons so selfish and supercilious, and of so equivocal an importance, that they fancy any compliance with the wishes of the many would tend to lessen their dignity in the eyes of their companions, and who foolishly imagine that a good coat places them above the necessity of conciliating the feelings of the multitude by the performance of an act of courtesy. It is evident there cannot be a greater mistake, since even the lower classes (whatever their own practices may be) keenly appreciate, and gratefully acknowledge, the slightest consideration shown to them by their superiors.

You, of course, will never offer a person the chair in which you are sitting, unless there is no other in the room; and you will be careful not to sit down in a chair which you know to be the one in which the lady or gentleman of the house usually sits, even though they are absent. Many persons would just as soon see a stranger using their tooth-brush, as sitting in the chair which they always occupy themselves.

It is bad manners to satirize lawyers in the presence of lawyers, or doctors in the presence of one of that calling, and so of all the professions. Nor should you rail against bribery and corruption in the presence of politicians, (especially of a New York politician,) or members of Congress, as they will have good reason to suppose that you are driving at them. It is the aim of politeness to leave the arena of social intercourse untainted with any severity of language, or bitterness of feeling. There are places and occasions where wrong must be exposed and reproved, but it is an unpardonable piece of rudeness to attempt such things at your own or another's social party, where every thing is carefully to be avoided that can in the least disturb the happiness of any one. For this reason all kinds of controversies are, as a general rule, to be avoided at such times.

If you would render yourself pleasing in social parties, never speak to gratify any particular vanity or passion of your own, but always aim to interest or amuse others by themes which you know are in accordance with their tastes and understandings. Even a well-bred minister will avoid introducing his professional habits and themes at such places. He knows that the guests were not invited there to listen to a sermon, and there may be some who differ with him in opinions, who would have good reason to feel themselves insulted by being thus forced to listen to him.

Avoid restlessless in company, lest you make the whole party as fidgety as yourself. "Do not beat the 'Devil's tattoo' by drumming with your fingers on the table; it cannot fail to annoy every one within hearing, and is the index of a vacant mind. Neither read the newspaper in an audible whisper, as it disturbs the attention of those near you. Both these bad habits are particularly offensive where most common, that is, in a counting or news-room. Remember, that a carelessness as to what may incommode others is the sure sign of a coarse and ordinary mind; indeed, the essential part of good breeding is more in the avoidance of whatever may be disagreeable to others, than even an accurate observance of the customs of good society."

It is a great thing to be able to *walk like a gentleman*—that is, to get rid of the awkward, lounging, swinging gait of a clown, and stop before you reach the affected and flippant step of a dandy. In short, nothing but *being a gentleman* can ever give you the real air and step of one. A man who has a shallow or an impudent brain will be quite sure to show it in his heels, in spite of all that rules of manners can do for him.

Never address a person by his or her initial letter, as "Mr. C.," or "Mr. S." It is as vulgar as a fishmonger's style. What can be more abominable than to hear a woman speak of her husband as "Mr. P.!" as though he had become whittled down, in her estimation, until there is nothing left of him but a single letter.

If you should ever be introduced to the family of a foreign nobleman who happens to be travelling in this country, be careful not to address them as "My Lord," or "My Lady," which is only customary among servants in their own country. "Your Lordship," and "Your Ladyship" would be proper; but even these, good taste will dictate that you should use sparingly, just often enough to show that you are aware of the position they occupy at home.

Be careful not to be over-nice and particular, or you will impress people with the idea that your life began in vulgarity, and you are now trying so hard to get away from it, that you rush to the opposite extreme. Not long since, we heard a lady call Spiten-devil creek "*Spiten du vel creek;*" and, some time ago, we saw one horrified beyond description, because some one used the word "*breeches*" in her hearing. But there was a legend among the old settlers in the neighborhood that she was not always so particular in other days when she was a milliner. These clumsy and affected attempts at refinement are generally taken as signs that those who practise them began life very near the bottom of the hill.

There is a vulgar custom among some women of this country, of using their husband's titles as marks of distinction for themselves, which they sometimes have even printed on their cards, as " Mrs. Capt. Smith," " Mrs. Col. Brown," " Mrs. Governor Bibbs," " Mrs. Alderman Tibbs." Not long since, we saw a large trunk, with one whole end occupied with the following label: " MRS. LIEUTENANT SPRAGUE, U. S. A., San Francisco." A man who was looking at this queer sight, asked a bystander the meaning of those letters, and received this wicked and impolite answer : " Why, those letters generally mean *United States Army*, but *there* I suppose they must mean *Ugly, Silly Ass*." The above *parvenu* custom was borrowed from the North of England, but has never been practised by really well-bred people in this country.

It is not well to use the words " genteel " and " gentility," in speaking of fashionable and refined people, as these words are now generally used as a sneer by the vulgar, to indicate what they regard as finery and affectation in polite society.

An excessive suavity of manners is not only displeasing—it is disgusting—for it is generally a sign of insincerity and deception.

There is nothing more offensive to a gentleman than the puppyism of many young gallants, who are perpetually boasting of the attentions which are bestowed upon them by the fair sex. A well-bred man not only never boasts of such attentions, but he never even admits that he has received them. In this particular the young Japanese lad, Tommy, showed his good breeding, when a lady, in a private box at Niblo's theatre, said to him, "Tommy, they say the ladies are all very fond of you;" to which he replied, "No, ma'am, I speak American language. Ladies like to speak to me—so do gentlemen; they understand me, I understand them. They say, 'How do, Tommy?'—shake hands, and I say, 'Very well, sir, ma'am'—shake hands, too. No more." It will be seen that Tommy sought for a proper reason why the ladies were fond of speaking to him.

No gentleman will stand in the doors of hotels, nor on the corners of the streets, gazing impertinently at the ladies as they pass. That is such an unmistakable sign of a loafer, that one can hardly imagine a wellbred man doing such a thing.

In walking with a lady, it is customary to give her the right arm; but where circumstances render it more convenient to give her the left, it may properly be done. If you are walking with a lady on a crowded street, like Broadway, by all means give her the outside, as that will prevent her from being perpetually jostled and run against by the hurrying crowd.

A well-bred man will not take a seat by the side of a lady with whom he is unacquainted, in a railroad car, unless there is no other seat for him; and if he is compelled to take such a seat, he politely apologises to the lady for doing so, in some such manner as saying that he is very sorry to disturb her, but there is no other vacant seat in the car.

Do not pretend to be what you are not, for no pretension can long hide what you in reality are. The thin veil is soon seen through, and by trying to deceive, in relation to your deserts, you will be judged an impostor in all things, and, as such, kicked out of society.

Do not assume too much for yourself and your family. For the man who gives himself airs of importance only exhibits the credentials of his own insignificance. It is known that the man of real position does not talk about it.

Affectation in anything that belongs to you is only holding a candle to your own defects. Besides, by affectation you insult every company you are in, for you assume that they are shallow enough to be deceived by your flippancy.

Exhibiting yourself as better and more pious than other men is another way of insulting your associates. The devout man never affects any remarkable degree of piety—it is the hypocrite who puts on godly airs.

It is a mark of ill-breeding to refuse praise where praise is evidently due; and, on the other hand, nothing can be more vulgar than indiscriminate and insincere praise. It is the next thing to abuse.

A proud and disdainful deportment is insulting to every company you may be in, and to every man you meet. Every one owes affability and good-nature to society.

It is a mark of weakness and sycophancy to run indiscriminately after every notoriety that comes along. It shows a lack of judgment, as well as of taste, for it will not do to be always led in the current of popular applause. Esteem and admiration are not always bestowed on those who best deserve them. They are often stolen from the public by those who have the art of setting off moderate qualifications, which frequently gives more reputation than real merit.

Nothing detracts more from the character of a gentleman than the exhibition of envy. He that perpetually manifests this bad spirit, not only tells everybody about him that he knows himself to be despised, but he renders himself the annoyance of every company.

Giving advice when it is not asked, is an impertinence that a gentleman is never guilty of. It is assuming a superiority on your part which even the firmest friendship will find it difficult to forgive.

Avoid going into company when you are what is called *out of sorts*, or peevish and dull. People get together in company to enjoy themselves, and if you are not in a condition to *enjoy* nor to be enjoyed, by all means stay at home.

There is no part of personal manners which is more significant than the mode of shaking hands. A country bumpkin seizes your hand with as much violence as though he were catching a pig, and if he does not break your fingers it is a mercy. The fop languidly gives you his hand, and you may shake it if you will, but it cannot be said that he grasps yours. The consequential and impertinent stripling holds out, in a patronizing manner, two fingers, or, perhaps, only his forefinger, which you may touch, unless you prefer to use the toe of your boot. It is needless to say that no *gentleman* is found shaking hands after either of these fashions.

The following witty remarks we copy from the Parisian Code of Politeness: " Propriety in the carriage of the body is especially indispensable to ladies. It is by this that, in a ball, a walk, or any assembly, people who cannot converse with them judge of their merits and their good education. How many dancers move off, and how many persons sigh with pity to see a beautiful woman, who has a mincing gait, affects grace, inclines her head affectedly, and who seems to admire herself incessantly and invite others to do the same! Who ever makes up his mind to enter into conversation with an immovable lady, and one who is formal and precise, lengthening out the body, pressing the lips, and carrying back the elbows as if they were fastened to her side?"

"It is not good *ton* for a lady to speak too quick or too loud. When seated, she ought neither to cross her legs nor take any vulgar attitude. She should occupy her chair entirely, and appear neither too restless nor too immovable. It is altogether out of place for her to throw her drapery around her in sitting down, or to spread out her dress for display, as upstarts do, in order to avoid the least rumple."

In walking, a lady ought to have a modest and measured gait; too great hurry injures the grace which ought to characterize her; a flaunting carriage betrays *étourderie*, or boldness; she should not turn her head, or stare about her; such a habit seems an invitation to the impertinent.

Immoderate laughter is exceedingly unbecoming in a lady; she may affect the dimple or the smile, but should carefully avoid any approximation to a horse-laugh. Laughers have been ranged under the following heads:—

>THE DIMPLERS.
>THE SMILERS.
>THE LAUGHERS.
>THE GRINNERS.
>THE HORSE-LAUGHERS.

The dimple is practised to give a grace to the features, and is frequently made a bait to entangle a gazing lover. This was called by the ancients the chain-laugh.

The smile is for the most part confined to the fair sex and their male retinue. It expresses our satisfaction in a sort of liberal approbation; it does not too much disorder the features, and is practised by lovers of the most delicate address. This tender emotion of physiognomy the ancients called the Ionic-laugh.

The laugh among us is the common *risus* of the ancients, and is simply an expansion of the smile, accompanied by a slight cachination.

The grin, by writers of antiquity, is called the Syncrusian, and was then, as it is now, made use of to display a beautiful set of teeth.

The horse-laugh is an undue expansion of the laugh, accompanied with a boisterous noise, and is not allowable in polite society. It may be, however, and often is, made use of in all kinds of disputation. Those who are proficient in it, by a well-timed laugh, will often baffle the most solid reasoner. This, upon all occasions, supplies the want of reason; is always received with great applause in coffee-houses, disputes, and wranglings; and that side which the laugh joins with, generally gets the better of its antagonist.

ON TALKING IN COMPANY.

A man is quite sure to show his good or bad breeding the instant he opens his mouth to talk in company. If he is *a gentleman* he starts no subject of conversation that can possibly be displeasing to any person present. The ground is common to all, and no one has a right to monopolize any part of it for his own particular opinions, in politics or religion. No one is there to make proselytes, but every one has been invited, to be *agreeable* and *to please*.

At such times you should avoid appearing dogmatical and too positive in any assertions you make, which can possibly be subject to any contradiction. He that is peremptory in his own story, may meet with another as positive as himself to contradict him, and then the two Sir Positives will be sure to have a skirmish.

You will forbear to interrupt a person who is telling a story, even though he is making historical mistakes in dates and facts. If he makes mistakes it is his own fault, and it is not your business to mortify him by attempting to correct his blunders in presence of those with whom he is ambitious to stand well.

If a man is telling that which is as old as the hills, or which you believe to be false, the better way is to let him go on. Why should you refuse a man the pleasure of believing that he is telling you something which you never heard before? Besides, by refusing to believe him, or by telling him that his story is old, you not only mortify him, but the whole company is made uneasy, and, by sympathy, share his mortification.

Avoid raillery and sarcasm in social parties. They are weapons which few can use; and because you happen to have a razor in your possession, that is no reason why you should be allowed to cut the throats of the rest who are unarmed. Malicious jests at the expense of those who are present or absent, show that he who uses them is devoid both of the instincts and habits of a *gentleman*. Where two individuals or the whole company agree to banter each other with good-natured sallies of wit, it is very pleasant, but the least taint of ill-nature spoils all.

If you are really a wit, remember, that in conversation its true office consists more in finding it in others, than showing off a great deal of it yourself. He who goes out of your company pleased with himself is sure to be pleased with you. Even as great a man as Dr. Johnson once retired from a party where everybody had spent the evening in listening to him, and remarked, as he went out, "We have had a pleasant evening, and much excellent conversation."

A sure way to please in conversation is to hunt up as many of each others' excellencies as possible, and be as blind as possible to each others' imperfections. There is no compromise of principle in this, for you are to consider that a social party is not intended as a school for reform, or a pulpit to denounce sin in.

Talk as little of yourself as possible, or of any science or business in which you have acquired fame. There is a banker in New York who is always certain to occupy the time of every party he gets into, by talking of his *per cents*, and boasting that he *began life without a cent*—which every one readily believes ; and if he were to add that he *began life in a pig-pen*, they would believe that too.

Even if you are not a good talker, try to sustain some share of the conversation ; for you as easily insult a company by maintaining a contemptuous silence, as by engrossing all the talk.

Listen attentively and patiently to what is said. It is a great and difficult talent to be a good listener, but it is one which the well-bred man has to acquire, at whatever pains.

If you meet an ill-bred fellow in company, whose voice and manners are offensive to you, you cannot resent it at the time, because by so doing you compel the whole company to be spectators of your quarrel, and the pleasure of the party would be spoiled.

Don't talk of " the opera " in the presence of those who are not frequenters of it. They will imagine that you are showing off, or that you are *lying*, and that you have never been to the opera twice in your life. For the same reason, avoid too frequently speaking of your acquaintance with celebrated men, unless you are a public man yourself, who would be supposed to have such acquaintance.

By all means, shun the vulgar habit of joking at the expense of women. All such tricks as refusing a lady a piece of tongue, because "*women already have tongue enough,*" are as vulgar as they are old and stale. The man who does not respect woman, exposes himself to the suspicion of associating generally with the fallen portion of the sex. And besides, he has no right to make a respectable parlor or drawing-room the theatre of such vulgar jokes and railing against the sex as go down in low society.

ON INTRODUCTIONS.

The custom which prevails in country places of introducing everybody you meet to each other, is both an annoying and an improper one. As a general rule, introductions ought not to be made, except where there is undoubted evidence that the acquaintance would be mutually agreeable and proper.

It is customary, in introducing people, to present the youngest person to the oldest, or the humblest to the highest in position, if there is any distinction, thus: "Mr. Thompson, allow me to present to you Mr. Smith;" or, "I wish to make you acquainted with Mr. Smith." The gentleman is always presented to the lady, as, "Mrs. Johnson, I have the pleasure of presenting to you Mr. Simpson." When you introduce parties which you are quite sure will be pleased with each other, it is well to add, after the introduction, that you take great pleasure in making them acquainted, which will be an assurance to each that you think they are well matched, and thus they are prepared to be friends from the start.

In introducing parties, be careful to pronounce each name distinctly, as there is nothing more awkward than to have one's name miscalled; for instance, for a man whose name is Morehead to be called *Molehead*, or Grimshaw to be called *Grimshanks*. Mistakes quite as unpleasant as these are constantly occurring, in consequence of indistinct introductions.

When you are introduced to a person, be careful not to appear as though you had never heard of him before. If he happens to be a person of any distinction, such a mistake would be unpardonable, and no person is complimented by being reminded of the fact that his name is unknown.

If by any misfortune you have been introduced to a person whose acquaintance you do not desire, you can merely make the formal bow of etiquette when you meet him, which, of itself, encourages no familiarity;

but *the bow is indispensable*, for he cannot be thought a gentleman who would pass another with a vacant stare, after having been formally presented to him. By so doing, he would offer a slight which would justly make him appear contemptible even in the eyes of the person he means to humble.

What is called " cutting " another is never practised by gentlemen or ladies, except in some extraordinary instances of bad conduct on the part of the individual thus sacrificed. An increased degree of ceremony and formal politeness is the most delicate way of withdrawing from an unpleasant acquaintance. Indeed, what is called " cutting" is rarely ever practised by well-bred ladies and gentlemen.

Letters of introduction are to be regarded as certificates of respectability, and are therefore never to be given where you do not feel sure on this point. To send a person of whom you know nothing into the confidence and family of a friend, is an unpardonable recklessness. In England, letters of introduction are called " tickets to soup," because it is generally customary to invite a gentleman to dine who comes with a letter of introduction to you. Such is also the practice, to some extent, in this country, but etiquette *here* does not make the dinner so essential as *there*.

In England, the party holding a letter of introduction never takes it himself to the party to whom it is addressed, but he sends it with his card of address.

In France, and on the continent of Europe generally, directly the reverse is the fashion. In America the English custom generally prevails; though where a young gentleman has a letter to one who is many years his senior, or to one whose aid he seeks in some enterprise, he takes it at once himself.

When a gentleman, bearing a letter of introduction to you, leaves his card, you should call on him, or send a note, as early as possible. There is no greater insult than to treat a letter of introduction with indifference. After you have made this call, it is, to some extent, optional with you as to what further attentions you shall pay the party. In this country everybody is supposed to be very busy, which is always a sufficient excuse for not paying elaborate attentions to visitors. It is not demanded that any man shall neglect his business to wait upon visitors or guests.

Letters of mere introduction are not sealed by the parties who write them; but the parties taking them may seal them or not, as they please, before delivering them.

ON DRESS.

Well-bred people do not often dress in what is called the "heighth of fashion," as that is generally left to dandies and pretenders. But still it is undoubtedly a great point gained to be well dressed. To be fancifully dressed, in gaudy colors, is to be very badly dressed, however, and is an example of ill taste which is rarely met with among people of substantial good breeding.

Cleanliness and neatness are the invariable accompaniments of good breeding. Every gentleman may not be dressed expensively, he may not be able to do so; but water is cheap, and no gentleman will ever go into company unmindful of cleanliness either in his person or apparel.

Did any lady ever see a gentleman with an embroidered waistcoat, and a profusion of chains, rings, and trinkets adorning his person?

Avoid affecting singularity in dress. Expensive dressing is no sign of a gentlemen. If a gentleman is able to dress expensively it is very well for him to do so, but if *he is not able* to wear ten-dollar broadcloth, he may comfort himself with the reflection that cloth which costs but three dollars a yard will look quite as well when made into a well-fitting coat. With this suit, and well-made shoes, clean gloves, a white pocket-handkerchief, and an easy and graceful deportment withal, he may pass muster as a gentleman. Manners do quite as much to set off a suit of clothes as clothes do to set off a graceful person.

Avoid what is called the "ruffianly style of dress," or the *nonchalant* and *slouching* appearance of a half-unbuttoned vest, and suspenderless pantaloons. That sort of affectation is, if possible, even more disgusting than the painfully elaborate frippery of the dandy.

Gentlemen never make any display of jewelry; that is given up entirely to the dominion of female taste. But ladies of good taste seldom wear it in the morning. It is reserved for evening display and for brilliant parties.

ON EVENING PARTIES.

Invitations to evening parties are sent several days before the party is to take place, and the answers should invariably be returned immediately, *accepting* or *declining, with regrets.*

In most of the American cities nine o'clock is the hour which custom has established as the time for the lady to be in her parlor, ready to receive her guests, and by ten o'clock all the guests should arrive. It is an affectation, not entirely devoid of assumption and impudence, for people to purposely delay their appearance till a very late hour.

In large and formal parties, it is generally customary for the servant to announce the names of the guests as they enter the room, but this is a ceremony well enough dispensed with, except on occasions of very large and formal parties.

It is the business of the lady of the house to be near the door to receive her guests: if she is not there, you need not go hunting through the crowd after her. We were once at a brilliant party in Philadelphia. where a young man, who had evidently read in some book on politeness that it was his duty to make his first address to the lady of the house, went tearing through the crowd after her, like an engine, carrying with him one side of a lady's dress, and overturning a small table that held a pitcher of lemonade, until he brought up against, and nearly unseated, a young lady who was presiding at the piano :---an incident which shows that without good sense it is impossible to be a gentleman.

In leaving a party, if you go before it breaks up, seek the lady of the house, and bid her good-night as quietly as possibly, and retire without attracting the notice of the remaining guests.

If a gentleman dances at a party, he does not kick and caper about like a monkey, nor sway his body to and fro like a public dancer upon the stage. He particularly avoids showing off at such times, unless he is ambitious to be taken for a dancing-master, between whose manners and those of a *gentleman* there is the widest difference.

I have already said that really well-bred people are never guilty of the abominable sin of backbiting ;

but yet there are thousands of people in the world who think themselves well-bred, whose mouths are guillotines to every good name that gets into them. Aaron Burr, who was one of the most refined and accomplished gentlemen that ever lived, used to say, that "the gulf between Dives and Lazarus was not greater than that between a *gentleman* and a *calumniator*." Parton, in his interesting life of this extraordinary man, relates the following characteristic anecdote:

"Some gentlemen were in his room one evening, when the conversation took a severer tone than he liked. Now, speaking ill of any one, or the use of denunciatory language, he never relished. After one of his guests had finished some severe remarks, the lady of the house stepped forward, and in a quick, graceful manner peculiar to her, repeated the lines from Burns' Address to the Unco Gude:

'Then gently scan your brother **man**,
   Still gentler sister woman;
Though they may gang akennin' wrang,
   To step aside is human:
One point must still be greatly dark,
   The moving *Why* they do it,
And just as lamely can ye mark
   How far, perhaps, they rue it.

'Who made the heart, 'tis He alone
   Decidedly can try us;
He knows each chord—its various tone,
   Each spring—its **various** bias;

> Then at the balance let's be mute—
> We never can adjust it;
> What's done we partly may compute,
> But know not what's resisted.'

Good-humor was restored, and a better spirit prevailed in the company. Burr, who had lain silent up to this time, now expressed the keenest delight. '*How good!*' he kept whispering—'how *very* good. So like you, my dear; *so* like you!' He was exceedingly pleased, and often alluded to the scene and the lines afterwards."

Remember, that if *good fortune* get you the esteem of the public, still nothing but *merit* can procure the respect and confidence of men of sense and virtue.

Of all the sinners against the laws of politeness, the *braggar* or the *liar* is one of the greatest. False pretending is one of the sure signs of ill-bred rascality. Not long ago, a family moved from the city a few miles out into a small country village, where the father, mother, sons, and daughters all commenced boasting of their associations and splendor in the city. But it soon became known that the head of this swaggering family was, a few years ago, a roper-in for a gambling hell, and a decoy-duck for a still more disreputable place, in Philadelphia; and afterwards a keeper of a vile den in California; and, finally, the proprietor of a faro-bank, and a manufacturer of illegal and indecent wares in New York city, where he brought up his daughters as shining lights of a free-love club.

Every member of this leprous family at once set up to be censors of the village manners, and slanderers of the moral excellence which they naturally enough hated. But vain are the thin disguises in which low vice tries to hide itself! Every well-bred person at once detects all false pretending to respectability. The true coin of good breeding is so indelibly stamped with unmistakable grace and naturalness, that no counterfeit can ever be made to imitate it. The only sensible thing for people of the character described above is, to keep as quiet, and remain as much in the dark, as possible.

The man who has no merit himself will always be envious of the merit of others ; and, therefore, by abusing others, you expose yourself to the suspicion of being destitute of character.

Modest people seldom fail to gain the good-will and respect of those with whom they converse, because nobody is envious of those who make no pretension to any especial claims upon their respect.

Do not forget that no matter how eloquent you may be, you will please most people more by listening to them than by talking yourself.

An overdone politeness is the next thing to rudeness, for it presumes upon your own superiority, or upon the inexperience of the one to whom you address yourself.

ON EVENING PARTIES.

The reason why we meet with so few people who are really agreeable in conversation is, because men generally think more of what they shall say themselves, than they do of properly answering what is said to them.

You cannot be too careful of the company you keep, because bad manners are as catching as infectious diseases.

Great talents for conversation, if not accompanied with the most vigilant politeness, will get a man many enemies; because, if you eclipse others in conversation, you must pay them great civilities to keep from wounding their pride.

Remember that there are but few good story-tellers, and that unless you are a rare exception to the generality of mankind, it will be a hazardous thing for you to attempt to tell stories in company.

If you have been abroad in foreign lands, avoid alluding to the fact, or relating what you saw and did there, except in the company of friends who you are sure are anxious to hear you; for it is very easy to arouse the envy and hatred of those who have enjoyed less advantages in seeing the world than yourself.

MARRIAGE.

I have already said, that when a man marries, it is understood that all former acquaintanceship *ends*, unless he intimate a desire to renew it, by sending you his own and his wife's card, if near, or by letter, if distant. If this be neglected, be sure no further intercourse is desired.

In the first place—a bachelor is seldom *very particular* in the choice of his companions. So long as he is amused, he will associate freely enough with those whose morals and habits would point them out as highly dangerous persons to introduce into the sanctity of domestic life.

Secondly—a married man has the tastes of *another* to consult; and the friend of the *husband* may not be equally acceptable to the *wife*.

Besides—newly-married people may wish to limit the circle of their friends, from praiseworthy motives of economy. When a man "*sets up*" in the world, the burthen of an extensive and indiscriminate acquaintance may be felt in various ways. Many have had cause to regret the weakness of mind which allowed them to plunge into a vortex of gayety and expense they could ill afford, from which they have found it difficult to extricate themselves, and the effects of which have proved a serious evil to them in after life.

DANCING.

With the etiquette of a ball-room, so far as it goes, there are but few people unacquainted. Certain persons are appointed to act as stewards, or there will be a " master of the ceremonies," whose office it is to see that everything be conducted in a proper manner: if you are entirely a stranger, it is to *them* you must apply for a partner, and point out (quietly) any young lady with whom you should like to dance, when, if there be no obvious inequality of rank, they will present you for that purpose; should there be an objection, they will probably select some one they consider more suitable; but do not, on any account, go to a strange lady by yourself, and request her to dance, as she will unhesitatingly " decline the honor," and think you an impertinent fellow for your presumption.

Any presentation to a lady in a public ball-room, for the mere purpose of dancing, does not entitle you to claim her acquaintance afterwards; therefore, should you meet her, at most you may lift your hat; but even that is better avoided,—unless, indeed, she first bow,—as neither she nor her friends can know who or *what* you are.

Lead the lady through the quadrille; do not *drag* her, nor clasp her hand as if it were made of wood, lest she, not unjustly, think you a bear.

You will not, if you are wise, stand up in a quadrille without knowing something of the figure ; and if you are master of a few of the steps, *so much the better.* But dance quietly ; do not kick and caper about, nor sway your body to and fro ; dance only *from the hips downwards ;* and lead the lady as lightly as you would tread a measure with a spirit of gossamer.

Do not pride yourself on doing the " steps neatly," unless you are ambitious of being taken for a dancing-master ; between whose motions and those of a *gentleman* there is a great difference.

If a lady should decline civilly to dance with you, making an excuse, and you chance to see her dancing afterwards, do not take any notice of it, nor be offended with her. It might not be that she *despised* you, but that she *preferred* another. We cannot always fathom the hidden springs which influence a woman's actions, and there are many bursting hearts within white satin dresses ; therefore, do not insist upon the fulfilment of established regulation " designer."

Besides, it is a hard case that women should be compelled to dance with everybody offered them, at the alternative of not being allowed to enjoy themselves at all.

If a friend be engaged when you request her to dance, and she promises to be your partner for the next or any of the following dances, do not neglect her when the time comes, but be in readiness to fulfil your office as her cavalier, or she may think that you have studiously slighted her, besides preventing her obliging some one else. Even inattention and forgetfulness, by showing how little you care for a lady, form in themselves a tacit insult.

If a lady waltz with you, beware not to press her waist; you must only lightly touch it with the palm of your hand, lest you leave a disagreeable impression not only on her *ceinture*, but on her mind.

Above all, do not be prone to quarrel in a ballroom; it disturbs the harmony of the company, and should be avoided if possible. Recollect, that a thousand little derelictions from strict propriety may occur through the ignorance or stupidity of the aggressor, and not from any intention to annoy: remember, also, that the *really well-bred women* will not thank you for making them conspicuous by over-officiousness in their defence, unless, indeed, there be some serious or glaring violation of decorum. In small matters, ladies are both able and willing to take care of themselves, and would prefer being allowed to overwhelm the unlucky offender in their own way.

If, while walking up and down a public promenade, you should meet friends or acquaintances whom you don't intend to join, it is only necessary to salute them the first time of passing; to bow or nod to them at every round would be tiresome, and therefore improper; have no fear that they will deem you odd or unfriendly, as, if they have any sense at all, they can appreciate your reasons. If you have anything to say to them, join them at once.

ETIQUETTE AT WASHINGTON.

The rules of social intercourse in the city of Washington, the capital of the United States, though in accordance with the customs of general good breeding everywhere, are nevertheless destitute of that unity and completeness which may be found in other American cities. What is called "society" in Washington is made up chiefly of foreign diplomats and our own statesmen and politicians, and the rules of etiquette practised there are, to some little extent, varied or modified by all the various European and American localities which are represented in its community.

But, for all this, there is no place in our country where etiquette is more inexorable, or exacting, than in Washington. All small cities, which happen to be capitals of great states, are sure to get intoxicated with self-importance—to put on airs, and become wise in their own conceits. The well-bred man will not be long in Washington before he will have occasion to smile at the truth of this remark; and if he perceives a few things in their etiquette which are peculiar and pedantic, he will not, of course, either disregard or attempt to reform them, but readily fall in with the customs of fashionable life there.

There is a small pamphlet on the "Etiquette of Washington," published in that city, all the essential matter of which is condensed in the remaining pages of this book.

DRESS.

"The very idea of a gentleman excludes that of a fop or dandy. A gentleman will dress well, but never gaudily. This rule alone, if properly attended to, might serve for all that we have to say under this head; but, for the benefit of the young and inexperienced, whose welfare we have most at heart, we will suggest a few things to be done, and others to be omitted. We say, therefore, eschew an excess of jewelry. A breast-pin, or gold button with a chain, is very well. A ring is also worn by some. Avoid gaudiness and singularity. Adapt your dress to your complexion. Washington, though a small place, is, in one respect, quite metropolitan. During the winter its society is made up of materials gathered from all parts of the country, and all the styles as well as all the politics of the country are represented here. A gentleman, therefore, may suit his taste in respect to the shape and material of his hat, coat, etc. The same remarks apply to the dress of ladies, but they, in the nature of things, are allowed greater variety of colors, ornament, style, etc., etc."

INTRODUCTIONS, CARDS, VISITING, &c.

It is not in good taste to give introductions, as a matter of course, as is the custom in the country. The reason of this restriction upon the natural dictates of polite and amiable natures can be best understood by those who live in cities. In the country, where everybody knows everybody, and everybody's business, the proverb that "a man is known by the company he keeps" loses much of its significance; but in cities it is literally true, and hence the disinclination of city people to make acquaintances, whom it might become inconvenient or distasteful to recognize on all occasions.

It is safest, therefore, to omit introductions, without a previous understanding with the parties, even at the hazard of seeming rude. But common sense and a knowledge of the parties will teach any one the proper course to pursue.

Letters of introduction should never be given unless the writer is well and favorably known to the person addressed, and he should be sure that the party introduced is worthy of respect and trust, in the capacity in which he is introduced. The latter may present the letter or not, as may suit his convenience. The letter should be left unsealed by the writer.

The bearer of a letter of introduction should send it with his card. He would thus avoid the awkwardness of waiting for a recognition while the party to whom it is addressed reads it. The latter may find it inconvenient to receive company, and the card would afford him an opportunity to decline.

But if the letter be on business, it should be presented in person. Business dispenses with ceremony. If you receive a letter introducing a gentleman, you should at once leave your card for him at his lodgings.

Cards are indispensable to the intercouse of polite society; but we are constrained by our limited space to omit specific directions for their use.

Visits of ceremony should be in the morning, and should not last more than five to twenty minutes. A card left at the door suffices for a morning call, among very fashionable people. It is to be borne in mind that in the fashionable world, morning never breaks earlier than eleven o'clock, and usually lasts until three. The lady who receives calls should do so at once, or send a servant to excuse her. When the call is intended for both the gentleman and lady, the name of the latter only should be mentioned. In making a morning call, a gentleman should retain his hat in his hand, which the lady will not notice. But if a longer visit is intended, the hat, overcoat, &c., should be deposited in the hall before entering the room.

The lady of the house should never trouble her guests with her household derangements, nor the gentleman with his business. The topics selected for conversation should be general, and of an agreeable nature. If the company agree in politics or religion, it is delightful to interchange sentiments and impressions of passing events; but it is always awkward, if not disagreeable and rude, to introduce controverted questions. Very intelligent and polished people may discuss politics without offence, but it requires the utmost skill and delicacy to do so; and, as a general rule, all such discussions run into unpleasant disputation.

It is the custom in Washington for two or more ladies, during the day, to visit the Capitol, the Patent Office, the Smithsonian Institution, &c., unattended by gentlemen, as otherwise they might be debarred many enjoyments. Where it is inconvenient for a lady to find a female companion in such a walk, it is sufficient to have the attendance of a child.

EVENING PARTIES.

Evening parties are most appropriate to the winter. They are discontinued during Lent, but may be resumed afterwards. Cards of invitation should be sent to guests some days beforehand, and the latter should immediately accept, or decline with regrets. The cards should be in the name of the lady, either written or engraved. Fashion has established nine o'clock as the hour at which the lady should be in her parlor to receive her guests; and from that hour to ten the guests are expected to arrive.

The lady should have everything arranged, so that she will not be compelled to leave her guests to superintend her household. The guests will be conducted to the dressing-rooms, and the ladies, having adjusted their toilets, will be attended to the drawing-room by the gentlemen who accompany them. A servant sometimes announces the names of the guests as they enter the room. The lady will precede the gentleman, or lean on his arm. The lady of the house will be near the door to receive them, and after a few words of greeting, they will pass on, and join in conversation with any of their acquaintances who may be present.

Gentlemen will not get together in groups to the neglect of the ladies.

When a table is spread, the host will precede his guests, in company with one of the ladies, followed by the hostess. The gentlemen present will conduct the ladies in a like manner.

When no table is spread, the refreshments will be handed around, and the guests will help themselves. At intervals, iced beverages will be passed around the rooms for the refreshment of the guests. White or very light-colored kid gloves are worn during the evening, except at supper.

DINNERS.

Invitations to dinner-parties may be sent out from two days to a fortnight before the appointed time. They should be in the name of the lady, and the acceptance or declination should be sent immediately, addressed to her. It is also necessary that the lady should be informed if any guest, after accepting the invitation, will be prevented by subsequent circumstances from attending. The invitations should specify the hour of dining, and the guests should be punctual in arriving. In Washington, the hour for dinner-parties is from four to seven o'clock. When dinner is announced, each gentleman should offer his left arm to a lady, if the dining-room is on the same floor; but if they are to descend the stairs, the lady should be on the wall side. The host should lead the way, and the lady should follow the company, on the arm of a gentleman of the party. She will, of course, take the head of the table, and should have a gentleman on either side to assist her in carving. Her husband should sit opposite to her, with a lady on each side of him. These positions next to the host and hostess are considered the places of honor. Soup will constitute the first course, which must be noiselessly sipped from the side of the spoon. It is impolite to ask for a second plate. Fish usually follows soup. It is helped with a silver fork, and eaten with a silver fork, assisted by a piece of bread held in the left hand.

A knife of the usual metal is deemed highly inju-
11*

rious to the flavor of fish. After this course, meat, fowls, &c., are served. The napkins are to be unfolded and spread upon the knees. Finger-glasses will be brought on with the dessert. They contain warm water, with a bit of lemon in it. It is usual to dip a corner of the napkin in the water, and wipe the lips; also to dip the fingers in and wipe them on the napkin. It is highly disgusting to spit or blow the nose with a loud explosive noise at the table. The knife is never used to convey food to the mouth; the fork being generally sufficient for the purpose; or it may be assisted by a piece of bread in the left hand. The servants should each be furnished with a clean white napkin, with which to handle the plates of the guests. Clean white gloves are sometimes used. Wine is not drunk until the second course is over. The ladies are helped to the kind of wine they prefer by the gentleman next to them. When the ladies retire, the gentlemen should rise with them, and stand until they leave the dining-room. Coffee may be served either in the dining-room or parlor.

DEPORTMENT IN THE STREET.

The toilet should be thoroughly adjusted before leaving the house, even to the putting on the gloves. The great point in walking is to be natural. All affected airs are contemptible. On the other hand, an awkward or slovenly gait should not be mistaken for a natural one.

A gentleman meeting a lady acquaintance should wait to be recognized by her, and should raise his hat while bowing to her. Also, in meeting a gentleman of your acquaintance who is accompanied by a lady, you should raise your hat out of respect to her, and he should respond in a like manner to your salutation. If a gentleman salutes the lady you accompany, you should return it, if she recognizes it. It is not necessary to take off the gloves in shaking hands with a lady, neither should a gentleman make the advances. In walking, the gentleman should keep next to the carriage-way.

A gentleman should never omit a punctilious observance of the rules of politeness to his recognized acquaintances, from an apprehension that he will not be met with reciprocal marks of respect. For instance, he should not refuse to raise his hat to an acquaintance who is accompanied by a lady, lest her escort should, from ignorance or stolidity, return his polite salutation with a nod of the head.

It is better not to see him, than to set the example of a rude and indecorous salutation. In all such cases, and in all cases, he who is most courteous has the advantage, and should never feel that he has made a humiliating sacrifice of his personal dignity. It is for the party whose behavior has been boorish to have a consciousness of inferiority.

A gentleman meeting a lady acquaintance on the

street, should not presume to join her in her walk without ascertaining that his company would be entirely agreeable. It might be otherwise, and she should frankly say so. A married lady usually leans upon the arm of her husband; but single ladies do not, in the day, take the arm of a gentleman, unless they are willing to acknowledge an engagement. Gentlemen always give place to ladies, and gentlemen accompanying ladies, in crossing the street.

BALLS.

Balls, to which anybody who chooses may go, and take whom he pleases, by buying a ticket, are avoided by many ladies, and with good reason. But select balls, under judicious and responsible management, are not liable to this objection. In such cases the ladies are invited, and none others go. The gentleman who accompanies a lady will dance the first set with her. She may then dance with other gentlemen. At a private party, a gentleman may offer to dance with a lady without an introduction, but at balls the rule is different. The gentleman should respectfully offer his arm to the lady who consents to dance with him, and lead her to her place. At the conclusion of the set he will conduct her to a seat, offer her any attention, or converse with her. A gentleman should not dance with his wife, and not too often with the lady to whom he is engaged.

VISITS TO OFFICIAL PERSONS ON BUSINESS.

Calls upon the cabinet and other administrative officers in Washington upon official business, should be made during business hours, at their respective offices. The visitor should be provided with a card, which the messenger will deliver. He should briefly state his business, and remain not a moment longer than is necessary. Members of Congress may be seen at their lodgings, or at the capitol while the Houses are in session. Very little ceremony is necessary if the visitor be an influential constituent.

THE PRESIDENT.

The President has a grand levee on the first of January, when people crowd to the executive mansion in such numbers, that of late years it has been found necessary to shut the doors, and only admit as many at one time as can be conveniently accommodated with space within. After this opening levee, which occurs in the morning, the President has periodical levees on a certain evening of each week, or, since Mr. Buchanan's term commenced, every fortnight. These are also well attended. The public are admitted indiscriminately on these occasions, but no refreshments are offered. The marshal for the district introduces the public. The President has also a sort of weekly summer levee in the south grounds, in which the performance of the marine band is the principal attraction.

The President is accessible to private individuals who desire to see him on business, and he has also set apart an hour or two on certain days in each week for receiving the friendly visits of the public. These regulations are often varied, and we therefore refrain from giving them. The President never accepts invitations to dinner, or makes social visits. An invitation to dine with the President is accepted, notwithstanding a previous engagement. It is proper to address him as *Mr. President.*

On New Year's day the New York custom prevails in Washington of keeping open-house. Not only the President and cabinet, but many other gentlemen, official and private, have adopted it, and furnish their voluntary guests with refreshments.

We have thus given the leading rules and principles of Washington etiquette. To supply all the details of ceremony in social and official life would require a volume, and compel us to depart from the plan which we had marked out for ourselves."

TABLE WIT AND ANECDOTES.

ALL men are bound to be especially amiable at table, and every thing tart and ill-natured is, therefore, carefully avoided. But yet, the graceful sally and happy retort are often among the most spicy and mirth-provoking events at a feast. A celebrated scholar and wit was selecting some of the choicest delicacies on the table, when a rich friend said to him, "What! do philosophers love dainties?" "Why not?" replied the scholar; "do you think all the good things of this world were made only for blockheads?"

This would be sure to "set the table in a roar," because it was a tilt between two friends and equals, and the question was asked for the purpose of provoking a wit's reply.

Once when Lord Chesterfield came late to dinner, an illustrious guest said to him, "What, my lord, you so late! we have already drank six bottles of wine." "That," said his lordship, "is more than I can *swallow*."

An English traveller dining at a French ordinary in Soho, seeing a large dish of soup with about half a pound of mutton in the middle of it, began to pull off his coat and vest, at which a French gentleman asked him what he was going to do? "Why, monsieur," said he, "I am going to see if I can swim through this ocean of porridge to yon little island of mutton."

A party of wags and *littérateurs* were lately dining at Delmonico's, when, after the bottle had made its tenth round, one of the company proposed this toast—"To the man whose wife was never false to him!" upon which a wag of an old bachelor jumped up and said, "Gentlemen, as I am the only unmarried man at this table, I suppose that that toast was intended for me."

Monsieur Charles Nalo, an eminent French translator, being employed on an American work, came to the words, *moose deer;* he flew to his dictionary, but could find no such word as *moose*, but finding the word *mouse*, he concluded that that was the word, which had been misprinted *moose*, and so he translated *moose deer*—'great mice, six feet high, with antlers.'

A Frenchman, having been but a short time in New York, was invited to partake of a large bowl of punch, a liquor which he had never tasted before. The next day, speaking of his entertainment, he asked, "Vat de call dat liqueur dat be all *contradiction:* where is de brandy to make him strong, and de water to make him weak, de sugar to make him sweet, and de lemon to make him sour?" "I suppose you mean *punch*," said one. " Aye, *punch!*" said monsieur ; " it almost punchee out my brains last night !"

A witty gentleman was dining with a nobleman, and as the company was talking of a voyage to India, some glasses of cape wine were handed round the table. All the guests expressed their praises of its exquisite flavor, and wished much to have a second taste of it. But when the gentleman found it was in vain to indulge this hope, he turned to the person who sat next to him, and happily alluding to the voyage to India, said, " As we cannot *double the cape*, suppose we go back to Madeira."

Dean Swift, having dined with a rich miser, pronounced the following grace after dinner :

"Thanks for this miracle! it is no less
Than finding manna in the wilderness.
In midst of famine we have found relief,
And seen the wonder of a chine of beef!
Chimneys have smoked that never smoked before:
And we have dined where we shall dine no more."

A nobleman once asked a clergyman, who was dining at the bottom of the table, " Why the goose was always placed next to the parson ?" " Really," said he, " I can give no reason for it ; but your question is so odd, that I shall never see a goose again without thinking of your lordship."

The great Scythian, Anacharsis, said, that " The vine produces three sorts of grapes : the first, of pleasure ; the second, of intoxication ; the third, of repentance."

A French officer, demanding his salary from the minister of war, declared that he was in danger of dying of hunger. The minister, who saw that his visage was full and ruddy, told him his face gave the lie to his statement. "Ah! sir," said the officer, "don't trust that—this face is not mine ; it belongs to my landlord, who has given me credit for a long time past."

A vintner, to whom Ben Jonson was indebted, invited him to dinner, and told him if he would give him an immediate answer to the following questions, he would forgive him his debt : "What is God best pleased with ; what is the devil best pleased with ; what is the world best pleased with ; and what am I best pleased with ?" Ben, without the least hesitation, gave the following reply :

"God is best pleased, when men forsake their sin;
The devil's best pleased when they persist therein;
The world's best pleased when thou dost sell good wine;
And you're best pleased when I do pay for mine."

In a company where Cardinal Pole was, the conversation turned on a young man who was very learned, but very noisy and turbulent. The cardinal remarked, that "Learning, in such young men, is like new wine in the vat; but after it is put into a vessel, having gathered its strength together, it settles, and is quiet and still."

Lord Chesterfield complained very much at an inn where he dined, that the plates were dirty. The waiter, with a degree of pertness, observed, that "Every one must eat a peck of dirt before he dies." "That may be true," said his lordship; "but no one is obliged to eat it all at a meal."

A noble bibber was one day asked which could drink the most wine, himself or his brother—a good three-bottle man, but also famous for taking care of his money. "Oh," said his lordship, "I have no chance with my brother—he will drink any *given* amount."

The author of "The Parson's Daughter," when surprised one evening in his arm-chair, two or three hours after dinner, is reported to have apologized by saying, "When one is alone the bottle *does* come round *so* often." On a similar occasion, Sir Hercules Languish, on being asked, "Have you finished all that port (three bottles) without assistance?" answered, "No, not quite that; I had the assistance of a bottle of Madeira."

A wit was at an entertainment, where at first they gave him excellent wine, but after the fourth or fifth glass some sour stuff. "These people," said he, "I suppose, take me for a cannon, which has to be washed with vinegar after every three or four rounds."

A tavern-keeper, who opened an oyster-shop as an appendage to his other establishment, was upbraided by a neighboring oyster-monger as being ungenerous and *selfish*. "And why not?" said he; "would you not have me *sel-fish?*"

In a company of *bon vivants*, as the toast circulated, a delicate gentleman simpered out, *Mirth and innocence*. The jolly dog, whose sentiment followed, gave in a similar tone of voice, *Milk and water*.

A country booby boasting of the numerous acres he enjoyed, Ben Jonson peevishly told him, that "For every acre you have of land I have an acre of wit." The other, filling his glass, said, "My service to you, Mr. *Wiseacre*."

The Cretan philosopher, Demonax, was asked if it was allowable for wise men to drink wine. "Surely," said he, "you cannot think that nature made grapes only for fools."

A man, reeling out of an ale-house, was hiccoughing out the praises of porter, which was, he said, both *meat* and *drink*. He shortly after tumbled into a ditch, on which his companion observed, it was also *lodging* and *washing*.

A lady tendered a dish of fruit to a gentleman at table, with this compliment: "Sir, this is not forbidden fruit, if you please to eat." He replied, "Madam, by one sign infallibly it should be, for I see it comes just now from paradise."

Erasmus, on account of a sickly constitution, obtained a dispensation for eating meat in times of abstinence. Being reproached by the pope for not observing lent, he replied, "I assure your holiness that I have a *Catholic heart*, but I must confess that I have a *Lutheran stomach.*"

Voltaire said to a beautiful lady with whom he was dining: "Your rivals are the perfection of art, but you are the perfection of nature."

Zeno, the philosopher, was once asked if wise men ever fall in love. He answered, "If wise men do not fall in love, beautiful women must be very unfortunate."

Louis XII. one day reproached a prelate with the luxury of his manner of living, and told him that the clergy did not live so splendidly in the early ages. "No, sire," said the prelate, "not in the times of the *Shepherd Kings.*"

It was wittily said of a great calumniator, and a frequenter of other people's tables, that he never *opened his mouth* but at another man's *expense.*

Two ladies, of high fashion, as they entered the rooms of a hotel at a watering-place, met a fat lady coming out who was finely dressed. "See," said one of them in a half whisper, "there is *beef a-la-mode* going out." "Yes," answered the other, "and there is *game* coming in."

A friend asked Crebillon why he had introduced so much terror into his tragedies. "I had no alternative," said he; "Corneille has taken the heavens, Racine the earth, and I had nothing left but the infernal regions."

La Lande was one day dining with a gentleman whose beer was better hopped than malted; and when the host asked the poet how he liked his beer, he replied, "By the faith of my body it is very well *hopped;* but if it had *hopped* a little further, it had *hopped* into the water."

A party of black-legs were at a coffee-room at Epsom, during the races, dining at the same time. Warren Hastings was taking his dinner. A gentleman present said, in a low voice, "What a wretched set is here!" "And yet," replied Hastings, "they are your *betters.*"

Lord Summerville, in a party of ladies and gentlemen, propounded his plan for cultivating the wastes of Africa, when a witty old maid present whispered, loud enough to be heard, that she thought it a most uncharitable idea, while so many *waists* remained unimproved at home.

Three gentlemen, going into a hotel together, one said to the waiter, "Bring me a glass of brandy-and-water, *I am so hot!*" Another said, "Bring me some gin-and-sugar; I have just *had a chill.*" The other cried out, "Bring me a rum-punch, because *I like it.*"

Fox, during the early part of his political career, once became terribly enraged at a tradesman, who insolently urged the payment of a bill, and threatened to "kick him to hell." "If you do," was the reply, "I will tell your father how you are spending his money."

A poor wit, who was told that his jokes had furnished daily food for conversation—"Then," said he, "conversation has thrived better on them than I have."

"War," said an ugly old woman, "is *a keen ravisher*." "Faith," replied a wit, in an undertone, "he must be, if he meddles with you."

A nobleman, who was about to marry a lady of great fortune, was asked one day at dinner, how long he thought honeymoon would last, and replied, "Don't talk of honeymoon, it is *harvest-moon* with me."

An abstemious nobleman, chiding one of his workmen for inebriety, observed, "It is very odd that all good workmen are addicted to drunkenness." "Then," answered the man, "I presume that your lordship is not a good workman."

Two friends at table,—one said, reading the paper, "There was a man hanged this morning—one *Vowel*." "Well," said the other, "let us be thankful that it was neither *U* nor *I*."

An English gentleman, entertaining his friends with some excellent claret, remarked that he sent a couple of hounds over to France, and received in return a hogshead of this wine. "Then," said one of the company, "it is *dog cheap*."

A poor man was once asked what three things he would have, if he could obtain them by wishing. "First," said he, "I would have as much fat bacon as I could eat; next, I would have as much ale as I could drink." Puzzled for a third object of happiness, he at last said, "Hang it! I will have a little more ale!"

A man with eleven daughters was complaining to a friend that he found it hard to live. "You must husband your time," said the other, "and then you will do well enough." "I could do much better," was the reply, "if I could husband my daughters."

When Cobbett kept a stationer's shop at Philadelphia, and was writing under the name of "Peter Porcupine," a young sub went to buy some quills, and thinking to pass a joke upon Peter, asked him if they were not Porcupine's quills? Upon which Cobbett, taking up the red-coat's money, dryly replied, making at the same time a very profound bow, "Oh! no, sir! they are a goose's!"

"Sally," said an amorous lover, speaking, the other day, to his intended, "give me a kiss; will you, Sally?" "No, I sha'n't," said Sally—"help yourself."

The evening before a battle, an officer asked Marshal Toiras for permission to go and see his father, who was at the point of death. "Go," said the Marshal, who saw through his pretext—"honor thy father and mother, that thy days may be long in the land."

Dr. Johnson treated Mrs. Siddons, who called upon him in Bold Court, with the most marked politeness. Frank, his servant, could not immediately bring her a chair. "You see, madam," said the Doctor, "wherever you go, how difficult it is to find seats."

Milton, that glory of British literature, received not above £10, at two different payments, for the copyright of "Paradise Lost," yet Mr. Hoyle, author of a treatise on the game of whist, after having disposed of all the first impression, sold the copyright to a bookseller for 200 guineas.

There is a young man in Cincinnati who is so modest that he will not "embrace an opportunity." He would make a good mate for the lady who fainted when she heard of the naked truth.

The late witty Samuel William Kiley, author of the "Itinerant," seeing a proud and sullen calf of sixty swelling down Lord street, Liverpool, accosted him politely, touching his hat—"Excuse me, sir, stopping you in the street, but I just wished to inquire the rent of the house No. 10 Great George street?" "Sir," replied his haughtiness, "I have no house in Great George street." "Oh! I beg a thousand pardons, sir," said Mr. R., "I thought all the town belonged to you."

Washington was visiting a lady in his neighborhood, and on his leaving the house a little girl was directed to open the door. In passing the child he said, "I am sorry, my dear, to give you so much trouble." "I wish, sir," she replied, "it was to let you in."

A gentleman looking at his watch, just after midnight, remarked, "It is to-morrow morning; I must bid you good-night."

Horne Tooke, being asked by George III. whether he played at cards, replied, "I cannot, your Majesty, tell a king from a knave."

Not long since, a person threw the head of a goose on to the stage of the Belleville theatre. Cortru, advancing to the front, said, "Gentlemen, if any among you has lost his head, do not be uneasy, for I will restore it on the conclusion of the performance."

An amiable enthusiast, a worshipper of nature after the manner of Rousseau, being melted into feelings of universal philanthropy by the softness and serenity of a spring morning, resolved that, for that day at least, no injured animal should pollute his board; and, having recorded his vow, he walked six miles to a hamlet famous for fish dinners, where, without an idea of breaking his sentimental engagement, he regaled himself on a small matter of crimped cod and oyster-sauce. This reminds one of a harmless piece of quizzing in the "Quarterly Review,"—that although the Pythagorean Sir Richard Phillips would not eat animal food, he was addicted to gravy over his potatoes.

It was suggested to a distinguished *gourmand* what a capital dish all fins (turbots' fins) might be made. "Capital!" said he; "dine with me to-morrow." "Accepted." Would you believe it? when the cover was removed, the sacrilegious dog of an amphitryon had put into the dish, "*Cicero de finibus!*" "There is a work all fins," said he.

The voice, if very strong and sharp, will crack a drinking-glass. One evening, at a party at the London Coffee-house, Ludgate Hill, Mr. Broadhurst, the well-known tenor, by singing a high note, caused a wine-glass on the table to break, the bowl being separated from the stem.

Dr. Franklin pleasantly observed, that the only animals created to drink water are those who, from their conformation, are able to lap it up on the face of the earth; whereas, all those who can convey their hands to their mouth were destined to enjoy the juice of the grape.

One of Lord Byron's odd fancies was dining at all sorts of out-of-the-way places. Somebody popped upon him in a coffee-house in the Strand, where the attraction was, that he paid a shilling to dine with his hat on. This he called his "*hat-house.*"

Talleyrand being asked if a certain authoress, whom he had long since known, but who belonged rather to the last age, was not "a little tiresome." "Not at all," said he, "she is perfectly so."

Salutation is the touchstone of good-breeding. There have been men, since Absalom, who have owed their ruin to a bad bow.

A bow (says La Fontaine) is a note drawn at sight. If you acknowledge it, you must pay the full amount

Perhaps the best retort upon a lie is to outwit it, as Galba did, when a courtier told him that he had caught eels in Sicily five feet long. "That," replied the emperor, "is no wonder, for there they are so long that the fishermen use them for ropes."

What the bottle tells, (and it is generally a great tell-tale,) perhaps it is the duty of friendship to keep secret.

Johnson is somewhat cynical upon the above maxim of the ancients. A man who is well warmed with wine will speak truth ; "this," he observes, "may be an argument for drinking, if you suppose men in general to be liars; but I would not keep company with a fellow who lies as long as he is sober, and whom you must make drunk before you can get a word of truth out of him."

"I have nothing to give," is a thoughtless reply to a street-beggar, for we forget the old moralist: "It is not necessary that alms should always come out of a sack. A man may be charitable, though he hath not an expanding plenty." Of the undeserving poor, when one blamed Aristotle for giving to a man of dissolute habits, he answered, "I gave not to the manners, but to the man."

The most celebrated wits and *bon vivants* of the day graced the dinner-table of the late Dr. Kitchiner, and, *inter alia*, the late George Colman, who was an especial favorite. His interpolation of a little monosyllable in a written admonition which the doctor caused to be placed on the mantel-piece of the dining-parlor, will never be forgotten, and was the origin of such a drinking-bout as was seldom permitted under his roof. The caution ran thus: "Come at seven, go at eleven." Coleman briefly altered the sense of it; for, upon the doctor's attention being directed to the card, he read, to his astonishment, "Come at seven, go in at eleven!" which the guests did, and the claret was furnished accordingly.

It being reported that Lady Caroline Lamb had, in a moment of passion, struck down one of her pages with a stool, the poet Moore, to whom this was told by Lord Strongford, observed: " Oh! nothing is more natural for a literary lady than to double down a page." "I would rather," replied his lordship, "advise Lady Caroline to turn over a new leaf."

Charles Lamb said once to a brother whist-player, who was a hand more clever than clean, and who had enough in him to afford the joke: "M., if dirt were trumps, what hands you would hold!"

Kennet, Lord Mayor of London, in the year 1780, began life as a waiter, and his manners never rose above his original station. When he was summoned to be examined before Parliament on "the riots," one of the members observed: "If you ring the bell, Kennet will come, of course." On being asked why, on the breaking out of the riot, he did not send for the *posse comitatus*, he replied, he did not know where the fellow lived, else he would. One morning, at the Alderman's Club, he was at a whist-table, and Mr. Alderman Pugh, a dealer in soap, was at his elbow: "Ring the bell, soap-suds," said Kennet, in his coarse way. "Ring it yourself, bar," replied Pugh, "you've been twice as much used to it as I have."

A lady, complaining how rapidly time stole away, said: "Alas! I am near thirty." Scarron, who was present, and knew her age, said: "Do not fret at it, madam, for you will get further from that frightful epoch every day."

Lord North, when contemptuously alluded to by Fox, as "That thing termed a minister," replied: "The honorable gentleman calls me *a thing*, and (patting his ample stomach) an unshapely thing I am; but when he adds, *that thing termed a minister*, he calls me that which he himself is most anxious to become; and, therefore, I take it as a compliment."

When Lord Bath was told of the determination of turning out Pitt, and letting Fox remain in the ministry, he said it put him in mind of a story of the Gunpowder Plot. The Lord Chamberlain was sent to examine the vaults under the Parliament House, and returning with his report, said "He had found five-and-twenty barrels of gunpowder—that he had removed ten of them, and hoped the other fifteen would do no harm."

Madame Dacier remarks, that Homer makes no mention of any boiled meats; and in all the entertainments described by him, (as in the dinner given by Achilles in the ninth Iliad,) the *pièce de résistance*, or principal dish, undoubtedly is a broil, from which it may be inferred that the Greeks had not as yet discovered the art of making vessels to bear fire. This discovery is supposed to have reached them from Egypt, and they rapidly turned it to the best account; for the Athenians, in particular, seem to have as much excelled the rest of Greece in gastronomy, as the French, the modern nation most nearly resembling them, excel the rest of Europe in this respect.

Among the witty aphorisms upon an unsafe topic, are,—Lord Alvanley's description of a man who "muddled away his fortune in paying his tradesmen's bills;" Lord Oxford's definition of timber, as "an excrescence on the face of the earth, placed there by Providence for the payment of debts;" and Pelham's argument, "That it is respectable to be arrested, because it shows that the party once had credit."

Henderson, the actor, was seldom known to be in a passion. When at Oxford, he was one day debating with a fellow-student, who, not keeping his temper, threw a glass of wine in the actor's face, when Henderson took out his handkerchief, wiped his face, and coolly said: "That, sir, was a digression; now for the argument."

Theodore Hooke's Code of Card-table Signals, in his clever novel of *Gilbert Gurney*, might be very effectually reduced to practice. "Never," says he "let man and wife play together at whist. There are always family telegraphs; and if they fancy their looks are watched, they can always communicate by words. I found out that I could never win of Smingsmay and his wife. I mentioned this one day, and was answered; 'No, you never can win of them.' 'Why?' said I. 'Because,' said my friend, 'they have established a code.' 'Dear me,' said I, 'signals by looks?' 'No,' said he, 'by words. If Mrs. Smingsmay is to lead, Smingsmay says, "Dear, begin;" dear begins with a *d*, so do diamonds, and out comes one from the lady. If he has to lead, and she says, "S., my love," she wants a spade. Smingsmay and spade begin with the same letter, and, sure enough, down comes a spade. "Harriet, my dear, how long you are sorting your cards!" Mrs. Smingsmay stumps down a heart, and a gentle "Come, my love," on either side, produces a club.'"

There has been in all governments a great deal of absurd canting about the consumption of spirits. We believe the best plan is to let people drink what they like, and wear what they like; to make no sumptuary laws either for the belly or the back. In the first place, laws against rum, and rum-and-water, are made by men who can change a wet coat for a dry one whenever they choose, and who do not often work up to their knees in mud and water; and, in the next place, if this stimulus did all the mischief it is thought to do by the wise men of claret, its cheapness and plenty would rather lessen than increase the avidity with which it is at present sought for.—*Sydney Smith.*

Thalwall and Coleridge were sitting once in a beautiful recess in the Quantock hills, when the latter said: "Citizen John, this a fine place to talk reason in!" "Nay, citizen Samuel," replied he, "it is rather a place to make a man forget that there is any necessity for treason."

In 1517, Sigismund de Pietrichstein established a Temperance Society, under the auspices of St. Christopher; a similar association was formed in 1600 by

Maurice, Duke of Hesse; the rules of which allowed a knight to drink seven *bocaux*, or glasses, at each meal, but only twice in the day!

Talleyrand not only said but *did* many witty things. On the death of Charles X., he drove through Paris for a couple of days, wearing a white hat. He carried a crape in his pocket. When he passed through the Fauxbourg of the Carlists, the crape was instantly twisted round his hat; when he came into the quarter of the Tuileries, the crape was instantly slipt off and put into his pocket again.

It is not only ill-breeding, but a sign of bad taste, to be late. It may sound very fine to be called *the late Mr. So-and-so*; it is an easy mode of attracting attention to drawl out an inquiry about the soups of the season, as if you had never had the good fortune to be present at a first course; but it is far from pleasant to find the woman you wish most to sit by monopolized, and yourself *planted* between the *bore* and the *gap*, as we once heard a lady describe her position, with Sir A——— on her left and an unoccupied chair upon her right.

The most unpunctual persons ever known were two brothers, celebrated time immemorial in the place-holding world. The late Lord Dudley used to say of them, that if you asked Robert for Wednesday at seven, you would have Charles on Thursday at eight.

An illiterate person, who always volunteered to " go

round with the hat," but was suspected of sparing his own pocket, overhearing once a hint to that effect, replied: "Other gentlemen puts down what they thinks proper, and so do I. Charity's a private concern, and what I give is *nothing to nobody.*"

Some young Americans, travelling on horseback among the White Mountains, became inordinately thirsty, and stopped for milk at a house by the roadside. They emptied every basin that was offered, and still wanted more. The woman of the house at length brought an enormous bowl of milk, and set it down on the table, saying: "One would think, gentlemen, you had never been weaned."

Coleridge relates: "I have had a good deal to do with Jews in the course of my life, although I never borrowed any money of them. The other day I was what you call *floored* by a Jew. He passed me several times, crying out for old clothes in the most nasal and extraordinary tone I ever heard. At last, I was so provoked that I said to him: "Pray, why can't you say 'old clothes' in a plain way, as I do now?" The Jew stopped, and looking very gravely at me, said, in a clear and even fine accent: "Sir, I can say 'old clothes' as well as you can; but if you had to say so ten times a minute, for an hour together, you would say 'ogh clo,' as I do now;" and so he marched off. I was so confounded with the justice of his retort, that I followed and gave him a shilling, the only one I had.

"Once I sat in a coach opposite a Jew—a symbol of old clothes-bags—an Isaiah of Holywell street. He would close the window; I opened it. He closed it again; upon which, in a very solemn tone, I said to him: "Son of Abraham! thou smellest; son of Isaac! thou art offensive; son of Jacob! thou stinkest foully. See the man in the moon! he is holding his nose at that distance; dost thou think that I, sitting here, can endure it any longer?" My Jew was astonished; he opened the window forthwith himself, and said, "He was sorry he did not know before, I was so great a gentleman."

Swift is characterized by Coleridge, as the soul of Rabelais dwelling in a dry place. Can anything beat his remark on King William's motto, (Recepit, non rapicet,) "that the receiver was as bad as the thief"?

After all, clubs are not altogether so bad a thing for family-men. They act as conductors to the storms usually hovering in the air. The man forced to remain at home, and vent his crossness on his wife and children, is a much worse animal to be with than the man who grumbles his way to Pall Mall, and, not daring to swear at the club-servants, or knock about the club-furniture, becomes socialized into decency. Nothing like the subordination exercised in a community of equals for reducing a fiery temper.

A shoemaker in Piccadilly, determined to astonish the world, had put up a motto from Euripides over his window. Bannister happened to be passing with Porson. "That is Greek," said Bannister. "What! are you acquainted with Greek?" asked the professor, with a laugh. "I know it by sight," was the reply.

George Selwyn, happening to be at Bath when it was nearly empty, was induced, for the mere purpose of killing time, to cultivate the acquaintance of an elderly gentleman he was in the habit of meeting at the Rooms. In the height of the following season, Selwyn encountered his old associate in St. James street. He endeavored to pass unnoticed, but in vain. "What, don't you recollect me?" exclaimed the *cuttee*. "I recollect you, perfectly," replied Selwyn; "and when I next go to Bath I shall be most happy to become acquainted with you again."

Drinking *super nagulum*, or on the nail, was a northern custom, which consisted in having only one drop in the cup, which was poured upon the thumb-nail to prove that justice had been done to the toast; or, to use the language of modern drinkers, the glass was cleared. The custom is alluded to by Bishop Hall, in his *Mundus alter et Idem*, in which the Duke of Tenderbelly exclaims, "Let never this goodly-formed goblet of wine go jovially through me;" and then he set it to his mouth, stole it of every drop, save a little remaining, which he was by custom to set upon his thumb-nail, and lick off. In Fletcher we find the phrase, "I am thine *ad ungeum*;" which meant, he was ready to drink with him to this extent.

Some one remarked to Mrs. Siddons that applause was necessary to actors, as it gave them confidence. "More," replied the actress, "it gives us breath."

A *bon vivant* being observed by a friend, who had not seen him for a long time, to be downcast in his countenance, and very unlike himself, was asked whether anything serious had befallen him. "Nothing of that sort," was his reply, "but I am quite an altered character; I have left off drinking." "Indeed!" replied his friend, rather astounded at the assertion, "and since when?" "Since two o'clock this morning," was the facetious reply, the speaker's countenance resuming its usual cast of good-humor and mirth.

Hobbs once said to a celebrated book-worm: "If I had read as many volumes as you have done, I should have been as ignorant as you are."

The pleasures of the table have never been incompatible with the gifts of genius, or the investigations of the understanding. "I cannot conceive," says Dr. Johnson, "the folly of those who, when at table, think of every thing but eating; for my part, when I am there, I think of nothing else; and whosoever does not trouble himself with this important affair at dinner, or supper, will do no good at any other time."

Lady Blessington remarks, that people who wear creaking shoes or boots are precisely those who are most addicted to locomotion.

An English gentleman, wanting a dessert-service of porcelain made after a particular pattern, sent over to China a specimen dish, ordering that it should be exactly copied for the whole service. It unfortunately happened that in the dish so sent over the Chinese manufacturer discovered a crack; the consequence was, that the entire service sent over to the party ordering it had a crack in each article, carefully copied after the original.

Hooke dedicated the first volume of his Roman History to Pope, which, he said, was "like hanging out a sign with a great flourish at the bottom of it, to catch the traveller as he goes by."

Old Dick Baldwin stoutly maintained that no man ever died of drinking. "Some puny things," he said, "have died learning to drink, but no man ever died of drinking." Now B. was no mean authority, for he spoke from great practical experience, and was, moreover, many years treasurer of St. Bartholomew's hospital.

Mr. Bentham has thus formally refuted the common fallacy as to the cruelty of skinning live eels: "No eel is used to be skinned successively by several persons; but one and the same person is used successively to skin several eels."

The meeting of two gentlemen in the theatre lobby is a happy illustration of the confusion a similarity of dress occasions. Coming from different points, each in a great hurry, one addressed the other with, " Pray, are you the box-keeper ? " " No," replied the other, " are you ? "

The French, a very sober people, have a proverb :—

> " Qu'il faut, à chaque mois,
> S'enivrer au moins une fois ;"

which has been improved by some, on this side of the water, into an excuse for getting drunk every day in the week, for fear that the specific day should be missed. It would, however, startle some sober persons to find this question made a grave argument, yet : " whether it is not healthful to be drunk once in a month," is treated of by Dr. Carr in his letters to De Quincey.

Lord Bolingbroke shrewdly notes : " I have observed, that in comedy the best actor plays the part of the droll, while some scrub is made the hero, or fine gentleman. So, in this farce of life, wise men pass their time in mirth, whilst fools only are serious."

Nothing is a courtesy unless it be meant for us, and that friendly and lovingly. We owe no thanks to rivers, that they carry our boats ; or winds, that they be nourishing ; for these are what they are, necessarily. Horses carry us ; trees shade us ; but they know it not.—*Ben Jonson.*

Sheridan had a Bardolph countenance, with heavy features ; but his eye possessed the most distinguished brilliancy. Mathews said it was very simple in Tom

Moore to admire how Sheridan came by the means of paying the price of Drury Lane Theatre, when all the world knows that he never paid it at all.

A gentleman from Ireland, on entering a London tavern, saw a countryman of his, a Tipperary squire, sitting over his pint of wine in the coffee-room. "Blood an' ounds! my dear fellow," said he, "what are you about? For the honor of Tipperary, don't be after sitting over a pint of wine in a house like this." "Make yourself aisy, countryman," was the reply; "its the seventh I have had, and every one in the room knows it."

Though an habitual valetudinarian, Moliere relied almost entirely upon the temperance of his diet for the reëstablishment of his health. "What use do you make of our physician?" said the king to him one day. "We chat together, sire," said the poet. "He gives me his prescriptions: I never follow them; and so I get well."

Horace Walpole relates: "At a great supper t'other night at Lord Hertford's, Lady Coventry said, in a vulgar accent, 'If she drank any more, she should be muckibus.' 'Lord!' said Lady Mary Coke, 'what is that?' 'Oh! its Irish for sentimental.'"

In the reign of Henry VIII. it was a recommendation for a servant if he could bear a quantity of strong drink; part of his good character, in times when it was accounted a point of hospitality, that the guests in the kitchen should be made as drunk as their masters in the dining-hall.

Ude, when in Paris, had fallen in love, and matters were nearly brought to matrimony. Previous to this conclusion, Ude, however, prudently made a calculation (he was an excellent steward) of the expenses of married life, and in the estimate set down Madame's expenditure at so many louis. Now, Ude customarily conveyed his billets in an envelope of patés, and he intended to shroud his offer in a paté d'Amande, but, unfortunately, in the confusion of love and cookery, the estimate of house-keeping was sent instead of the proposal. The next day Ude was apprised of his mistake by a letter from his mistress, stating the high estimation in which she held M. Ude; but that as —— louis were too small an allowance for a woman of fashion, she must decline the honor of becoming Madame Ude. The story got wind, and by a sort of *lusus a non lucendo* analogy, the name of Paté d'Amande was changed into Paté d'Amour.

The Count Altamira, a splendid little man, four feet two inches high, could boast of the title of Prince, with three dukedoms, although he used the ancient title as the chiefest honor. He would never bow his neck to the yoke of Napoleon; and he it was who made the appropriate reply to Wittol, Charles IV., when he said, " Cousin, what a little fellow you are!" " Yes, sire; but in my own house I am a great one."

Cambacérès, second consul under the French republic, and arch-chancellor under the empire, having one day been detained in consultation with Napoleon beyond the appointed hour of dinner, begged pardon for suspending the conference, as it was absolutely necessary for him to dispatch a special messenger immediately; then seizing a pen, he wrote this billet to his cook: "Sauvez les entremets—les entrées sont perdues."

A patriotic Frenchman has observed: "I regard the discovery of a dish as a far more interesting event than the discovery of a star, for we have always stars enough, but can never have too many dishes; and I shall not regard the sciences as sufficiently honored, or represented among us, until I see a cook in the first class of the Institute."

Alexander Newell, Dean of St. Paul's, and Master of Westminster School, in the reign of Queen Mary, was an excellent angler. But, says Fuller, whilst Newell was catching of fishes, Bishop Bonner was catching of Newell, and would certainly have sent him to the shambles, had not a good London merchant conveyed him away upon the seas. Newell was fishing upon the banks of the Thames, when he received the first intimation of his danger, which was so pressing, that he dare not go back to his own house to make any preparation for his flight. Like an honest angler, he had taken with him provision for the day; and when in the first year of England's deliverance, he returned to his country, and his own haunts, he remembered that, on the day of his flight, he had left a bottle of beer in a safe place on the bank: there he looked for it, and "found it no bottle, but a gun—such the sound at the opening thereof: and this (says Fuller) is believed (casualty is mother of more invention than industry) the original of bottled ale in England."

Mrs. Molesworthy, who was the daughter of the Right Honorable Lord Molesworthy, of Ireland, was a fine wit and poetess in her day, which was about the time of Milton. She was quite as free in some of her jokes as some of our modern strong-minded women. The following epigram on a gallant lady is hers:

> "O'er this marble drop a tear,
> Here lies fair Rosalinde;
> All mankind was pleased with her,
> And she with all mankind."

In a poem entitled Runaway Love, she makes Venus offer the following extraordinary reward for the apprehension of her son, Cupid:

> "And he that finds the boy shall have
> The sweetest kiss I ever gave;
> But he that brings him to my arms,
> Shall master be of all my charms."

At a literary party at Strawberry Hill, 12th September, 1734, Mr. Walpole remarked that, at a certain time of their lives, men of genius seem to be *in flower*.

Said he: "Gray was in flower three years when he wrote his Odes;" and he added, laughing, "had Gray lived a hundred years longer, perhaps he would never have been in flower again."

Dominico, the harlequin, going to see Louis XIV. at supper, fixed his eye on a dish of partridges. The king, who was fond of his acting, said: "Give that dish to Dominico." "And the partridges, too, sire." Louis being pleased at his wit, replied: "And the partridges, too." The dish was gold.

A French wit being very ill, his landlord begged him to settle his account. The poor author, who saw that everything was charged exorbitantly high, wrote at the bottom of the account, "*If I die, let it pass—if I live, for revisal.*"

A marquis said to a financier: "I would have you to know that I am a man of *quality.*" "And I," replied the financier, "would have you to know that I am a man of *quantity.*"

Some astronomers, who had been making observations, thought they perceived several spots on the sun. Voiture happened shortly afterwards to be in company, when he was asked if there was any news: "None," said he, "but I hear very bad reports of the sun."

A gascon being at the play, was seated in the pit, and as he kept constantly fidgeting about, his sword got entangled in the legs of those who sat beside him. "Sir," said an officer, fiercely, "your sword annoys me." "Very likely, sir," said the gascon, coolly, "I believe it has annoyed a good many."

The Duchess Dowager of Bolton, who was a natural daughter of the Duke of Monmouth, used to divert George I. by affecting to make blunders. Once when she had been at the play of "Love's Last Shift," she called it, "*La dernier chemise de l'Amour.*"

At another time she pretended to come to court in a great fright, and the king asking the cause, she said she had been at Mr. Whiston's, who told her the world would be burnt up in three years, and, for her part, she was determined to go to China.

The Abbé Regnier, secretary of the French Academy, was collecting in his hat from each member a contribution for a certain purpose. The president, Roses, one of the forty, was a great miser, but had paid his quota, which the Abbé not perceiving, he presented the hat a second time. Roses, as was to be expected, said he had already paid. "I believe it," answered Regnier, "though I did not see it." "And I," added Fontenelle, who was beside him, "I saw it, but I do not believe it."

Cardinal de Bernis, when only an Abbé, solicited Cardinal Fleury, then four-score, for some preferment. Fleury told him fairly he should never have anything in his time. Bernis replied : *Monseigneur j'attendrer,* "My lord, I shall wait."

Francis I. was one day playing at ten-pins, when a monk, who was playing on his side, by a successful stroke insured the victory to the king's party. " Well done!" said the king ; " a brave stroke for a monk !" " Sire," replied the monk, " your majesty can make it the blow of an Abbé when you please." Soon afterwards the Abbaye of Bourmazen became vacant, and the king gave it to him.

An advocate of the king, in pleading, used to put his arms in such a position that he seemed to be levelling them at the court. The president, a man of humor, tired of this eternal gesture, said to him one day, " Raise your piece a little, sire ; you will hurt somebody."

On the 18th of October, 1609, the daughter of the Count de Crequi, aged nine, was married to the Marquis de Rohan, the son of the Duke de Sully. The minister, Dumoulin, seeing the bride approach, said, " Do you present this child to be baptized ?"

When Fox came last into power, he was one day talking to Mr. Sheridan about new taxes. " Why," said Mr. Sheridan, " that is not my department ; all I think is, that we should be careful not to meddle with any that reach ourselves." " Aye!" rejoined Mr. Fox, " what then think you of one on *receipts !*"

The Abbé de la Riviere was praising very highly the Duc d'Orleans, the uncle of Louis XII., in the presence of his daughter. Among other things, he said, "He was a very wise and pious prince, and a man of great *worth*." "True," replied Mademoiselle d'Orleans, "you ought to know better than any one, for you have sold him often enough."

Louis XII. one day looking at himself in his mirror, was astonished to see a number of grey hairs on his head. "Ah!" said he, "these must be owing to the long speeches I have listened to; and it is those of M. le —— in particular, that have ruined my hair."

M. Bossuet, Bishop of Meaux, at eight years of age, preached a sermon at the Hotel de Rambouillet. It was nearly midnight when he closed, and Voiture, who was present, said, as he rose to go, "I have never heard a sermon so early—or so late."

Bantin, in presenting a poet to M. d'Hemery, said, "Sir, I present you a person who can give you immortality; but you must give him something to live upon meanwhile."

Augustus Nicholas died just at the time when a poll-tax was about to be levied, and the wits, who knew his avaricious disposition, said he died to avoid it, and made an epigram on him to that effect, declaring that, when Charon asked him for his fare, he exclaimed:

"O cruel fate! in vain I fled!
We pay a poll-tax when we're dead!"

mmm

An admirer of some of our modern poets said to the learned Professor Porson, about fifty years ago, that Wordsworth and some others of his school would be read after Milton, Dryden, and Pope were forgotten. "Yes," replied the professor, "*but not before.*"

During our Revolutionary war, an interview took place at Ward's Point, between Lord Howe and Dr. Franklin. Lord Howe was profuse in his expressions of gratitude to the State of Massachusetts, for erecting a marble monument, in Westminster Abbey, to his elder brother, Lord Howe, who was killed in America in the last French war, saying, "he esteemed that honor to his family *above all things in this world.* That such was his gratitude and affection to this country, on that account, that he felt for America as for a brother, and if America should fall he should feel and lament it like the loss of a brother." Dr. Franklin, with an easy air, and a collected countenance, a bow, a smile, and all that *naïveté* which sometimes appeared in his conversation, and is often observed in his writings, replied: "*My Lord, we will do our utmost endeavors to save your lordship that mortification.*"

Le Père Arius said, "When le Père Bourdaloue

preached at Rouen, the tradesmen forsook their shops, lawyers their clients, physicians their sick; but when I preached the following year, I set all to rights, *every man minded his own business.*"

Scipio Nasica, the cousin of the great Scipio, called one day on Ennius, the poet, whose servant (though his master was at home) denied him. Soon after, Ennius returned the visit, and was told by Scipio himself that he was not at home. "Nay," said Ennius, "I know you are, I hear your voice." "You are a fine fellow, indeed," replied Scipio. "When I called the other day on you, I believed the maid who told me you were not at home, and now you will not believe me, although you have *my own word for it.*"

The learned professor and principal of the Academy of Saumur, used to spend five hours every morning in his study, but was very punctual at dinner. One day, on his not appearing precisely at the dinner hour, his wife entered his study and found him still reading. "I wish," said the lady, "that I were a book." "Why so?" replied the professor. "Because you would then be constant to me." "I should have no objection," rejoined the professor, "provided you were an almanac." "Why an almanac, my dear?" "*Because I should then have a new one every year.*"

In the times of Diogenes, an infamous character, of great intellectual note, had the following inscription written above his door. "Let nothing bad enter this door." "And where," said Diogenes, "shall the master of the house enter?'

Joshua Barnes, the famous professor of Greek at Cambridge, was remarkable for a very extensive *memory*, but also for the weakness of his *judgment;* and when he died, the wits wrote,

"Hic jacet Joshua Barnes,
Felicissimæ memoriæ,
Expectans judicium."

Here lies Joshua Barnes of most happy memory, *waiting for judgment.*

The Marquis del Carpio, a grandee of Spain, was once giving the holy water to a lady, who presented him a skinny, ugly hand, ornamented with a costly diamond, and he said loud enough to be heard, *Quisiera mas la sortija que la mano: i. e.,* "I had rather have the ring than the hand." The lady, taking hold instantly of the golden collar of his order, said, *Ego el cabestro que el asno: i. e.,* "And I the halter, rather than the ass."

Mr. Pye, who was made poet-laureate at the beginning of this century, was a man of great learning, and much was therefore expected of him. His first ode was on the *king's birth*, and it was distinguished for nothing but its frequent allusions to *vocal groves* and *feathered choir.* George Stevens, a facetious wit of the times, read it, and immediately exclaimed :—

"When the Pye was opened
The *birds began to sing!*
And was n't that a dainty dish
To set before a *king?*"

Queen Margaret, of France, wife of Henry IV., was provoked by one of many beggars, to say *Pauper ubique jacet*—" the poor lie everywhere!" when the mendicant, to her surprise, exclaimed :—

"*In thalamis, Regina, tuis hac nocte jacerem,
Si foret hoc verum, Pauper ubique jacet—*"
Thy bed then, Queen! this night I should lie there,
If it were true, "The poor lie everywhere!"

To which the Queen retorted :—

"*Carceris in tenebris plorans hac nocte jaceres,
Si foret hoc verum, 'Pauper ubique jacet—*'"
A prison dark! this night you should lie there,
If it were true, "The poor lie everywhere."

When Dante was at the Court of Il Signore della Scala, the sovereign of Verona, the prince said to him one day: "I wonder, Signor Dante, that a man so learned as you are should be hated by all my court, and this fool," pointing to his favorite buffoon, who stood by him, " should be by all beloved." Dante replied : "*Your Excellency would wonder less, if you considered that we like those best who most resemble ourselves.*"

Cicero one day sent for Pophilius Cotta, a professor of civil law, to be a witness in a case which he was trying. The professor came, but on entering the court, declared that he "*knew nothing of the matter.*" "Don't be in a hurry," exclaimed Cicero; "you think, perhaps, that I am going to examine you in jurisprudence."

One of the wits of Queen Elizabeth's time wrote the following quaint lines on the Queen and Sir Francis Drake:

> "O Nature! to old England still
> Continue these mistakes;
> Still give us for *kings* such *queens,*
> And for our *Dux* such *Drakes.*"

PREAMBLES AND RESOLUTIONS.

A PREAMBLE is simply an introduction to a resolution, or to a set of resolutions, and is intended to give reasons why they should be offered.

The opening clause of the Declaration of Independence of the United States partakes of the nature of a *preamble*, and is as follows:—

"When, in the course of human events, it becomes necessary for one people to dissolve the political bands which have connected them with another, and to assume among the powers of the earth the separate and equal station to which the laws of nature and of nature's God entitle them, a decent respect to the opinions of mankind requires that they should declare the causes which impel them to the separation."

The above simple and brief statement of the reason why the *declaration* which follows it is made, is a model *preamble* in consequence of its *brevity* and *simplicity;* and the *declaration* itself partakes of the nature and intent of a series of resolutions, justifying the act of independence.

A *preamble* should be as brief a statement as is possible of the character and propriety of the resolutions to which it is an introduction.

There is on record an amusing history of the manner in which our pious New England fathers justified their seizure of all the lands of the natives of the country, which they accomplished by preamble and resolutions in something like the following form:

"*Whereas*, 'The earth is the Lord's, and the fulness thereof'—

"1st, It is *Resolved*, That this land belongs to the Lord.

"2d, *Resolved*, That *we* are the Lord's people.

"3d, Therefore, *Resolved*, That this land belongs to us."

And they took it.

Preambles and resolutions are sometimes introduced, with great effect, on convivial occasions, to give a sort of mock dignity and importance to some common event, and may be made a source of a great deal of amusement. A New York gentleman who was about starting for the city of Washington where he was to be married, gave a supper to his bachelor friends, at which, after the party was considerably warmed with champagne, the following preamble and resolutions were introduced, as a concluding act of an evening of merriment:

Whereas, Marriage has been held in the highest esteem by all refined and civilized nations; and has the sanction of divine command, as the only authorized means of multiplying and replenishing the earth;—and

Whereas, Our worthy and obedient host, moved with a sincere and pious desire to obey this command to the utmost of his distinguished ability, has resolved to enter at once upon the arduous and responsible duties of matrimony;—therefore,

Resolved, That this meeting tender to him congratulations, and express its high sense of the fidelity and ability with which he will prosecute his laudable undertaking.

Resolved, That a committee of nineteen be appointed to accompany him on his journey as far as the city of Baltimore, to support, comfort, aid, and encourage him, and thereby keep him from faltering in his matrimonial intentions.

Resolved, That we generously allow our worthy host to pay all the expenses of said committee.

At a convivial party of journeymen tailors, the evening was concluded with the following preamble and resolutions:

Whereas, Every profession is to be respected according to its importance to mankind,—

Resolved, That there is no profession or trade which deserves more the respect and gratitude of society than that of the tailor.

Resolved, That the tailor is the most charitable of men, inasmuch as he makes it his business to hide the *imperfections* and cover up the *faults* of mankind.

Resolved, That to the tailor society is indebted for its greatest propriety and decency, as without him all men would be obliged to appear naked in the public streets.

Resolved, That the tailors' trade is the oldest and most respectable on earth, it having originated in the Garden of Eden, where, after the devil had exposed our first parents' nakedness, a tailor kindly stepped in and made them garments of fig-leaves.

Resolved, That we, tailors, no longer submit to the disgraceful appellation of "*ninth part of a man,*" but boldly show the world that, individually, we possess the full measure of manhood.

Resolved, That any tailor who uses a short yardstick, and refuses good and honest measure to his kind customers, disgraces his craft.

Resolved, That these resolutions be published in all the family newspapers in the city of New York.

The preamble and resolutions may be made to convey the most terrible rebuke to rascality and hypocrisy; an instance of which occurred some time ago, in a small village about thirty miles distant from the metropolis. A man who had been, all his life, a gambler of the most scandalous description, and who brought up his daughters in a "free-love" club, and from their childhood familiarized them to the society of black-legs and licentious adventurers, was rebuked by the indignant villagers in the following manner:

Whereas, All such practices as gambling and the manufacturing of obscene and indecent wares are opposed to the best interests of society, and can not exist without more or less destroying the foundations of morality and religion;—and

Whereas, It is every man's duty to protect society from all such associations as have a tendency to corrupt good manners and good morals;—

Resolved, That the man who offends against society by the practice of such aggravated and indecent vices forfeits all claim to the respectful notice of decent and upright people.

Resolved, That no man can familiarly associate with gamblers, black-legs, and venders of obscene articles, without subjecting himself to the suspicion of conniving at these monstrous and disgusting vices.

Resolved, That young women who are brought up in such licentious and abominable society as "free-love" clubs, and who associate from their infancy with the most impure and abandoned of men and women, are unfit and dangerous associates for the sons and daughters of respectable and well-conducted families.

Resolved, That any man who would open the doors of respectable families to such loose-minded and corrupting associations, is a foe to the well-being and virtuous manners of refined society, and deserves to be regarded with suspicion and dread by all prudent and right-minded parents.

Resolved, That it is neither proscription nor persecution to refuse the ordinary intercourse of respectable social life to those who disregard the sacred rules of decency, morality, and religion.

We scarcely need add that the above preamble and resolutions had the desired effect upon the obnoxious family, and completely banished it from every avenue of prudent and respectable social intercourse.

The remedy was a truly severe one, and one that could not be approved by the charitably disposed, except under circumstances where the greatest alarm was felt for the good manners and pure morals of the young of both sexes.

DUTIES OF CHAIRMAN OF A MEETING.

ELECTION, OR APPOINTMENT.

1. On this officer, of course, depend mainly the order and the efficiency of a meeting. It is too much the custom to confer the office as a sort of compliment, as a mark of respect to the man. And as rank and the possession, or reputed possession, of wealth are held in respect, so some one of the persons present more distinguished than the rest by a quality of this kind is usually selected. A reputation for learning, or for talent, comes in for its share of consideration; and ripeness of years, and gentlemanly deportment and conduct have their weight. All this is very well. Men do look, will look, and, indeed, ought to look, among the possessors of these distinguishing characteristics for their leaders, their representatives, and their presidents. And if they find in one of these possessors the qualities which fit a man for the office in question, they will act wisely in selecting him.

2. To confine ourselves, however, to the selection of a man for the office of chairman of a meeting in which a debate is to be held,—

3. It is desirable, nay, it is necessary to the good conduct of the meeting, that the chairman be regarded with confidence. It will not do to nominate a man for such an office, as is not unfrequently done, out of mere personal compliment; done, too, frequently, by some pert and forward hanger-on, sometimes to repay obligations already received, or to bespeak expected favors. It will not do thus to suffer impertinence to usurp the office, to place its idol in the chair, and to lower the respectability, to consume the time, and to impair or destroy the efficiency of the meeting.

4. The chairman ought to be a man previously held in respect; but at all events he must be treated with deference whilst he is in the office; and his authority, his decisions, should be upheld and enforced by the meeting, or there can be no order. At any rate, the chairman must be held in respect.

5. There is something, nay, there is much in the personal appearance and in the years of a man by which the respect of an assemblage is to be raised and preserved; his known station and habits of life come next into consideration; and then his fitness for the office, which is instantly perceived and felt by the meeting.

6. This fitness for the office is certainly the main thing. Imposing and gentlemanly appearance, habits of command in private life, the possession of a standing in society, of learning, and even of talents, sink, all sink,

into nothing, when the man is placed in a situation for which he is not, and for which he and every person present feel that he is not fitted. Whilst, on the contrary, the fitting man, although devoid of all external aids of person and of fortune, without reputation for talents or for learning, but having a knowledge of the duties, of the business of the office; having a mind clear, not liable to be disturbed; a man thus self-possessed, with appearances and prepossessions against him, will often disperse and emerge from the difficulties, and make the assemblage forget the man in the dignity and the importance of the office.

7. Such entire fitness for the office of chairman is not, it must be confessed, often to be found. However, in every assemblage of our countrymen we may find some of these qualities, some of these mental qualifications. And if we find them in a man respectable for his years and his personal appearance, let them be preferred; if with these we find wealth, honorably inherited or acquired, and liberally enjoyed, still better; and lastly, if in addition to all these excellent qualifications we can find for our chairman a man in the enjoyment of a high station in society, then shall we have every reasonable security for the pleasant, the orderly, and the efficient conduct of a meeting. Whilst, on the contrary, when a man is thrust into the office just to subserve the views of an officious individual, or party, without any natural or acquired personal fitness for it, —his incapacity stands in need of so many advisers; so many volunteer their aid; he gets so many participa-

ELECTION, OR APPOINTMENT. 303

tors in his office; petty and self-appointed chairmen spring up in every quarter of the meeting, which soon, instead of becoming an orderly assemblage, degenerates into a disorganized mob; and would, after wrangling and quarrelling, disperse as such, were it not for the determined perseverance of some few energetic men who may take the imbecile chairman into their hands, and, by poking him about, through one step after another, get through the business of the meeting with or without the knowledge or the concurrence of the greater part of the persons present.

8. To avoid catastrophes of this kind, and to obtain at least some of the satisfactory results and attendant circumstances of an orderly and well conducted meeting, let every man, on his first entrance into it, and until the chairman be appointed, cast about him, and be prepared instantly to name the most suitable person, in his estimation, for the office. Thus will each man be prepared to do his duty on this preliminary and important point. Being thus prepared, each individual may wait until the lapse of the moment when the appointment is to take place. Then, of course, some person ought to propose a chairman; or, if there be some sufficient reason for deferring such proposition for a short time, it will be an act of acceptable kindness on the part of any gentleman, in an audible voice to address a few words to the assemblage, stating, in his opinion, such reason, and proposing, in distinct terms, not an indefinite time, not "*a few minutes,*" nor "*ten minutes, or a quarter of an hour,*" but a definite

time : so that the persons present may know exactly their time ; may know the moment to which the business of the meeting is adjourned, and not be left at the mercy of any tricky party, who might mould the meeting to almost any shape or purpose by taking advantage of an indefinite adjournment; which is, in fact, and ought always to be regarded, as a breaking up or dissolution of the meeting.

9. The moment for business having arrived, the moment for the appointment of a chairman, some one of the meeting names a gentleman for the office. Let not this disconcert any man. It is the moment on which the order and respectability of the meeting depend more than on any other ; and let each man, who is a lover of order, be prepared to do his duty. If he be the man on whom you have fixed, second the nomination with all decent expedition ; but if not, if you think you have set your eye on a more eligible man, just allow time, and not an instant longer than is requisite ; just allow time for such a seconding, and then, whether the first nomination be seconded or not, in as firm a voice as you are master of, nominate the gentleman whom you have chosen.

10. Let it not be imagined that such a nomination of a second, a third, a fourth, or a fifth gentleman for this office is any mark of disrespect towards any one. I may not know the gentleman or gentlemen already nominated ; or knowing may know nothing of his or of their fitness for the office; whilst I do know that

the gentleman on whom I have fixed is a very eligible person, perhaps a very able chairman. I submit his name, therefore, to the meeting, desirous that this meeting, of which I am a member, should have the benefit of his skill and impartiality. The nomination of a second, of a third, or a fourth gentleman for the office, whilst it is the best service that any man at this time can render to the meeting, seeing that it offers to that meeting a choice, on a point of so much importance; whilst it is the best service that any man can render to the meeting, is, as before stated, no mark of disrespect towards any gentleman previously named. There can be no honor in being appointed to an office where there is no choice. So let me be elected from among others, says every man who is at all qualified for the office, and worthy of presiding among his neighbors.

11. To return to the important process of appointing a chairman. A gentleman has been named; I have allowed time — a distinct moment must be sufficient — for the nomination to be seconded; and then, having previously fixed on a gentleman whom I know to be qualified for the office, or whom I prefer, in a distinct and audible voice I name him. A moment's pause, such as was before allowed, in courtesy, in decency, in justice, ought to be allowed for the seconding of my nomination; and then another gentleman may with perfect propriety be nominated in like manner; and another, and another. The meeting will now have a choice. And if these pauses be allowed, and the nominations be made distinctly, it will soon be

seen, soon be heard, on which gentleman the choice of the meeting rests. And such a course of proceeding, which, even if four or five gentlemen be thus nominated, will not require more than a single minute, will be a happy passage of an orderly course of proceeding throughout.

12. As it is a duty incumbent on the persons assembled to listen to the nominations, and to allow the moment's silence requisite for the seconding, so does this state of things impose a duty on the persons who may be nominated to the office of chairman. This duty, without the observance of which there will be disorder; this duty is silence, and an acquiescence in the decision of the meeting. Disclaimers, protests of unfitness, of indisposition, of the superior claims of others; in short, speeches of any sort, however short, ought to be carefully avoided until there be a chairman seated and the meeting thereby organized. It does not follow that because a gentleman is nominated to the office of chairman that he will be appointed. So that each gentleman so named may with perfect propriety, and indeed ought to remain silent, leaving it to the meeting, who best know whom to prefer, to make its choice. If, indeed, it do happen that, owing to the state of health or to any other circumstance, the gentleman selected have some insuperable objection to undertaking the duties of the office, as it is desirable above all things that the meeting be organized with as little delay as possible, still let such gentleman take the chair, and from that position, as briefly

as he please, state or allude to the objection, begging the meeting to choose another chairman, during which he will preside and render his best assistance. There being now a chairman, the meeting, being now organized, may and ought to have the question, on each nomination, put to it, and its vote taken on each nomination; just as its vote is to be taken on any other question. But, before proceeding to take the votes, the chairman should allow time for all the nominations likely to be made.

13. It is an awkward and unpleasant thing for a gentleman called upon to fill the office of chairman of a meeting, on the occasion of his first taking the chair to have to make his way towards it alone. No gentleman ought to be left in this situation, whether the meeting be large or small. On the election of the Speaker of the House of Representatives, he is, with great propriety, accompanied and handed to his chair. And something of this ought to be observed and practised, of ushering to his seat for the first time the chairman of any company.

14. Thus far I have treated of cases in which the chairman is to be chosen by the meeting on its assembling. And it is in such cases only that precepts or advice can be required. There are other cases, in which meetings are convened, and the intended chairman is named in the requisition, or document, by which the meeting is convened. Such meetings are, of course, the result of some previous meeting, great or small, at

which this appointment of chairman, and other arrangements have been made. All this is very proper, desirable, and even necessary, in the case of a large meeting. To such previous appointment of a chairman there could be no reasonable objection, even if it did not come recommended to us by its tendency to forward the business of the meeting; there could be no reasonable objection to it, in point of order, at least, seeing that it is previously and openly announced; and the man who entertains insurmountable objections to the chairman, may stay away.

15. It must be proper and desirable, on occasions of large meetings, to have the chairman previously appointed. Five hundred persons are probably as large an assemblage as can be expected, on the instant, to elect a chairman in a satisfactory manner; and it may, therefore, on all occasions on which a meeting is reasonably expected to exceed this number, be desirable for some smaller number, including among them, of course, unless it be impracticable, the originators of the proceedings; it may, in all such cases, be desirable and proper for some such body of persons to select and appoint a chairman: the mode of doing which ought, however, to be attended with at least all the observances and forms that are inculcated in paragraphs 9, 10, and 11; and ought, likewise, to be influenced by the considerations suggested in the few previous paragraphs, beginning with that numbered 4.

16. A smaller body may thus, with perfect propriety

and, indeed, very laudably, take upon itself to appoint a chairman to a larger body of persons. And this it may do, either in time to have it duly announced, previously to the assembling of the larger body, or just at the moment appointed for the commencement of business; such smaller body being assembled and known to be assembled, in some contiguous and duly accessible place; and known, indeed, by the great body of the meeting, to be so assembled for the purpose of making this and other arrangements for the orderly and efficient conduct of the meeting.

17. One word here as to the PRINCIPLE on which this and the other rules are laid down; the principle on which all proper rules and observances must be founded. This principle is, simply, JUSTICE; it is, in another word, EQUITY. That is to say, equality of right. A number of persons are called together to discuss, to debate, to resolve, to determine. If there be some previous arrangement by which one man, in virtue of his office, or by due election, shall preside; and if, as in cases of shareholders, some of the parties assembling are, by due and previous agreement, to have two or more votes, whilst others are to have only one; if there be cases of this kind, there can be no inequity in such appointed officer or chairman taking his place; nor any in the larger holders having a plurality of votes; because, as predicted, all has been duly and previously arranged and appointed. But, where no such arrangement or appointment has been made, or agreed to; where a meeting is called without any

previous and explicit distinction of persons and of powers, all are to be understood as equal; that is, equal in point of rights. In this state of things every man who has a right to be present, and, of course, every man who comes within the description of the requisition has such right; every such man has a right, and an equal right with any other man, to assist in the nomination of a chairman, or to be himself nominated and elected; and, of course, an equal right to make, and to second, and to vote for or against, motions and amendments. This is the principle, this is the rule. And on the due observance of this principle, throughout the whole of its proceedings, must the peace, and the order, and the final success of every meeting proceed.

18. Nor is there the slightest reason for any rational or just man to wish that it were otherwise. Are we to be told that there is a difference in the education, in the understanding, in the rank and station, and in the moral and intellectual qualities of men; and that, on this account, they ought not to be equally treated? Is this the plea for distinctions, for preferences, and for exclusions, at meetings such as these of which we are treating? Show me your gauge for measuring, for ascertaining the exact worth, the intellectual rank, of men; and for exhibiting with precision the estimation in which a man is held, and in which he ought to be held, by his neighbors and his fellow-countrymen; show me this gauge, and then will I consider of the plea for distinctions and exclusions.

19. But, indeed, we have this gauge. And we see it applied as completely as human infirmities and prepossessions will permit us to apply it, in the case of a public meeting. It is indubitable that when any man offers himself, for any purpose, to the attention of an assemblage of his neighbors, that assemblage applies the gauge. It takes into consideration all his qualities and pretensions, and, bating that leaning towards wealth and power and established reputation, to which we are all of us prone, it generally forms a tolerably accurate estimate of a man. At all events, this is the best gauge we have. The decision is apt to be greatly in favor of the influential and the educated; and he who wants more than this for them, must be an irrational devotee.

20. So much for the principle on which we ought, and, indeed, on which, if we would preserve the peace and order and secure any good effects from a meeting, so much for the principle on which, throughout the whole of the affair, we must proceed; that is to say, a principle of equity towards every man duly entitled to be present.

21. To resume: We left our subject with paragraph 16, in which the appointment of a chairman to a large meeting, by a smaller preparatory meeting, had been considered and concluded. The chairman, then, is selected and appointed. The next step to be taken is, to introduce him to the larger meeting, and to install him in his office; which may be done with great propri-

ety and effect by a brief address from some gentleman who is acquainted with the merits and the fitness of the chairman elect. And this, may we not venture to pronounce, is the only occasion on which a speech of any description can with propriety be addressed to a meeting previous to the installation of its chairman and to its consequent organization.

THE REQUISITE POWERS AND DUTIES OF HIS OFFICE.

22. These duties, when a discussion is to be carried on, when motions are to be made, and amendments moved, and eager speakers to be restrained, and sometimes turbulent auditors to be ruled; these duties are not within the scope of every man. And yet, when we call to mind the considerations by which assemblages of men often seem to be guided in the selection of a chairman, we might very fairly conclude that this office, one of the most difficult that a man can be called on to sustain, is, in their estimation, the very easiest thing in life. However, it is not our business to expatiate on the difficulties, but to remove or to surmount them.

23. The chairman ought, in reality, to have a chair, and this chair ought, if the assemblage be of any considerable number, to be raised, and by all means so placed as to detach, in some slight degree, the gentle-

man, who is on every occasion to be observed ; who is to be first addressed ; who is to be appealed to first and last by every speaker ; whose rising is, on the instant, whatever may be going forward, to be the signal for the most silent attention ; who is, in fact, whatever he be in his individual and private character, now the selected depository of all the authority, and, indeed, of all the dignity of the meeting. This gentleman, who ought never to be out of sight, ought by no means to be kept standing whilst others are speaking. And this arrangement, although due to him, is not to be regarded as designed solely for his ease, and in compliment to the man, but as one of the requisite means for preserving the order of the assemblage.

24. How, indeed, can any man preserve this order, among contending parties and rival speakers, unless he have this, and every other arrangement that can be devised, to make the duties of the office less difficult?

25. There is, we believe, a becoming disposition among us to pay deference to the chairman, but then he must be A CHAIRMAN. He must not be one among a knot of men, surrounded by them, talking with them scarcely visible to the greater number of persons present. How is any man to preside, if he be one of a cluster of men, some of them, possibly, rivals and opponents, and for any thing that even he or the meeting knows, caballing against him? The thing is not to be expected ; is impossible.

26. Besides, for another important reason, the chairman is not to be spoken with save by his secretary or clerk, and ought to hold none but indispensable communications even with him, during debate. Setting aside the unseemliness of communicating, in private conversation, with individuals of the meeting, there must be always sufficient to occupy the whole mind of the chairman in the business of the meeting, the object of which he must keep constantly and clearly in view so as to detect, and be ready to check on the instant, any, the slightest aberration from it. He is to know, is to see, and to hear every thing that is going on; he is to bear in mind all that has passed, and to have a clear view of what remains to be done, so as to be able to suggest with promptitude the next step to be taken, and thereby to keep the attention of the meeting to its purpose. To insure attention and order, he must himself set the example, and must listen with marked attention to every speaker.

27. With this arrangement the office of chairman becomes much less difficult than it would otherwise be. The gentleman appointed ought, as was before intimated, to be accompanied or handed to his chair by some one or two others, so that every one sees and feels that his taking upon himself the office is not a piece of assumption on his part.

28. No gentleman will require to be reminded that on taking the office of chairman, in a meeting in which different and opposing measures may be pro-

pounded, he resigns all thoughts of promoting any particular views or course of proceeding to which he himself may be inclined. If a gentleman can not thus resign his views—and there are cases in which a man ought not—his duty will be to take the chair to which he is elected, and from that situation to state to the meeting the obligation he is under to advocate and to maintain a particular course of proceeding, and to beg that they will select another chairman, during which selection he will gladly assist by presiding.

29. On entering upon the duties of his office, the chairman will have to address himself to the meeting, very briefly but distinctly adverting to the purpose for which it is assembled, and if there be a requisition or other document under which the meeting is convened, he will do well to read it; or, if it be of any length, to cause it to be read in a distinct and audible voice. After this, if it be not indicated in the requisition, the chairman may with great advantage point to the course of proceeding intended to be pursued by the gentlemen who have projected and convened the meeting; the course by which they mean to pursue their object, if he be informed of that course; and thus will the meeting have the whole matter before them. Whatever may be his opinions or his wishes with regard to the proposed measures, it will be his duty to abstain from the slightest expression of them, leaving the advocating of the measures, and the objecting to them, to the several speakers. If there be seats for the

company, and they are not seated, it is highly expedient that the chairman require them to be so. And if he think that some of them require instruction on this head, it will be equally expedient in him to request that gentlemen will keep their seats during the business of the meeting, save when they rise to speak ; and that each gentleman, on the conclusion of whatever he may have to say, instantly resume his seat, affording thereby a fair opportunity for any other gentleman to rise. Observations of this kind, according to the taste and judgment of the chairman, concluding with a recommendation to the meeting to give a patient hearing to the several speakers, will form a very suitable prelude to the business of the meeting. On resuming his seat, the chairman, both now and on every other occasion, intimates his desire that the business of the meeting should proceed.

30. A motion will now, of course, be submitted to the meeting ; and this motion, having been read, generally by the mover, will doubtless be seconded. After the moving and the seconding, the words of the motion in writing being handed to the chairman or to his secretary, ought again, in an audible voice, to be read to the meeting, either by the chairman or by some person of his appointment: and immediately after this, for any objection to be made on such motion, or any amendment moved thereon. If, after a reasonable and sufficient pause, no objector present himself, the chairman will proceed to put the motion to the meeting, taking the votes for it, and then against it, in the

manner usual at meetings of the same description. This is by a show of hands, or by the ayes and noes.

31. If, however, an objection to the ORIGINAL MOTION, as the first motion is called, be raised, that objection must take one of the following shapes: it must be an AMENDMENT, or it must go to NEGATIVE the motion, or it must go to POSTPONE the consideration of the motion, or it may be for the PREVIOUS QUESTION, or, lastly, it may be a motion to ADJOURN the meeting. And it is a duty incumbent on the chairman to see that the objector shape his course distinctly to one of these ends. If the objector do not, pretty early in his speech, disclose to the assembly to which of these ends he is shaping his course, the chairman may, with great propriety, rise from his seat and ask him the question as to what end he is aiming. The understanding and the patience of a number of men are not to be trifled with, and their purposes frustrated by indefinite and aimless harangues. The chairman, I say, under such circumstances, may inquire as to the course intended to be pursued. But he will, doubtless, use his judgment as to this point. If the speaker be listened to with eager attention by a part of the meeting, and with patient attention by a decided majority, then will there be no propriety in interrupting him; for such attention is the best test of his being right. It is, in short, to save the meeting from a waste of its time and a trespass on its temper that the chairman, in a case of this kind, is to interfere. And he will do it, of

course, with all due courtesy; with firmness and authority when required.

32. Of these four modes of raising an objection to an original motion, it is of the utmost importance that we obtain a clear understanding. So let us treat of them severally, in due order.

33. But, first; of an ORIGINAL MOTION. There is a duty here incumbent on the chairman with regard to this motion; a duty due to his own character and to the character of the meeting. Although such a case seldom occurs, yet, as it might occur, we ought to be prepared for it. A motion, even an original motion, may be framed on an oversight, or in error, with regard to the express purpose of the meeting. In this, as in other cases, it is the duty of the chairman to be vigilant; and if such a case occur he ought to point it out.

34. However, this, after all, may be only matter of individual opinion, as every proposition is to be regarded until it have been determined on by a vote of the meeting. The chairman may misapprehend the motion; or he may even be under some error with regard to the express purpose of the meeting. Either of these is possible—but we ought to be very careful in admitting and acting on such a presumption; however, it is possible that the chairman, in objecting to a motion on this ground, may be in error; in which case, with becoming deference to his office, he may be

reasoned with. If his objection be not removed, then it will be his duty to set such erroneous motion aside; or, if susceptible of correction, to have it corrected. If, however—as it is of course possible—the chairman be, in such a case, manifestly, and in the opinion of a majority or near a majority, in error, and his error be not corrected, then ought he, as due to himself and to the meeting, to entreat that meeting to select another chairman, and thus to permit him to resign an office in which no man ought to be called on to do any thing or to suffer any thing to be done which he does not deem perfectly consonant to order. What has been just stated with regard to the course to be pursued by a chairman in the case of an original motion, is equally applicable to an amendment on a motion.

35. Second; of AN AMENDMENT on a motion. This, as the term imports, is designed by the mover as an *improvement* on a previous motion. There are cases in which we may very properly entertain a wish that nothing should be done; cases in which we may not only be opposed to a motion just made, but altogether opposed to any thing of the nature of such a motion; opposed to any step whatever being taken in any such direction; and, indeed, opposed to any movement whatever. In a case of this kind we do not propose an amendment; unless, indeed, we might choose, as a means of awakening the attention of the meeting to our own view of the case, to propose an **ironical amendment**; except in such a case as this, if

we be opposed to any thing being done in the direction proposed, we do not move an amendment, but object to, argue directly against, the motion, and seek to persuade the meeting to reject it by voting it out. We do not move "*as an amendment*" that the step proposed in the foregoing motion be not taken; nor that the motion be rejected. We do not, in such a case, make a motion of any description; but, as before stated, we argue against the motion. There can, in short, be no motion properly framed to put a direct *negative* on any thing. Motions, propositions of any sort, must never be in the *negative*, but always in the *affirmative* form. They must always affirm that something IS, or SHALL BE; never the contrary. And it is part of the duty of the chairman to see that all motions be put in the proper form.

36. An amendment, then, like an original motion, must be in the affirmative form; and, professing as it does to be an improvement on such motion, it ought, ostensibly at least, to be shaped towards the same end; unless, indeed, that in the opinion of the mover of the amendment the original motion be not conformable to the purpose of the meeting, in which case he may, on that ground, offer his amendment for the avowed purpose of superseding that motion altogether.

37. Third. Sufficient has been said in the last paragraph but one on the mode of proceeding in order to put a negative on a motion. Of the methods of resisting the adoption of a motion, as enumerated in

paragraph 31, the *third* is by a motion postponing its consideration, the meaning of which is too obvious to require a word of explanation.

38. Fourth; of THE PREVIOUS QUESTION. A motion to this effect is resorted to in order to set aside a motion without either amendment, postponement, negation, or further discussion thereon. There are propositions which we may deem useless or unwise, but which we can not absolutely pronounce to be unsuitable and irrelevant to the purpose of the meeting, and which, therefore, the chairman can not take upon himself to prohibit and put down. The motion for *the previous question* is a contrivance to get rid of a proposition of this sort, without either calling on the chairman to do so ungracious a thing as to prohibit its discussion, or on the meeting to vote upon it. It is, in short, a contrivance to elude a further discussion of a proposition. Its nature is this: A motion, being made and seconded, is to be put to vote if no person rise to oppose it. Well, no person may like to place himself in the situation of an opponent to such a proposition: for it may affirm a series of undeniable truths, but lead to no practical result, and it is for results that men meet in debate; or it may be irrelevant to the purpose or purposes of the meeting, and yet have a semblance of propriety so as to make its impropriety questionable; or, lastly, it may be incomprehensible, nonsensical, or absurd.

39. Now a man of sense and spirit does not like

to place himself in opposition to a proposition such as any of these which we have supposed. And yet he, and a majority of the meeting, may wish to get rid of it. The step then to be taken is to move the previous question; which question, although never directly put save in a case of this kind, is always understood to have been put, and carried in the affirmative, previous to a meeting entering on the discussion of any motion. And the moving of "the previous question" is the moving "That this meeting do now proceed with the discussion of the motion before it." The mover of this wishes, of course, that the meeting shall decide that it will not proceed with the discussion, and thereby throw out the proposition. But, as laid down in paragraph 35, all motions must be made in the affirmative form, and a negative vote may thus be obtained under that form.

40. Thus may a meeting at any time, if it please, in a regular and orderly manner, and without throwing the ungracious office on its chairman, set aside a motion which it may deem useless, or otherwise unworthy of discussion. "The previous question," however, must wait its turn ere it be moved. The motion against which it may be employed, besides being moved, must be seconded, and put to the meeting by being read by the chairman or by some person under his direction. Because, until this be done, "the previous question" is premature, is unnecessary, is out of order.

41. Fifth, and last. A motion to ADJOURN. This

may be made at any time, and may be again and again repeated. Nor is it an easy matter to devise a rule by which the making of it can be restrained, without subjecting a meeting to very great inconveniences. The usual restraint, the obligation not to make a motion for an adjournment lightly and inconsiderately, or for factious purposes, consists in the great responsibility, in the odium to which the mover would subject himself, unless countenanced by the general sense of the meeting. But this odium, this responsibility, is generally sufficient, and is the chief or only security for orderly conduct in any part of a public meeting.

42. Thus, then, have we before us the several motions and forms of motions which any member and every member, entitled to be present at a meeting, has a right to make; and that which each individual has a right to do, it is the business and the duty of the chairman to protect him in the performance of.

43. Is it necessary to observe that these rights are little liable to be abused? They never, in fact, are abused. Our citizens generally are but too diffident of themselves to be troublesome in making superfluous motions. And no one will call in question the salutary nature of these rights, save persons of peevish and ungovernable tempers, who would have every thing their own way. However, salutary or not, the rights do exist, and must exist, where a number of men are assembled for the purpose of debating on any prop-

osition, and there can be no order unless all parties be equally protected and aided by the chairman in the fair exercise of these rights.

44. But these are rights to make motions merely. Every individual entitled to take part in the proceeding, that is to say, entitled to be present and to vote, is fully entitled to make motions, and to second motions, provided that such motions be conformable to the rules just laid down. But the making of speeches, the occupying of the time and attention of the meeting by making speeches, is another affair. Here, each man must make his own way to the favor and to the attention of a meeting. And the meeting ought to be allowed to choose whether it will hear him or not. It must be the duty of a chairman to forbid partial, and envious, and preconcerted interruptions of a speaker; but if a whole meeting have a distaste either for the man, or for his manner of speaking, or for the matter of his speech, it can never be the duty of a chairman to insist on their listening. The meeting ought to be allowed to choose whom and what it will listen to, in the way of speaking; and has a right, must have a right, to express its approbation, or its disapprobation, in any manner it may please. It is partial and preconcerted interruptions only that a chairman ought to repress, without being called upon to obtain a hearing for a tedious, incapable, or otherwise distasteful speech. But a motion is another matter. A man who can not obtain attention as a speaker, may move a proposition; and it must be the duty

of the chairman to protect him in this right, and to treat his motion with quite as much respect and attention as he would treat that of the most eloquent and favorite speaker.

45. I am supposing, of course, that a motion thus offered is duly adapted to the purpose of the meeting, and that it is, if amounting to any thing more than a simple proposition to postpone a decision, to adjourn a meeting, or something equally brief and clear; I am supposing, that if it be a motion requiring many words, it shall be handed to the chairman, duly and clearly written out, and then, being comformable to the purpose or purposes of the meeting, and to the business then in hand, it must be the duty of the chairman to receive it and to put it to the meeting as he would put any other proposition. For inability to make a speech, or inability to obtain a hearing, arise from what cause it may, can in no respect be regarded as disqualifying a man for making motions. To return:

46. A motion being fully submitted to a meeting, that is to say, being moved, seconded, and read or recited by the chairman, can no longer be deemed the mere proposition of the mover and seconder, to be, if they please, at any time withdrawn by them. On the contrary, it has become a sort of property of the meeting. There is no knowing, without a vote, who may be for it or who against it. It may be the pleasure of the meeting, or of a part of the meeting,

to pronounce its opinion on the proposition; and, having submitted it, the mover and seconder are not competent to withdraw it, save with the unanimous acquiescence of the meeting.

47. A motion being thus fully before a meeting, if no objector present himself, may be put to the vote without further speaking, although there can be no irregularity in a third or fourth speaker offering reasons in its support. But neither mover nor seconder ought again to be permitted to speak, save in explanation of some previous obscurity or manifest misapprehension, and to such explanation should any further words from either of them be very rigidly confined. But if an objector appear, if a debate arise, then may the mover speak a second time; or his seconder, as I apprehend, if no member object to it, may without impropriety speak on his behalf; such speech being strictly confined to a reply to the objections stated; to explanations as before spoken of; and to a summing up of the arguments previously used in support of the motion. No new matter ought to be suffered to originate in this second speech, for, if it were, the whole debate would be reopened, and the objectors to the motion would manifestly be entitled to answer such new matter, and bring forward new arguments and second thoughts on their parts against it. And thus would there be no end to a question.

48. This right of reply, as it is termed, exists in the mover of an original proposition; but belongs

not to the mover of an amendment, whose movements altogether, both speech and motion, are in opposition, are in answer to the original motion, and to the speech or speeches made in its support. There must be limits to a debate. Men who do not make speeches must not be kept in unlimited attendance on those who do; nor must speakers be permitted, by repeated answers, by replies, and rejoinders, to degenerate into a wrangle. The rule is: One speech for each man, if he please, on each motion, and no more, save to the mover of an original proposition; whose second speech is, also, to be kept from new matter, from second thoughts in favor of his motion, save such thoughts as clearly apply in answer to the objections just made to his proposition. It is, of course, the duty of the chairman liberally to interpret and to apply this rule.

49. With regard to the time of commencing his reply. This, as almost every thing else in these matters, must be in deference to the convenience and wishes of the meeting. When a number of men are assembled on business, that business ought to be done with promptitude, with spirit, but with due attention to order. There ought to be no loitering, nor any indecent haste. So the time for the mover to rise and to commence his reply is when a pause occurs in the debate; when no person appears eager to make objection; or when a meeting, impatient to come to a close, calls for an end to the debate. In either of these cases the chairman will handsomely fulfil his

duty by turning his eyes towards the person who made the original motion, thereby signifying to him that he is ready to hear any thing which such person may have to say in reply.

50. The debate being ended by the reply, or by the person who is entitled to reply declining to exercise his right, without permitting any further speeches or amendments the chairman ought to proceed to put the question, as it is called,—that is, to take the vote of the meeting; which vote he, of course, takes in the manner that is usual in meetings of the same description; commonly by a show of hands: but if there be a dispute or uncertainty about the decision, it must become his duty to divide the meeting, and, if necessary to a satisfactory decision, to have the persons on each side counted.

51. There must be no unfair proceeding in this part of the conduct of a meeting. There is a never-failing and a most admirable disposition in the people of this country to debate on their differences, to discuss their opposing claims; to meet for these purposes; and then all parties who have a right, and who choose to be present, being assembled, to put the point in dispute among them to the vote, and then to yield to that vote whether it be for or against them. This disposition in the great bulk of the people never fails us. And nothing in human nature can be more admirable, more salutary. They think not of fighting. Come, say they, let us discuss the difference between us; and, having duly

and fairly done that, let us take the opinions of all the parties concerned by a vote, and if we be outvoted we will yield. Men see things in different lights, their interests frequently oppose each other, therefore there will be differences of views, of opinions, and of feelings; but what can be more admirable than this disposition of our fellow-citizens, thus fairly to discuss and peaceably to settle those differences?

52. To ensure such peaceable settlement, however, the proceedings must be fair, must be equitable. Men must not be thus invited to meet, to discuss, and to vote, and then find that a little knot of people have predetermined what the decision shall be. Men who will yield with cheerfulness to a majority, become unruly when they find that they are assembled to be deceived, to be betrayed. This, of course, can never happen, save when the chairman is of the party who have predetermined the question, or when he, through weakness or through some culpable motive, lends himself to their unfair views. If the chairman do his duty; if, having excepted the office of chairman, he deal impartially; if, having duly received motions, and had them debated, he proceed to ascertain on which side the majority stands, and give his decision accordingly; if he do all this, as a man of honor always will do, however discontented some of the minority may be, the greater part of them will silently and even contentedly acquiesce, all will respect, the majority will zealously support him, and order and good temper will reign over the meeting.

53. But for the chairman to lend himself to the purposes of a party, what is it but to pervert his office, and to betray the confidence which men are accustomed to repose in that office? The least evil arising from such a course of conduct is the discontent and turbulence usually attendant on it. The ultimate and not very remote consequences of such behavior on the part of chairmen, were it to become prevalent, would be to drive our brave, our generous, our just countrymen from their habitual fair play and confidence in each other; to drive them from these, which, happily, are still a part of their nature; to drive them from their debating and voting, into the use of the knife and the dagger.

54. To return to the course of business which the chairman has to perform, the details of which we left in the taking of the vote, at paragraph 50.

55. If there be but one motion before the meeting, the chairman proceeds, the debate being ended, to take the votes FOR and AGAINST that motion. But if there be an amendment on that motion, he takes the votes for and against the amendment first; and, if there were a second or a third amendment, then would he have to take the votes on these severally, for and against each, beginning with the last, and ascending upwards towards the original motion.

56. When there is a motion and an amendment thereon to be voted on, it is a common practice to

take the vote simply for the amendment, and then that for the original motion, and so to decide the question between these two merely in favor of that which has the greater number of votes. But this is by no means correct. For, although one of these motions may have more votes than the other, it does not follow that it is to be adopted. A majority of the meeting may be averse to both, and have, therefore, voted for neither. It is their turn to vote. And to give them this turn, each motion must be put completely to the meeting, FOR and AGAINST. Thus—first, *for the amendment*, and then, *against the amendment*. When, if a majority be *for the amendment*, the question is settled, the amendment being carried, and the original question voted out; but if the majority be against the amendment, then comes the voting *for* and *against the original motion*. And this may be outvoted, likewise. It by no means follows that because two or three propositions are made to us, we must accept one of them. We may very wisely choose to remain as we are, rejecting every proposed alteration.

57. In the manner thus laid down may a number of motions, original, or amendments, be successively disposed of. And the rules laid down on this, and on all the other points, apply equally to large or to small meetings.

58. Having ascertained that the business of the meeting, and consequently the duties of the chairman,

are at an end, the chairman ought, with promptitude, to declare that the proceedings have terminated, and instantly to leave the chair; affording thereby an opportunity to the meeting to express its approbation or disapprobation of his conduct.

59. Thus far have we looked only to the duties and to the office of chairmen of occasional or single meetings, without referring to those of the chairman of a permanent society, council, or committee, which assembles, adjourns, and reässembles at stated and appointed periods.

60. It must be merely on the reässembling of a meeting of this kind that there can now remain any thing particular to observe on. On such occasions the chairman will have to refer to the minutes of the preceding meeting. Whether this assembling be a recurrence only of the ordinary and regular meetings, or the result of a special appointment, by adjournment or otherwise, it will, in the outset, be the business of the chairman to state. And then he will read, or cause to be read, from the minutes of former meetings, whatever may tend to lead the present into the business awaiting its attention.

61. There are one or two questions closely connected with this part of the subject, yet to be spoken of. The first of which, in point of interest and importance, is this:

62. Can a chairman, who has made himself obnoxious to a meeting, or who has lost its confidence, can a chairman thus circumstanced be removed? And if he can, in what manner is it best to be done?

63. I answer, that I do not see how a chairman can, according to any rules of order, be forced out of his office, and another placed in stead, and the business of a meeting be carried forward. When a meeting is so unfortunate as to have a chairman who will not act impartially, he is little likely to listen to a proposition for his own removal and for the election of another. Men ought, in the outset, to be careful whom they elevate to the office of chairman. But finding themselves hampered with a partial and perfidious person in that office, I know of no course that can be pursued, with a due regard to order, but that of determining to do no business under him. Let an adjournment *sine die* be moved; let it be put to the meeting in the best manner it can be put; see that a decided majority are in its favor, and then leave the obnoxious chairman with his partisans, if they choose to remain.

64. The question sometimes arises—Is there any occasion on which a person speaking may be interrupted by another person rising to address the chairman? This is a nice and important point. And I answer, that such interruption may with propriety take place. But the person offering the interruption takes upon himself the responsibility. If he offer it im-

properly, he will incur the disapprobation, the censure, and condemnation of the meeting. It can be proper only when a speaker is out of order; either making a proposition that is irregular in some particular, or wandering from the question before the meeting, or otherwise unnecessarily consuming the time, or endangering or perverting the just and reasonable purposes of the meeting. It is an ungracious office to interrupt a person who is thus irregular; the chairman may be inattentive to the irregularity, or, hoping it will soon terminate, may defer the exercise of his authority. In any case of this kind, an individual of quick discernment and great zeal for the success of the proceedings may, with commendable spirit, rise, and, addressing himself to the chairman, may point out the irregularity. That may suffice to put a stop to it. But if it do not, the meeting will most probably express its opinion.

65. An individual thus offering himself to the attention of the chairman, in the middle of a speech, ought to be listened to whilst he briefly points out what he conceives to be an irregularity. And the moment an individual thus rises, signifying, as he ought to do, that it is on a point of order, the person speaking ought, of course, to stop, awaiting the decision of the chairman, who alone, and not the meeting, is to be addressed and appealed to on all points of order.

66. When at once two or more persons rise, or advance, in order to address the chairman or the meet-

ing, the question as to which shall first speak is to be determined by the chairman, who will determine it in favor of the gentleman who first catches his eye. There can be no better rule devised than this. The chairman, as laid down in paragraph 23, ought to be so placed as to be able to see all, and to be seen of all; and, as it is part of his duty to avail himself of this, his favorable situation, so ought he best to see who first advances to speak. After the gentleman who first catches the chairman's eye, the second and third, according to the nomination of the chairman, ought to have the privilege of speaking.

67. The last point which, under this head, it may be advisable to notice is this--and it is designed for every individual member of a meeting. Let the chairman be the sole preserver of order. Any attempt to assist him in this part of his office, save by silent and respectful attention to him, must tend to create disorder. There are, certainly, extreme cases in which it may become expedient for a meeting to expel from its body some ungovernable and disorderly individual: this, of course, is a case to which the rule just laid down does not apply. It is the privilege of the chairman alone to call to "ORDER." Let no other individual presume to utter the call. But let the meeting at all times be ready to enforce attention to the wishes and to the commands of "THE CHAIR."

www.ingramcontent.com/pod-product-compliance
Lightning Source LLC
Chambersburg PA
CBHW032221010526
44113CB00032B/189